RADICAL PERTH MILITANT FREMANTLE

First edition 2017 by Black Swan Press
Second updated edition with new chapters 2019 by Interventions Inc

Interventions is a not-for-profit, independent left wing book publisher. For further information:
    www.interventions.org.au
    interventionspublications@gmail.com
    Trades Hall Suite 68
    54 Victoria Street
    Carlton VIC 3053

Red Swan Series Vol 2
Series Editor: Alexis Vassiley

Design and layout second edition by Viktoria Ivanova
Cover photo second edition courtesy of West Australian Newspapers (Image No. WAN-0031385)
Back cover photo second edition courtesy of West Australian Newspapers (Image No. WAN-0031387)

Editors: Fox, Charlie; Vassiley, Alexis; Oliver, Bobbie; Layman, Lenore
Coordinating editor: Fox, Charlie

Title: Radical Perth Militant Fremantle

ISBN: 978-0-9945378-7-4: Paperback

© Charlie Fox 2019
Individual chapters remain the property of their respective authors.

The moral rights of the authors have been asserted
All rights reserved. Except as permitted under the Australian Copyright Act 1968 (for example, a fair dealing for the purposes of study, research, criticism or review), no part of this book may be reproduced, stored in a retrieval system, communicated or transmitted in any form or by any means without prior written permission.

All inquiries should be made to the coordinating editor.

 A catalogue record for this book is available from the National Library of Australia

RADICAL PERTH MILITANT FREMANTLE

Edited by Charlie Fox, Alexis Vassiley, Bobbie Oliver and Lenore Layman

INTERVENTIONS
MELBOURNE

The editors wish to acknowledge the Whadjuk people of the Noongar nation and recognise their continuing connection to land, waters and community. We pay our respects to them and their cultures; and to elders both past and present.

We dedicate this book to all the fighters and dreamers who populate this book, and the fighters and dreamers of the future who will inspire us in the struggles to come.

CONTENTS

Acknowledgements — i
Preface — iii
Introduction by Charlie Fox — 1

PART 1: Walking Radical Perth — 13

1. Perth Chinese Community's Fight for Survival — 17
2. CAMP and Gay Rights — 25
3. Forrest Place Protests — 37
4. Occupy Perth — 47
5. Katharine Susannah Prichard and the Interwar Peace Movement — 59
6. Banners of Hope and Apron Parades — 71
7. Solidarity with the Pilbara Aboriginal Station Hands Strike — 83
8. Yugoslavs and Interwar Radicalism — 95
9. Monty Miller and other Early Perth Radicals — 105
10. The Red Dean and Rock Masses in the Long 1960s — 115
11. The 1931 Treasury Building Riot — 125
12. Art as a Weapon: The Workers' Art Guild — 135
13. Fighting for the Foreshore — 145
14. Annie Westbrook, Wobbly, Eliza Tracey, Stirrer — 155
15. Battle for the Barracks — 165

16	The Workers' Embassy at Solidarity Park	**175**
17	Goonininup versus the Old Swan Brewery	**189**
18	The Single Noongar Claim	**199**
PART 2: Walking Militant Fremantle		**211**
19	Chinese Seamen in Fremantle	**215**
20	War on the Waterfront	**231**
21	Fremantle's Bloody Sunday	**241**
22	John Curtin at the Worker	**251**
23	Hard Hats, Heritage and Hope	**263**
24	The Anti-Vietnam War Demonstrations	**275**
25	May Day: The Workers' Day	**291**
26	Fremantle's Counterculture: India and the Orange People	**305**
PART 3: Driving the Radical Suburbs		**317**
27	Red Square and the Flagpole	**321**
28	The Scarborough Snake Pit	**329**
29	Closing the Asylums	**339**
30	Student Radicalism in the 1970s	**351**
31	Wimin Writing: Perth's Radical Feminist Publications	**365**
32	Hope in the Wasteland: East Perth City Farm	**375**
33	The Pioneer Bookshop and Portnoy's Complaint	**385**
34	The Women's Peace Camp	**395**
	Select Bibliography	**405**
	Picture Credits	**429**
	Editors and Contributors	**431**

ACKNOWLEDGEMENTS

The editors wish to express their appreciation to all the authors for their contributions to both the first and second editions of *Radical Perth, Militant Fremantle*, and to everyone who reviewed and commented on entries. We are very grateful to Sandra Goldbloom Zurbo for her excellent work in copyediting this second edition. We also thank individuals and institutions who provided and permitted reproduction of images.

Publication of the first edition was made possible by a research grant from the School of Media, Culture and Creative Arts, Curtin University. Thanks are due to Professor Graham Seal, and especially to Dr Sue Summers, of the now defunct Black Swan Press, for publishing the first edition. We now thank Janey Stone and the staff at Interventions for publishing the second edition. We also acknowledge the interest and support of the Australian Society for the Study of Labour History, Perth Branch.

PREFACE

The first edition of *Radical Perth, Militant Fremantle* was published by Black Swan Press in 2017.

This second updated edition of has several changes from the first. It includes three new chapters: 'Chinese Seamen in Fremantle', 'Green Bans in the 1970s', 'Solidarity with the Pilbara Aboriginal Station Hands Strike'. The chapter on radical student activities at the University of Western Australia has been replaced by a new chapter that extends the story to include the Western Australian Institute of Technology (WAIT): 'Student Radicalism in the 1970s'. The other chapters are unchanged except for minor corrections and updates.

The chapters are now grouped into three sections: Walking Radical Perth, Walking Militant Fremantle and Driving the Radical Suburbs. The chapters can be read and enjoyed in any order. In addition, by using the maps included you can use this book to create self-guided tours of locations relating to the radical history of Perth and Fremantle. Chapters that cover events which occurred in Perth and Fremantle are marked on both maps.

For those wishing to join an organised tour, Charlie Fox conducts occasional guided walks of Perth and Fremantle. He can be contacted at charlie.fox@uwa.edu.au.

This revised edition is published by Interventions Inc. It is the second in the Red Swan series of books about radical history and politics in Western Australia. The first in the series, *A Natural Battleground* by Bobbie Oliver, published by Interventions in March 2019, extends the story of the Midland Railways Workshops (chapter 27).

INTRODUCTION

Perth, 1930s, in the midst of the Great Depression. On a hot summer Sunday James Riddle, magistrate, scourge of the lawless, defender of the righteous, gazes out on an unfamiliar city. This was not the city he knew, of work, life, colour, movement and wealth.

> But now the city lay in an exhausted sleep, empty and meaningless, sprawling like a dead monster among green living things. A few leisurely pedestrians, clad in loose, comfortable garments, passed to and fro over the pavements. The clangor of a tram two blocks away was the death rattle of a robot. Under the trees in the parks the unemployed lay gasping in their sweat-soaked rags: the ordure of the city. In the hot Sabbath sun the city slept amongst its ordure, amidst the excrement passed from its concrete bowels; and the church bells pealed slowly, echoing meaninglessly through the empty streets.

Thus did John Harcourt, the young communist novelist, portray Perth in his banned and long forgotten 1934 proletarian novel *Upsurge*. The story is in the title. It describes the revolutionary upsurge of Perth's starving, immiserated and oppressed unemployed and its brutal repression, put down by police, courts and government. Does it sound like Perth? Is it really Perth? Even in the midst of the Great Depression? When we first thought of writing a book called *Radical Perth*,

Militant Fremantle, and mentioned it to people, many of them laughed. 'Militant Fremantle yes. But radical Perth?' joked one. 'Surely that's an oxymoron.' 'Well, no,' we would patiently proclaim, 'we came up with seventy topics in no time at all and most of them weren't in Fremantle.'

Still, it's not surprising that people might think a history of radicalism in Perth would be a short one. For many years the dominant school of Western Australian history writing argued that WA was bound together by an informal but widely held belief that isolation had bred consensus, that discord and upset was the fault, not of Western Australians, but of outsiders: 't'othersider', gold seekers from Victoria in the 1890s, who brought dangerous ideas such as trade unionism and Labor Party politics with them, or communists in the Great Depression of the 1930s, who conned the local unemployed into demonstration and riot. Even as late as the 1999 republic referendum, in which Western Australians voted no more heavily than anybody else, the WA premier attributed this to resentment against a yes campaign run by 'eastern staters'.

Of course, referenda on certain proposals do give some comfort to this picture of consensus. In the conscription plebiscites in World War 1, Western Australia voted in favour most strongly to conscription. In the 1954 referendum to abolish the Communist Party, Western Australians voted most strongly in favour on this issue as well.

To conclude from such results that Western Australia was so profoundly conservative that radicalism was unknown is plainly wrong. Militant Fremantle is well known but then, taking the city as a whole, there is also a long history of radicalism in Perth, as the following chapters will attest. Those who think of it as inevitably conservative are probably not thinking of the more distant past, but of the recent past and the present. True, Perth is not known to be a radical city, often thought to be too laid back to encourage protest. That sunshine! Those beaches! That river! That listless and unconcerned search for pleasure! Author Robert Drewe summed up this view beautifully in 1977 when he wrote in the *Bulletin* of a stroll along the Swan at Crawley:

> I walked the length of the beach up to the Royal Perth Yacht Club, with its massed wealth floating serenely in the shallows, and back to Mounts Bay Road. On my right the city skyline stood out sharply against the sky, especially the letters 'BOND', in dark blue atop one building and on my left the tower of the university with its strikingly harmonious architecture and red ochre tiles was visible through the gum trees. A magpie carolled in the distance right on cue. It was quiet and still and as I strolled past where the old Crawley Bay tearooms once stood, two butterflies flapped lightly into my face. They were copulating on the wing, fused gently together and just too languid to get out of my way.

It is true that these are uncongenial times for radicalism in Australia and much of the Western world. In the last twenty years, political alternatives to the status quo seem to have faded away.

Perth has never been a radical city like Paris with its history of revolutions or Barcelona with its anarchist traditions. Nor does it have a strong radical tradition like, for example, Melbourne. But it would be silly to expect that those great waves of revolutionary politics that have swept the Western world had no local presence and, as we will see, they all did.

Liminal years around the end of an old century and the arrival of the new seem to encourage radical ideas. Workers' politics developed in Perth in the late nineteenth and early twentieth centuries, as it did in the eastern colonies and states. Indeed, such politics arrived in

Perth with the heavy immigration of gold seekers from Victoria who came to the eastern goldfields. The Western Australian working class organised into trade unions but they were often seduced into the new arbitration systems. Unions formed the Labor Party, which the institutions of parliament quickly tamed. Socialist and radical groups such as the Social Democratic Federation, the Henry George League and the Industrial Workers of the World (IWW, or the Wobblies) arrived late in the nineteenth and early in the twentieth centuries to shake up Perth's complacency and to press for more radical change. The women's movement arrived in Perth, too, to agitate for equality through women's suffrage and new institutions for women and staffed by women.

Inspired by the 1917 Bolshevik Revolution, a branch of the Communist Party of Australia appeared in Perth in 1921, but it failed and a permanent branch wasn't established until 1931, at which time it took over the mantle of radicalism from the Wobblies and, although always small, put itself at the forefront of radical causes for the next forty years. As shown in this book, communists had a hand in the unemployed campaigns of the Great Depression. They were behind Perth's fertile radical theatre scene in the 1930s and 1940s. Communist led unions supported striking Chinese seamen in Fremantle before and during World War Two. They supported the famous Aboriginal pastoral workers' strike in the Pilbara after World War 2. The Party's radical bookshops made available to Perth readers books no mainstream bookshop would sell. Long-time member Joan Williams wrote *The First Furrow*, the first history of the communist movement in Western Australia. In fighting for the release of Philip Roth's novel, *Portnoy's Complaint* in 1970, communists led the way in the battle against censorship. By then, communism was already being torn asunder by the fracturing of its own certainties and by the new ideas of 1960s radicals.

The 1960s swept through Perth as they did the rest of Australia, bringing with it a new, flourishing and youthful radical life. Student politics took a sharp turn to the Left, second wave feminists began to organise, as did early environmentalists. Aboriginal protesters took inspiration from the radical turn in the eastern states of Australia and the radical African American movements in the USA. Hippies and others began to explore the possibilities of an alternative society. The sexual revolution arrived; tuning in, turning on and dropping out – especially turning on – became a real alternative. Sydney's famous green bans had their Perth counterparts. In the 1970s gay activism arrived to fight for the repeal of laws outlawing gay sex. Together, to that brilliant soundtrack to the 1960s – rock'n'roll – these movements began to build a social and cultural revolution in Perth.

These histories could be those of any Australian city, but one thing that is peculiar to Perth is the late arrival of radicalism. Whereas Melbourne, Sydney and Adelaide can legitimately claim that their radical history began in their early days (Sydney's rebellious convicts, Melbourne's rebellious workers, Adelaide's Chartist origins), Perth did not have a sustainable radical politics until the late nineteenth century. Certainly there were radical critics of the early colony's policies regarding Aboriginal people: Robert Menli Lyon (or Robert Lyon Milne, which was his correct name) is a good example. Yagan, the Aboriginal warrior and leader, can be classed a radical. The Irish rebel convicts, the Fenians, had a fleeting presence, while radical newspapers such as the *Fremantle Herald* struggled to get traction.

It is not difficult to see why radicalism in early Perth struggled. For the first years of its life, it was little more than a village battling the elements, poor soil and little capital; sixty years after its foundation it was still a big country town, its 6500 people paling into insignificance when compared to Adelaide, which had 95 000. In 1901, on the day of Federation, and with a decade of heavy immigration from the east of people in search of gold, with 70 per cent of its population born outside the state, Perth's people numbered only 44 000 but ten years later there were 111 000. Perth had become a city. Thereafter it grew slowly until after World War 2, when the postwar baby boom and those great postwar immigration schemes saw its population rise rapidly. From a population of 268 000 in 1947, it had, by 1961, hit 475 000 and has continued apace ever since, overtaking Adelaide in the early 1980s and now threatening Brisbane to be the third largest city in Australia. Perth has long been the fastest growing capital city in the nation. Today its residents number about 2.2 million people.

Perth began its life as a village, became a market town, and then, after the goldrushes, a commercial city with its own suburbia spreading inexorably up and down the coast and inland towards the Darling Scarp. Until the building of the Kwinana strip in the 1950s, it had no heavy industry; rather, its manufacturing entailed repair, assembly and reconstruction: the Government Railway Workshops in Midland is one example, the Ford and General Motors car assembly plants in Mosman Park in the interwar years, another. Otherwise its biggest employers were in the commercial and finance sectors and the public service.

Perth became a finance city during the mining boom of the 1960s, when highrise office blocks began to replace those older, elegant Edwardian buildings that lined St Georges Terrace. As tightly packed suburbs spread the urban sprawl took over the surrounding hinterland. Then, in the boom of the 1980s, the Terrace was renewed again: inner city workers' suburbs began to become gentrified and increasing density finally came to the CBD itself as huge blocks of apartments were built. Like all cities Perth was built and rebuilt, its character changing with its skyline.

This potted history is important because radicalism is so often a phenomenon of the city. This is not to say that radicalism was unknown in the rest of Western Australia. Think of the Aboriginal resistance fighter, Jandamarra, in the Kimberley in the 1890s, the 1940s Pilbara Aboriginal pastoral workers' strike, and the hippie communes in the southwest in the 1970s and 1980s. Many of the stories in our book brought city and country together. The Wobblies had a strong presence in the eastern goldfields in the 1920s and their organisers walked their weary beat from the city to the country. Katharine Susannah Prichard wrote her major works about rural, pastoral and goldfields Western Australia. The anti-Vietnam war movement stirred passions all over WA.

We argue, however, that sustained radicalism needs the energy of the city, the collective experience of oppression or discontent among a critical mass of people. But the city need not be the size of Paris in 1789, Moscow or St Petersburg in 1917, or any of the other great European cities that revolted in 1848 and 1919. Nor need it be like the US cities that rioted and burned in the 1960s. Perth achieved that critical mass in the late nineteenth and early twentieth centuries. Critical mass intertwines with economic and social conditions and with the influx, ebb and flow of political ideologies. It is true that in Australia political ideologies were and are rarely home grown, rather they arrived from Europe, the USA and, in the 1960s and beyond, from India. However, despite the assertions of their opponents, they were never alien to Australia. They all found root here, sometimes shallow, more often deep, and ultimately took on an Australian character, drawing together hundreds, sometimes thousands, sometimes tens of thousands of followers.

What are the principles on which our radicalisms have been chosen? The first is that radicalism is contextual, a product of its time, defined by the political, social, economic and cultural context with which it conflicts. That it requires an assault on the status quo, advocates new and far-reaching changes in thinking and new ways of doing things or that, by overturning the system, it promises a better, fairer world, seems axiomatic. Of course, as the once radical becomes the status quo, what was radical then may seem anything but today. To give one example: in the 1890s, the Perth establishment was appalled at the prospect and reality of gold-digging Melbournians with their radical ideas about democracy, trade unionism and labour politics, demanding rights in pristine Western Australia. But labour quickly became Labor and its politics lost their radical tone as the party turned to the parliamentary way and moderated its demands in the search of electoral success. Soon, under sway to that rural behemoth, the conservative Australian Workers' Union (AWU), Labor's struggle came to be against those to its Right as well as those to its Left and too often joined with conservatives to crush its leftist enemies.

The second principle is that radicalism comes in a host of different forms. Thus we consider industrial and political radicalism in the field of working class politics. We also consider radical feminism, Aboriginal self-determination, environmentalism, peace movements, movements for sexual liberation and deinstitutionalisation. We consider the expression of radicalism in culture: from theatre, art, music, books and dance. We look at cultural forms that might otherwise be described as simply unruly, such as the Scarborough

Beach Snake Pit in the 1950s, for example.

The third principle we have tried our hardest to adopt is to give our choices a concrete edge, showing, where possible, the traces of our stories in Perth's urban landscapes. This has been difficult. Some buildings important to the history remain, used now for different purposes (shops, takeaways); others are long gone, replaced by office blocks and other new buildings, and carparks. The Perth Esplanade, home to demonstrations, protests and generations of orators, has also gone, replaced by glitzy highrise overlooking the water.

Some places remain. The intersection of St Georges Terrace and Barrack Street, where the 1931 Treasury riot took place, will never be lost. Miscellaneous houses and offices that housed headquarters of movements still remain, as do the floor of Red Square in the Midland Government Railway Workshops, and Solidarity Park, site of the Workers' Embassy behind Bullshit Castle – as the one-time communist and later union official Jack Marks liked to call Parliament House. Some buildings will surprise you. St George's Cathedral, that lovely old church on St Georges Terrace, was where in 1970 and 1971, the Red Dean, John Hazelwood, hosted five rock masses for peace, love, life, freedom and the environment. Of course, some protests were about buildings themselves: the 1966 campaign to save Perth's barracks, which stimulated Perth's heritage movement, the green bans on the Palace and Peninsula Hotels and Fremantle's Victoria Hall in 1973, and Bessie Rischbieth's quixotic protests against changes to the Swan River's foreshore.

Radical Perth, Militant Fremantle, then, explores the city's radical geography: the places where radicals habitually went to protest, the places associated with particular campaigns, the houses, shops and offices where they held their meetings, printed their papers and pamphlets and created their posters, the theatres and nightclubs where they staged their performances, the bookshops from which radical tracts were sold. If all roads led at one time or another to The Esplanade – Perth's Domain, its Yarra Bank, its Hyde Park Speaker's Corner – or to Parliament House and Forrest Place in the CBD, all feet walked to the flagpole when the Midland Government Railway Workshop workers decided to hold a meeting. The father of Western Australian radicalism, Monty Miller, walked from his home in East Perth to Green's Building, the Leisure Hour Club, the Mechanics Institute and the Hibernian Hall, buildings that were home to early movements such as the Theosophical Society, the Labour Church, Social Democratic Federation and the Wobblies. In Fremantle, generations of May Day marchers trooped off to The Esplanade, leaving from the Fremantle Trades Hall, where Fremantle Rajneeshees set up their ashram in 1981. In 1919 and 1998 waterside workers took on bosses and governments in dramatic and sensational disputes that had their own waterfront geography. In the 1970s feminists set up headquarters in Glendower Street, East Perth, as well as in the CBD, many moving on from The University of Western Australia (UWA), the centre of student protests in the 1960s and 1970s. Of course this radical geography changed shape with the times; there was little crossover between the geography of workers' radicalism and modern feminism, for example, and radical music has more to do with nightclubs and edge of the city festivals than with either of the above.

Why, then, a history of radical Perth? We could talk about good historians' reasons: to fill a gaping hole in Western Australian history writing, to challenge assumptions about the nature of Western Australian society, to redraw the boundaries and focus of writing about Western Australian culture and politics. It's also because these seem to be unpropitious times for radicals. Yet, radicals are always optimistic and the rise of Bernie Sanders in the USA and Jeremy Corbyn in Britain gives hope, although the rise of the Right, including the fascist Right, reminds us of the need for vigilance, which is why it is important to chart a history that can educate, inspire and exemplify the possibility of radical change.

We hope that this book will put Perth on the map in a new way. It was inspired by the publication of *Radical Melbourne: A Secret History*, published in 2001 by Jeff Sparrow and Jill Sparrow, which charted Melbourne's radical history in the years before 1939. A second volume, *Radical Melbourne: The Enemy Within*, followed in 2004 to bring the story up to the present. In the same year Ray Evans and Carole Ferrier published *Radical Brisbane: An Unruly History*, which traced Brisbane's radical history from its beginnings. In 2010 Terry Irving and Rowan Cahill added *Radical Sydney: Places, Portraits and Unruly Episodes*, covering the radical ground of Sydney's history. Then, in 2015, James Bennett, Nancy Cushing and Erik Eklund edited *Radical Newcastle*. Each book is, in effect, a walking tour of places and buildings, the visible traces of the cities' radical pasts. Inspired by these splendid examples we have decided that Perth too needs its own radical history and Australia needs its own radical Perth.

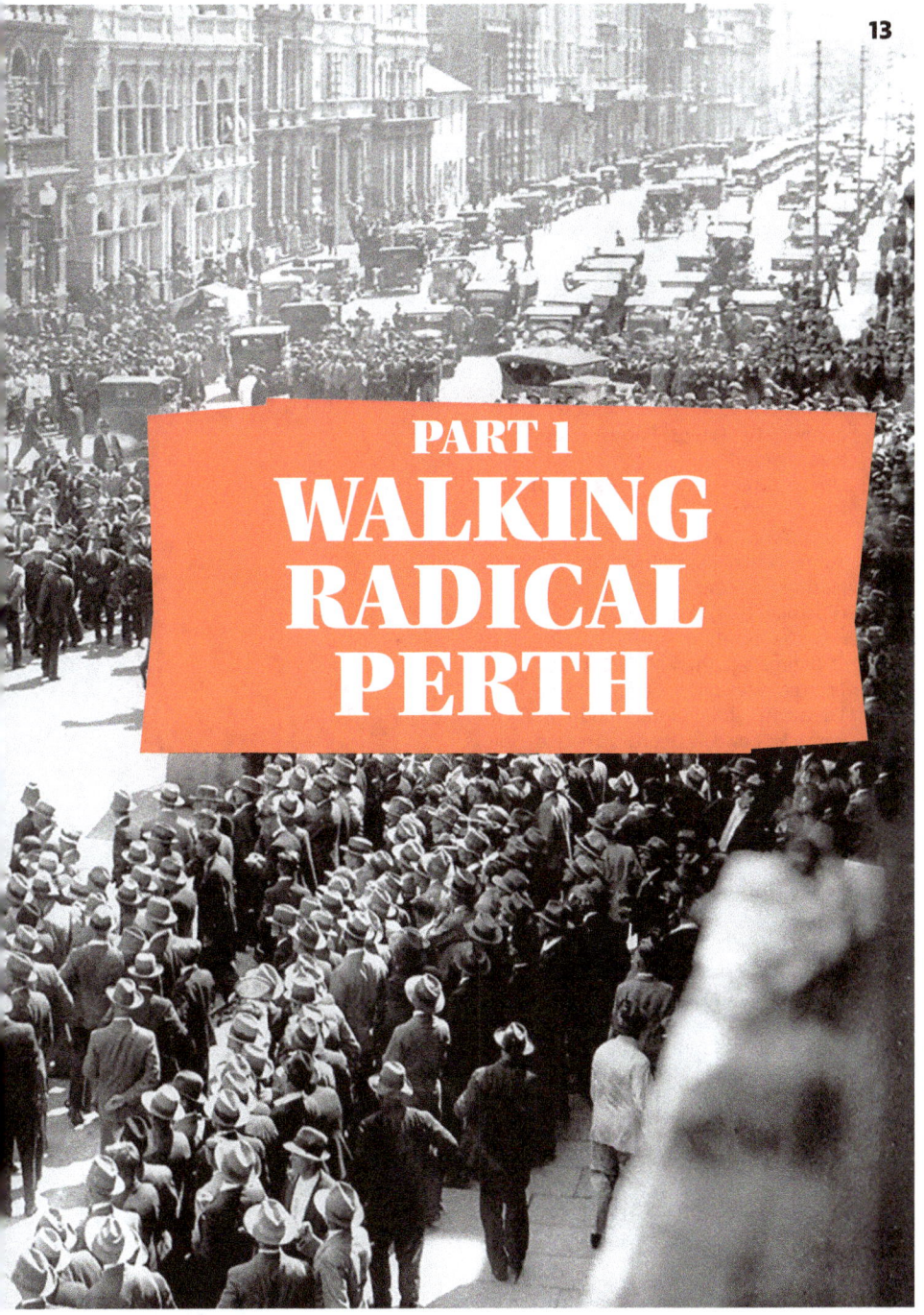

PART 1
WALKING RADICAL PERTH

LEGEND
WALKING RADICAL PERTH

1. Chung Wah Hall, James St (See chapter 1)
2. Connections Nightclub, James St (See chapter 2)
3. John Curtin at the Worker (See chapter 22)
4. Forrest Chase (see chapter 3)
5. Open area, Forrest Chase (See chapter 4)
6. Padbury Building, now walkway opposite GPO steps, Forrest Chase (See chapter 5)
7. Murray Street mall (See chapter 6)
8. Hay Street mall (See chapter 24)
9. Perth Town Hall (See chapter 7)
10. Young Australia League Hall, Murray St (See chapter 8)
11. Hibernian Hall, Murray St (See chapter 9)
12. St George's Cathedral, St Georges Terrace (See chapter 10)
13. Treasury Building, intersection of Barrack St and St Georges Terrace (See chapter 11)
14. Chancery Building, bottom of Howard St (See chapter 12)
15. Elizabeth Quay (See chapter 13)
16. Elizabeth Quay (See chapter 14)
17. Palace Hotel (See chapter 23)
18. Barracks Arch, St Georges Terrace (See chapter 15)
19. Solidarity Park, Harvest Terrace, behind Parliament House (See chapter 16)
20. Goonininup, Mounts Bay Road (See chapter 17)
21. Everywhere (See chapter 18)

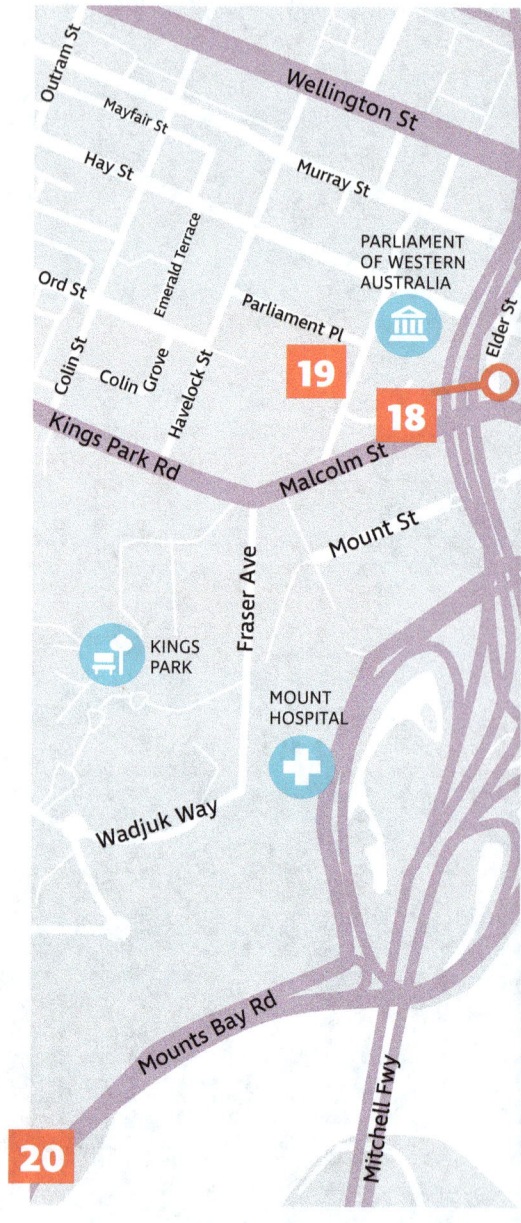

PERTH

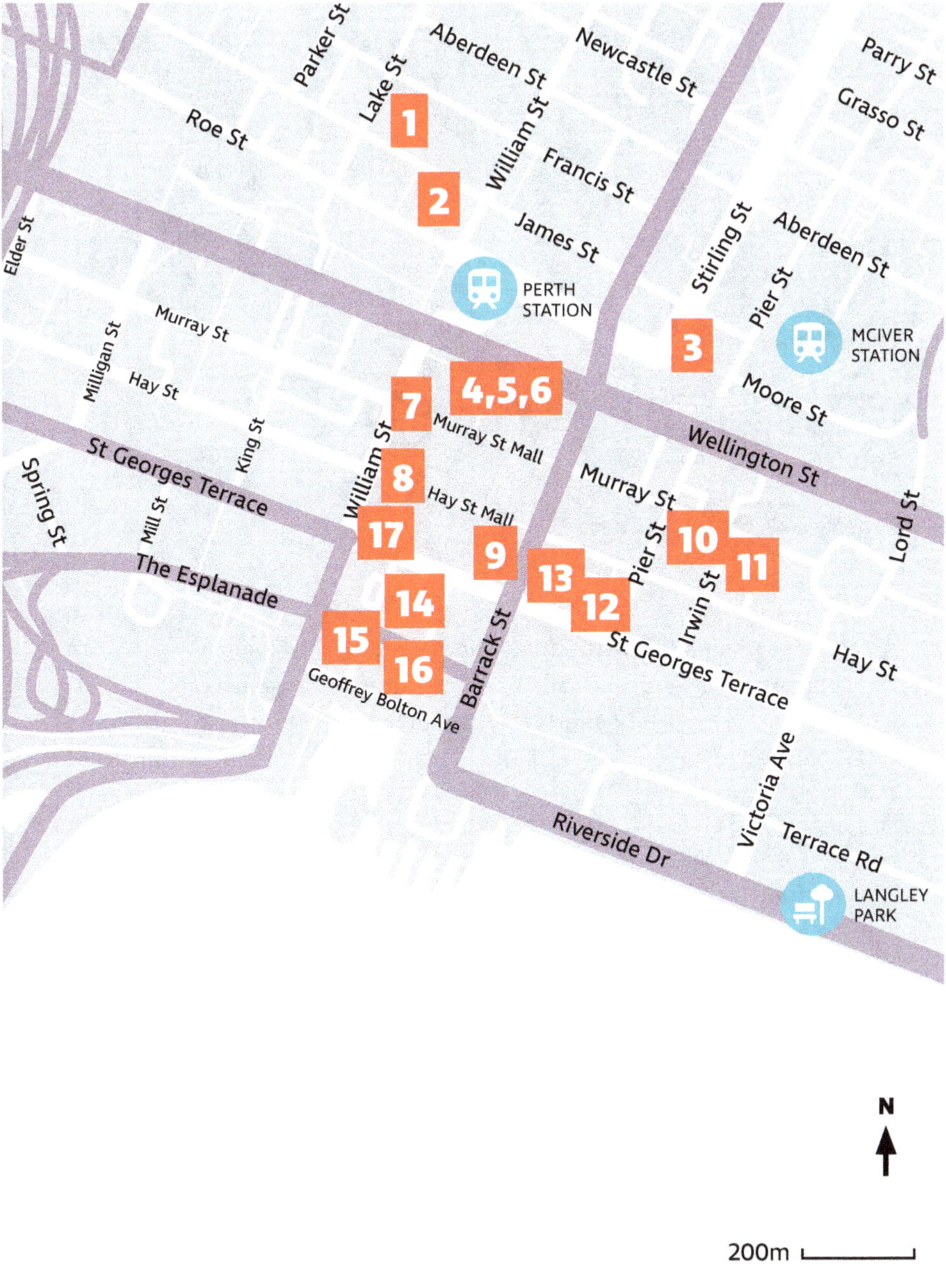

Parker St
Aberdeen St
Newcastle St
Parry St
Lake St
Grasso St
Roe St
William St
Francis St
Elder St
James St
Stirling St
Aberdeen St
Pier St
PERTH STATION
MCIVER STATION
Murray St
Milligan St
Hay St
Moore St
Wellington St
King St
William St
Murray St Mall
St Georges Terrace
Spring St
Mill St
Hay St Mall
Murray St
Lord St
Pier St
The Esplanade
Barrack St
Irwin St
St Georges Terrace
Hay St
Geoffrey Bolton Ave
Victoria Ave
Riverside Dr
Terrace Rd
LANGLEY PARK
1
2
3
4,5,6
7
8
9
10
11
12
13
14
15
16
17
N
200m

The Chung Wah Association's float, proudly displaying a large red silk and blue satin banner, featured in a parade on Trench Comforts Day, 9 September 1917

1
Perth Chinese Community's Fight for Survival

Lenore Layman

Situated on James Street in what is now the Northbridge heritage precinct is the Chung Wah Hall, opened in 1911 as the headquarters of the Chung Wah Association. It was, according to the association, to be 'a suitable place of resort for Gentlemen of the Chinese nationality residing in Western Australia for the purpose of providing and encouraging literature and education amongst the members of the Association'. Behind this reassurance of educational self-improvement, intended to soothe fears in the wider society, lay the aim of bonding Chinese residents more closely for their survival, improved welfare and protection of common interests. The new association insisted in 1909 that

> Unity is strength and an association is vitally necessary ... We are like scattered sand and it is no wonder that the Westerners are bullying us and passing stringent legislation aimed at displacing us.

By 'us', Chung Wah meant 'all Chinese' and the association promised that no regional or ancestral separations would divide members. Rather, all would be bonded – 'everyone together whoever you are'. Collectively, they would stand more chance of resisting discrimination and ensuring a fair go.

Built in Federation Free Style, the two storey Chung Wah Hall announced its permanent presence in Perth's urban landscape with its solid brick structure, balustraded parapet, iron filigree front balcony, elaborate detailing and an imposing front entrance with tessellated tiled floor and timbered staircase. Perth's Chinese merchants and shopkeepers who established the association and its hall, led by inaugural president Louis Wah Louey (1909–12, 1914–15), were determined to imprint a Chinese presence in Western Australia's overtly hostile social environment. While this presence was not assertive (indeed it was most often self-effacing) the Chinese community organised to insist on its own existence, legal rights and resistance to unequal treatment.

The Hall was located 'over the line' in James Street in the centre of the community's business and social life, surrounded by Chinese shops, restaurants and places of licit and illicit entertainment. Between Roe and James Streets were the major produce markets used by market gardeners. Goods imported from China could be easily purchased, letters written and translated, mail collected, meetings held and friends encountered. This Chinatown met the community's social and cultural needs and sustained its members who worked at market gardening, laundry work, shopkeeping, furniture making and domestic service, but lived in economic and social isolation from the wider society, on its margins.

From its establishment in 1909 the Chung Wah Association represented Perth's Chinese residents who sought fundamental change to Western Australian society and culture. Members did not march in the streets in protest, hold public rallies, make provocative speeches or confront the police in any way; rather, they eschewed all direct action and always avoided attracting public and media attention to themselves. Instead, members of the association utilised the tools of a democratic order – written appeals to authorities, petitions, court actions and letters to newspaper editors – to seek the elimination of discrimination. Could such a non-confrontational approach be called radical? The means may not have been but the goal certainly was: an end to discrimination against a racial minority and therefore greater equality and justice. Theirs was a quiet, tempered radicalism. It had to be, given the widespread hostility they faced.

By the early twentieth century, fierce anti-Chinese attitudes and policies prevailed in WA. Chinese people were virtually barred from entry to the country. When labour was in short supply after the end of convict transportation, the colony had imported Chinese indentured labourers and servants. With the aim of temporarily utilising Chinese labour without according them any recognition as settlers the *Imported Labour Registry Act*s of 1874, 1882, 1884 and 1897 established ever tighter controls on employers and contract workers. The last of these Acts confined these indentured labourers to the north of the colony. Colonial legislation to restrict Chinese immigration culminated in the *Immigration Restriction Act 1897*, which established the use of a dictation test that could be given to a prospective immigrant in any language to prohibit the entry of anyone deemed undesirable, a practice that foreshadowed the Australia wide legislation of 1901, commonly known as the White Australia Policy. WA had been slower than its sister colonies to erect 'great white walls' but, when they were built in the goldrush era, they were just as high.

Discriminatory colonial legislation aimed at those Chinese who were already resident in the country also escalated from the 1880s to the 1900s. The *Sharks Bay Pearl Shell Fishery Act 1886* barred Chinese from obtaining a shallow pearling licence, while the *Goldfields Act 1886* prohibited any 'Asiatic or African alien' from holding a miner's right or lease. Then the *Factories Act 1904* struck again at the survival of the Chinese community by harshly discriminating against Chinese owned and run furniture factories and laundries, where most Chinese enterprise was concentrated. The Act imposed more limited working hours and higher registration fees on Chinese businesses than on their non-Chinese competitors, blocked all new Chinese owners or occupiers from factory businesses and required that furniture be branded with the words 'Asiatic labour'.

This plethora of legislative discrimination resulted in shrinking Chinese businesses and an ageing community unable to renew itself because wives and relatives could not emigrate. Adding to these legislative shackles was intense anti-Chinese public sentiment, particularly in the press and growing labour movement. Their representations of Chinese residents as 'a giant evil in the land' hardened public opinion and made it more extreme.

Chinese residents responded determinedly but strategically to the legislative discrimination, avoiding anything that might inflame the febrile atmosphere within which they were forced to live. In 1886, sixteen Chinese Sharks Bay pearlers employed the Perth legal firm Stone and Burt and petitioned the governor, calling for a reversal of their exclusion from shallow pearling that had been instituted in the *Sharks Bay Pearl Shell Fishery Act*.

> Your Petitioners and others who have been engaged in this industry for years would be shut out from working the banks and would therefore lose our livelihood. Our boats and plant would be useless to us and we would be utterly ruined.

This petition did not bear fruit but persistent lobbying did result in a government payment of £1000 compensation for the loss of value of the fishing boats and other plant. Exclusion from the industry could not be reversed.

When the *Factories Act 1904* sought to exclude Chinese from WA factories and workshops, Chinese furniture makers and laundrymen employed lawyer C. J. R. Le Mesurier to petition the British government, asking that the Act be disallowed because it abrogated Britain's treaty obligations to China, which required that the Chinese be treated 'on the same footing as all other races, and that there shall be no disqualification of colour or race permitted against them'. The Act perpetrated 'a cruel wrong' for which, at the very least, there should be just compensation. The protest was also sent to the Chinese, Japanese, Indian and Afghan governments. When the press reported that the Colonial Office had confidentially requested reconsideration of the legislation it caused outrage in the WA parliament.

At the same time, Chinese businesses used the legal system to extend their resistance, challenging the *Factories Act 1904* clause by clause. In six cases between 1905 and 1912 Chinese firms that had been successfully prosecuted appealed their convictions; four cases were successful. WA Minister for Commerce and Labour J. S. Hicks commented in December 1905 on the outcome: 'There is no doubt that as the *Factories Act* stands, the Constitutional law will not allow it to have full force.' In 1912, the last year of overt protests against the *Factories Act*, Chinese businesses gained the support of the Chinese Consul-General in their campaign. He spoke to the premier about the registration fees and the regulation requiring furniture to be stamped. All this campaigning failed to change the wording of the Act, but there was some relief. Only the clauses relating to wages and hours of work in furniture factories were enforced; the rest were not.

In 1912 Perth's Chinese community established a Chamber of Commerce to try to strengthen their voice. And they protested again in 1920 when another discriminatory Act, the *Factories and Shops Act*, replaced the 1904 Act. The Chung Wah Association presented to parliament a petition signed by eighty members together with letters to all parliamentarians, while twenty-seven Chinese laundrymen submitted another petition, all without result.

In 1901 Western Australian Chinese had joined their fellows around Australia to protest the imposition of the new Commonwealth's *Immigration Restriction Act*. The Reverend Paul Soong Quong, a leader of WA's Chinese community, wrote a letter in protest to the prime minister:

> Speaking for the majority of my Countrymen in this State I can attest that they are industrious, frugal, honest and good living as any other class of citizen in the State, that they do not, as it is frequently asserted, work for a less wage than Europeans, but always demand fair remunerative payment.

In 1902 several businessmen petitioned the Chinese emperor for assistance to fight the Act. These appeals continued, with WA Chinese representatives calling on the Australian government in 1905 to treat them not as an enemy but as Australians.

Perth's Chinese people tried as best they could to show that they were Australians in everything but name. If allowed they joined in wider community events, taking part in celebrations for a Royal visit and coronation in 1910. Active in fundraising during World War 1, they provided a decorated float for a 1914 parade and carried the Chung Wah's large red silk and blue satin banner in parades on Trench Comforts Day and Rose Day in 1917, as they did later to celebrate war's end in 1918. They also contributed to local charities, including hospitals, the Red Cross, the Home of Peace and orphanages.

The Chung Wah Association provided an effective welfare service to all WA Chinese. In 1911 any old or sick member who requested help was given £4 to return to China. As the Association declined in strength in line with the community it represented, it was forced to reduce this assistance to £1. As well, money was collected to pay defence lawyers for Chinese who were caught in the legal system net. Community members were keenly bonded to their homeland, and contributed frequently to causes in China, particularly to disaster relief. They were nationalist in sympathy and strong supporters of the Kuomintang, giving generously to nationalist political causes, hoping that their political powerlessness in Australia might change as China became a stronger, united and more modern country.

Their hard work, self-effacement and financial generosity were to little avail. The existing Chinese community could only struggle on as the inability to renew its population with family immigration put more and more pressure on the community's viability. By 1947, of the 1539 who had been resident in 1901, just 385 Chinese remained. Demographic renewal by immigration and community revival required changes to public attitudes and an end to legislative discrimination, changes that were not evident until the mid 1960s with the beginnings of relaxation of the White Australia immigration policy. At the same time attitudes, especially among young people, were changing as endemic racism began to come under critical scrutiny. The Whitlam government's ratification of the UN's *International Convention on the Elimination of All Forms of Racial Discrimination* and its passing of the *Racial Discrimination Act*, both in 1975, were important milestones on Australia's path to becoming a multiracial society. That path has been rocky in places. During the 1980s, for instance, the Australian Nationalist Movement, led by Jack van Tongeren, fire bombed a number of Perth's Asian restaurants and businesses and preached race hatred until van

Tongeren was imprisoned in 1989. Despite such setbacks, Australia has moved steadily towards full multiculturalism. Indeed, by 1985 the WA Minister for Multicultural and Ethnic Affairs named the former immigration restriction policy as 'one of the darkest chapters in Australian history'.

In the early 1970s the Chinese population and the Chung Wah Association began to revive and the hall was restored and renovated. Welfare services recommenced and in 1974 Mandarin language classes began. By the 1980s the community was flourishing. It conducted all sorts of cultural activities to entertain the community itself and the wider society – a dragon boat club, a lion dance troupe, a literary and arts group, t'ai chi classes and a group for teaching Chinese dancing and singing; a youth group was formed in 1990. Chinese New Year and the Moon Festival became celebrations for everyone. In 1985, at the time of the Chung Wah Association's seventy-fifth anniversary, its president reflected on a turbulent history.

> The strong sense of community and family solidarity are the hallmarks of our community. These core values are those that help us overcome adversity in the search for a rightful role in this land which we have made our home and that of our children ...
>
> We strongly believe that retaining our culture, language and heritage, handed down to us through thousands of years, will enable us to participate and develop a truly multicultural Australia, one where minorities have the same rights as the majority as citizens.

In its own way it is a quietly radical history with much suffering and many defeats but eventual victory.

2
CAMP and Gay Rights
Charlie Fox and Bri McKenzie

Four unsuccessful legislative attempts were made – 1973, 1977, 1984 and 1987 – before homosexual sex in private between consenting adult males was decriminalised in Western Australia. After some dramatic politics in WA's Legislative Council the relevant Bill finally passed in 1989 but as a consequence of the compromises needed to get it through the parliament, it was an Act with significant limitations. Nevertheless, sex in private between consenting men over the age of twenty-one was henceforth legal in WA. More than anyone else, the organisation Campaign Against Moral Persecution WA, or CAMP WA, was responsible for decriminalisation. CAMP WA had been formed in Perth in May 1971 as part of a growing national movement of gay men and women. Headed in WA by Graham Douglas and Brian Lindbergh, it grew quickly and by the end of the year had at least 500 members. CAMP lasted for nineteen years.

Soon after its foundation CAMP organised the first law reform public meeting. The packed meeting, held at a small hall in Shenton Park, was chaired by a Catholic priest and supported by Ray Young, a Liberal member of the WA parliament. Its pressure on the Tonkin Labor government led to the 1974 Royal Commission on Homosexuality, which recommended decriminalisation.

The arrival of CAMP was an extraordinary moment in Western Australian history. There had never previously been a politics organised around an alternative sexual identity, although, as gay groups often pointed out, society itself was organised around heterosexuality and actively repressed alternatives. However, the sexual revolution of the 1960s did hit WA, relationships between sex, procreation and marriage were decoupled and spaces for different sexualities appeared openly. In addition, a new progressive politics of human and civil rights took up issues of sexuality. As the slogan said, the state had no business in what people did in their bedrooms.

Until 1989, male homosexual sex was illegal in WA and could, in theory, be punished by anything up to a twelve year prison sentence and a whipping, although in practice such sentences were no longer applied. (Lesbians were treated very differently; lesbian sex was never illegal.) Despite decriminalisation in 1989, police still entrapped and charged gay men on beats, places where gay men went for casual sex. Around the same beats, many young homophobic men still made a sport of what they called poofta bashing, in some cases to hide their own sexuality. Despite the progress in gay social and cultural life in Perth, there were still dangerous aspects of life as a gay person that remained even after decriminalisation. For CAMP WA, decriminalisation was necessary to give homosexual men the right to exercise the same rights to their sexuality as heterosexuals had.

In tandem with its active agitation for decriminalisation, CAMP was active from the outset in many other areas, including policing of homophobic violence, discrimination in employment, biased presentations in sex education and the portrayal of gay men in the media. CAMP held regular public meetings, appeared on television and radio, and addressed hundreds of social, political and educational groups, including high schools. It demonstrated against known homophobes, defended gays and lesbians and provided information, argument and myth busting. It was the most constant public voice of Perth's gay community.

CAMP also established subsidiary organisations. The most important was the Homosexual Counselling and Information Service (HCIS), later renamed the Gay and Lesbian Counselling Service and eventually Living Proud. HCIS grew out of its Dial-a-Friend Helpline and in 1974 began training counsellors. Volunteers worked the phones for callers who simply wanted to know what was happening in town, particularly those wanting advice and reassurance on coming out. CAMP was also associated with Gay Activities Groups Services (GAGS), an organising, resourcing and fundraising body that facilitated some of Perth's premier gay organisations and events. CAMP WA also ran its own newsletter, *West Campaigner*, produced by a group headed by Geoff Davis.

While getting issues into the public sphere was of prime importance, so was creating spaces where gay people could meet in comfort and safety. In 1971 CAMP set up the Spartan Club in its West Perth clubrooms, where it ran curry nights, discussions, indoor sports and other activities. Cocktail parties, cabarets, BBQs, car rallies and film and card evenings were also on the menu, all bringing a semblance of 'normal' social life to gays. CAMP also encouraged commercial outlets to get involved, so hotels, bars saunas and other venues opened their doors to gay patrons. Ultimately, CAMP's social doings enabled the emergence of an overt gay subculture in Perth.

The number of gay organisations grew. By the mid 1970s, there were associations of gay men and women at each of Perth's tertiary institutions: UWA, WAIT (later Curtin University) and Murdoch.

Gay Catholics and Gay Anglicans set up support groups. There were Hellenic and Jewish gay groups. Those interested in sporting activities formed the Gay Outdoors Group. A Gay Broadcasting Collective broadcast on WAIT's radio station 6NR. As time passed, the number of groups increased.

CAMP WA had only one rival. Perth Gay Liberation had arrived in Perth in 1977, with branches at all of the state's three university campuses. In effect a Perth branch of a militant tendency in gay politics in eastern Australia in the 1970s, it wanted to fight the wider politics of gay oppression, seek relationships with other liberation groups against common enemies and confront rather than negotiate. Clearly, Gay Liberation was more radical than CAMP. Its primary aim, as set out in a February 1980 meeting of the group, was 'political[,] ... organising and fighting against the oppression of Lesbians and Male Homosexuals in our society'. It thought 'a radical change in societies [sic] perception of sexuality and sexual roles' was needed. Thus, in 1978, it promoted gay identity, holding a Gay Pride Week and a Gay Pride march and sexuality weeks at UWA and WAIT. In 1980, it took part in a National Day of Action on gay issues. It was also very conscious of its maleness, aware that an inherent sexism might be found among its own members.

The relationship between gay men and women was an important issue for gay political groups. For many years, while CAMP still had an office and meeting space, Wednesday nights were always women's nights and where possible women counsellors were rostered to take counselling service calls. However, early in CAMP's history, it became apparent that, although there were female members and some women on the executive, men dominated. This led to a concerted effort by women members to create a space for themselves in the

CAMP clubroom and to develop their own politics. In 1975 a lesbian activists subgroup was set up in CAMP to agitate around women's issues generally, but particularly around issues concerning lesbians. The omission of sexual preference in anti-discrimination laws was an early one.

It isn't clear how long this group lasted, but later, CAMP women set up the Wimin's Room, describing itself as Perth's only all lesbian social group that organised women only trips to the country, skate nights, and film and discussion evenings. It was run from CAMP's offices but tended to portray itself as non-political, perhaps suggesting that Perth lesbians weren't as radical as their eastern states sisters, many of whom left the gay movement when radical feminism and lesbianism aligned in the late 1970s. In mid 1985 this group became more overtly political and renamed itself the Gay Women's Action Lobby, announcing in CAMP's *West Campaigner* that this was 'the first time in Perth that a group of gay women has got up and been vocal and political'. It aimed to raise awareness of gay women's interests; it retained a continuing connection to CAMP, which, in 1986, in its list of to do's, included developing the lesbian movement.

While CAMP's social group may have been responsible for Perth's openly gay subculture, the commercialisation of gay culture proved to be a double edged sword for the organisation. As commercial entertainment venues – especially Connections nightclub, established in 1974 – enticed gay people away from CAMP clubrooms, CAMP offerings fell away. At the same time, the number of organisations, events, entertainments and celebrations, gay friendly businesses and businesses run by gays seemed to increase every year, as business recognised the pull of the gay dollar.

Among the highlights of the gay calendar were the Arts Ball and the Gay Olympics. The Ball had elements of variety, burlesque, drag, cross-dressing and fancy dress, as fashions from the USA gay scene penetrated Perth. The Gay Olympics, sponsored by gay-friendly businesses, pitted teams against each other in events such as sprints and relays, fun team sports such tug of war, and more flamboyant events, such as handbag throwing and high-heeled races.

Over the years, new entrants appeared on Perth's gay entertainment scene: bars and hotels such as the Clarendon and the Red Lion, nightclubs, Beaufort 565 sauna, coffee shops, including Pinkles, not for profit social groups such as Society Seven, raunchy events such as the Sleaze Balls, and organised parties where male strippers and skimpily attired waiters mixed with drag queens and people in fancy dress. Some of these places and events were for men and women, but others were segregated into for guys only, ladies' nights and for wimin only.

From the 1980s new gay magazines also circulated. The older magazines, CAMP's *West Campaigner* and Gay Liberation's *Gay Images*, continued, looking more and more earnest against the backdrop of a newfound raunchiness in *Western Gay*, *Gay Call* and *Westside Observer*. Although active in one political campaign, as we will see, these new publications were less about gay politics and more about hedonism and sexuality. They were men's magazines that didn't seem much interested in the doings of gay women.

This new and growing gay subculture had profound implications for gay and lesbian politics. When Sydney activist Craig McGregor came to Perth in 1982, he identified one of the movement's greatest problems as 'a split between political gay men and women and those individuals who identify with what we call lesbian/gay subculture'. While the emergence of a non-political gay subculture was evident in

Perth, there were few debates about it.

If it didn't reach the level of debate, there were constant complaints in both men's and women's organisations about the political load being carried by a small body of activists. Even while the number of openly gay people was increasing there was a long term decline in CAMP's membership. In 1987, the Law Reform Coalition complained that, in trying to get a petition up to support law reform, it 'met with almost total disinterest by gay people'.

One issue of huge significance for all elements in the homosexual community was the advent of AIDS. For gay Australians, AIDS was never just a health issue; it was also deeply political. The disease – understood by the broader public in the early 1980s to affect only homosexual men – was an obvious threat to the gains of the previous decade.

Indeed, the acceptance of the fact of homosexuality was an enduring theme of Australia's response to AIDS and a significant part of the reason Australia was so successful at quickly bringing the disease under control. National AIDS infection rates peaked early. There were 2500–3000 new infections in 1982–83, which number dropped sharply to 1500 in 1985, and subsequently stabilised at about 500 per year after that. This success was the result of the partnership between gay activists and federal, state and territory governments, who worked together to fund a coherent safe sex message.

Importantly, campaigns around safe sex were delivered by the gay community to the gay community through the gay press and were presented so as to promote and normalise safe homosexual sex. On government committees and through AIDS councils, which were set up countrywide during the early 1980s, gay activists became respected sources of information and embodied a new status hitherto unknown to gay men.

The gay community in WA was quick to organise around the AIDS issue. In July 1982, before the first case of AIDS had even been reported in Australia, *West Campaigner* warned its readers about the risks of new sexually transmitted diseases (STDs) affecting gay men, including gay-related immunodeficiency disease, what was then known simply as GRID. From January 1983, public meetings about AIDS were held regularly in Perth. CAMP's counselling service designed an STD brochure that included information on AIDS prevention. Publications such as *Western Gay* and *West Campaigner* were active throughout 1983 and 1984 in bringing AIDS information to readers, and groups such as CAMP and GAGS were central in campaigning for HIV screening services. The state's first screening facility was established in April 1983 at Royal Perth Hospital's Clinical Immunology clinic, thanks in part to the lobbying undertaken by Perth's gay activists.

WA had its first confirmed case of HIV infection in late 1983; in 1984 there were fifteen new infections. The following year the number jumped to 100, including, for the first time, one woman. Rates peaked in 1986 at 104 new infections. The subsequent reduction in HIV infection rates across the state mirrored national trends and highlighted the success of the WA gay community in promoting HIV screening within at risk groups. In 1995 there were only thirty-nine new infections statewide, the lowest annual infection rate since the 1986 peak.

As deaths from AIDS began to increase during the 1980s, action on the disease at the national level intensified. In June 1983, the National Health and Medical Research Council (NHMRC) set up its first working party on AIDS and in September that year the first national community AIDS body, the Australian AIDS Action Committee was set up in Melbourne. In late 1984 the NHMRC established its National

Tel. 224561 (after 6pm)

CLUBROOMS
Well, the Clubrooms at 79 Outram St. West Perth are operating and many members are using them. They are open from 6pm to midnight, Sunday through to Thursday, and till 3.am on Friday and Saturday. BUT THEY NEED YOUR PATRONAGE!! Without the help of each and every member of the Campaign we cannot hope to maintain them. Come along as often as you can and bring your friends.
- (i) ROSTER: Not everyone has indicated that they are available for the roster -- have you responded?? Please let us know as soon as possible when you are able to help out of an evening.
- (ii) ATTENDANCE: The first two nights of operation, the rostered persons did not turn up(apologies received but at a late hour). Members cannot expect the senior officers of the club to be on "duty" every night. You must turn up when rostered, and you must notify the club well in advance(about a week), if you are unable to attend. Now, how about it: we have worked hard to get the premises, it's up to all of us to see that they don't fizzle out in the first month!!!

EVENTS
Notice of all events will be posted on the notice board in the hallway. Please read this regularly so that you do not miss out on anything. Please note the following coming events:-
- (i) The Club will open on Christmas Day if members want it. Let us know if you are likely to drop in and we will open it at about 10.am. Once again, this is up to YOU!
- (ii) BOXING DAY: A beach picnic for all members and friends. Everyone is welcome. We leave the Clubrooms at 10.30am sharp on Sunday 26th Dec. and travel about 20 miles north to a PRIVATE beach and large shack. Bring bathers, food, drinks etc. This is going to be a day to remember so let's have it well patronized. NO COSTS!
- (iii) NEW YEAR'S EVE: We will have a party in the Clubrooms for members only. Club opens at about 8.00pm(bring own drinks). Due to numbers, note members only!
- (iv) B-B-Q EACH SUNDAY: From Sunday 12th Dec., and every Sunday after, (excluding Boxing Day), we will have a B-B-Q in the backyard for members and friends. All you bring is your own drinks. NOTE: we urgently need someone to look after the small amount of organization required. We can't leave it up to the President and Secretary every darn week. Is there someone who hasn't offered his or her services and who can carry out this small task? It involves mainly buying meat and salads. Please let us know.

DONATIONS REQUIRED
The Clubrooms are in operation due to the generosity of a number of members who have offered donations and loans. There are still many members who have not contributed anything at this stage. We still need this money: please don't assume that because everything is in operation that we are financially secure- WE ARE NOT. Remember, we have a lot of loans to repay. How about it you wealthy members who have not given anything? Send your $25, $50, ect to the Clubrooms Committee.

MATERIALS REQUIRED
The following items are required for the Clubrooms and any member who can see his or her way to donating them should contact us soon.
- (i) A scrabble set.
- (ii) A large bookcase (in any condition)
- (iii) Books(old,new,bound, paperback,any type), magazines.
- (iv) Small tinkle bell (sounds like Peter Pan and Wendy!!). This is needed for the Coffee Shop.
- (v) A double-basin stainless steel sink! and a PLUMBER, repeat,

Front page of Campaigner, the first Gay publication in Perth, 1971

AIDS Taskforce, which coordinated the policy response of state and territory governments and worked with the gay community in devising and implementing prevention strategies, including promoting the safe sex message.

In WA the state Labor government had also begun taking more decisive action on HIV. In early 1985, two representatives of CAMP's counselling service were appointed to a state government subcommittee on AIDS education and publicity. The inclusion of the gay community in AIDS policy making came about after two years of lobbying the Health Department, which had hitherto insisted that AIDS was a medical matter and that community involvement was therefore not needed.

Despite such challenges, WA's gay community was among the most effective and active in reducing AIDS infections and bringing information to the local gay community. CAMP printed leaflets on safe sex that were distributed around the beats. Australia's first safe sex pamphlet was produced and distributed throughout 1983 at Connections nightclub. On the initiative of CAMP president Jeff Hayler and initially funded by GAGs, the Western Australian AIDS Council (WAAC) was established in May 1985. WAAC was unique in Australia in that it deliberately set out to be broadly community-based and included representatives from all the groups potentially affected by AIDS: the gay community, injecting drug users, haemophiliacs and sex workers. In 1986, WAAC set up the first AIDS helpline in WA, which educated members of the public about AIDS and HIV. The organisation was also involved in the provision of sex education at Perth schools and, from 1988, the distribution of condoms at Perth's sex onsite venues.

WAAC first received state government funding in 1986; the introduction of the National HIV/AIDS strategy in 1989 saw WAAC receive more. HIV drug treatments were becoming available in Australia and reductions in rates of AIDS infections and deaths from HIV have largely been attributed to these. But in WA, it was the work of the gay community that laid the groundwork for the effective management the crisis.

Meanwhile, CAMP kept up the pressure on law reform, forming a new body, the Homosexual Law Reform Coalition, to fight the battle for decriminalisation. This was not straightforward, however, and CAMP refused to support Labor MLC Bob Hetherington's attempts to reform the laws in 1984 and 1987, objecting to the differences in the age of consent for heterosexual and homosexual sex, notwithstanding that Labor policy called for a common age of consent of 16. There were also problems about the language of and penalties for 'indecency' and 'gross indecency', the former describing illegal heterosexual sex, the latter illegal homosexual sex. David Myers, one of the leaders of CAMP, wrote to Hetherington. The entire Bill, he said, 'underscores the attitude that homosexuals are second rate citizens, unequal before the law'.

Although gay groups were well aware of the consequences of criminalisation in the AIDS era, it was AIDS that led to the introduction of the 1989 reform bill. A group of doctors began to lobby for reform, pointing out how difficult it was to get gay men to admit to having HIV while gay male sex was illegal. The Gay Law Reform Group quickly jumped on board. This time the Labor government made sure it had the gay movement on side before it took the Bill to parliament. The usual conservative elements were still opposed, but reform already had the support of the major churches, legal groups and the media and opinion polls recorded majority support. Although some in the gay movement still opposed the proposed age of consent (still eighteen), most supported the Bill. But the movement seemed surprisingly insouciant. One spokesperson told the *West Australian* that 'it would make little difference to the gay community but would be an important step in winning wider public acceptance of homosexuality'. Gay culture was now so strong that the laws against homosexual sex were, for many, simply irrelevant.

Opposition MLC Peter Foss crossed the floor, giving the government the votes needed to pass the Bill. But Foss insisted on twenty-one as the age of consent, other inequitable amendments and a crude preamble stating that parliament didn't approve of homosexuality. The gay community and the government accepted these with gritted teeth but were underwhelmed. A spokesperson said: 'The bill's passage did not call for dancing in the street, but there would not be a funeral.' The (amended) Bill, became law.

CAMP WA continued its work long after its eastern states branches had disappeared, a longevity unparalleled in Australian gay politics. By the later 1980s, however, its time had come and in 1990 it was wound up. By this time the new expressive subculture dominated, interested more in identity, hedonism and entertainment than civic politics. When Perth's annual Pride March began in 1990, the public celebration of gay sexuality and culture had arrived.

But activism didn't disappear. The group Gay and Lesbian Equality worked with younger activists to keep law reform on the agenda. The Labor government elected in 2001 reduced the age of consent to 16 and in 2002 and 2004 repealed or amended a raft of other discriminatory laws. In 2017, after a 13-year struggle, in which Perth activists participated through Equal Love WA, marriage equality became law. We have achieved a lot, but with new attacks on LGBTI rights such as the Morrison Liberal government's Religious Discrimination Bill the struggle continues.

3
Forrest Place Protests
Lenore Layman

> *Political and personal passions both found their place.*
> *Deep-held emotions wanted their expression*
> *And democracy had to firmly put its case.*
> *Politicians spruiked here, rallies gathered.*
> *People expressed things that mattered most.*

Robert Drewe, 2012
Engraved in granite, paving at Forrest Place

Constructed in 1922 to house impressive federal buildings on a central Perth city site, Forrest Place quickly proved popular for protest rallies as well as official celebrations. The vantage point afforded by the imposing steps of the new General Post Office (GPO) became a magnet for public spectacle, and protesters of all kinds embraced a new space for collective action. When these protests were added to the CBD mix of shoppers, commercial activity and road traffic, congestion threatened and the authorities were more than ready to deal with it, using provisions in the *Traffic Act 1919*, which made traffic a state responsibility managed by the police. As a result, for the next six decades Forrest Place saw irregular but fierce conflicts between the forces of law and order and dissenters' assertion of their freedoms of speech, association and peaceful assembly.

The first came during the 1930s when the unemployed tried to include Forrest Place among their meeting venues, but the *Traffic Act* required prior police permission for meetings and it was not forthcoming. Those meetings that did go ahead in Forrest Place in defiance of the rules led to confrontations – some of them jocular, others not so much. A protest in June 1930 about the establishment of a camp for single unemployed at Blackboy Hill to push the men out of public sight saw small groups challenge the police using the anonymity of the crowd to unsettle their authority. The *West Australian* on 6 June described the fun.

> Protesters baited police by commencing mock struggles amongst themselves. When the constables attempted to push through the densely packed crowd to investigate the commotion that ensued, the unemployed would fall back, the mimic disputants would separate and a laugh would go up.

On the night of the Treasury Building demonstration in March 1931, around 500 unemployed and numerous spectators gathered to protest police actions that had occurred earlier in the day. One speaker, Ernest McWilliams, was arrested, and scuffles broke out with the police who used batons to break up the gathering. The *West Australian* on 7 March reported that

> Some of the crowd displayed a marked disinclination to be moved on and had to be hustled along. Three men who hampered the efforts of the constables to clear the streets were charged only with being under the influence of liquor.

Soapbox orators loved the GPO steps. One was Violet Wilkins, a fiery IWW member, who was frequently arrested in central Perth between

1930 and 1941 for speaking without a permit, being disorderly, creating a disturbance and using insulting language. She was a passionate advocate for the unemployed. Protesting from the steps in 1932 to a crowd of approximately 200 people about 'the starvation wages paid to girls' led to fourteen days imprisonment. Taken away by the police she shouted from the car: 'Fellow workers, there is plenty of food in the warehouses and stores. Go and get it. I will fight and keep on fighting until the red flag is flying in the workers' commonwealth.'

Protests continued through the 1930s. In 1938 labourer Patrick Kearney used the GPO steps without a permit to protest his continuing unemployment and 'misfortunes on the Goldfields … I have been victimised by this so-called Democracy', he shouted. He served three days in gaol in default of a 10 shillings fine but refused to desist so was imprisoned again – this time for seven days – for the same offence in January 1939. According to the *Mirror,* he was unrepentant.

> I fought in the last war, so did many of you. And here are recruiting posters telling us it would be manly to fight in the next. The same men sooling us as sooled us in 1914. It might be manly, but is it humane; is it Christian? Millions being spent on preparing defences. How much interest is being taken in your children in peacetime? Ask them for money for bread and they sneer at you; ask them for money for a uniform and you're a hero.

Released from prison undeterred, he spoke again from the steps, this time fined £5 or fifteen days imprisonment in default. His protests continued until 1941 when his comments on the war voiced on The Esplanade earned him six months imprisonment. According to the *Daily News* of 17 June Kearney declared: 'If Hitler took control of us it would only be a change of masters as far as I am concerned … I am not frightened of the bug-house. I've been there before.' Patrick Kearney, Violet Wilkins and others drew hundreds of Perth people to the spectacles they created through the 1930s until the total war effort after 1941 lost them their audience. How many listeners were influenced by the radicals' protests is unclear; what is clear is that authorities took seriously their threat to 'good order'.

This police control, making spontaneous protests impossible and hemming all demonstrations with multiple restrictions, fell particularly on communists in the postwar period. In December 1950, for instance, six months into the Korean War, five young people – 'Rivo' Gandini, Venie Holmgren, Ted Zeffert, George Cattermole and Brian Carey – were arrested in Forrest Place for carrying placards without permission. One read, 'Ban Atom Bomb, Not Beer', another, 'Withdraw Australian Troops From Korea'. Despite claims of victimisation – other groups, particularly religious ones, carried placards without interference – all five were fined; four were members of the Eureka Youth League and one a member of the University Labour Club.

Australia's involvement in the Vietnam war and the reintroduction of conscription, its requirement for overseas service introduced in 1965, precipitated another generation of radicals into confrontations with the police. Protests quickly escalated in size and turmoil. A jointly organised anti-conscription rally in Forrest Place on 11 June 1966 drew a crowd of 500 or so to swell the numbers of Saturday morning shoppers. 'One, two, three, four / We don't want another war' the crowd shouted as a young man (without a permit) began to address them and three others held aloft their burning draft cards. Adding to the disruption were those in the crowd who had come to oppose – not support – the rally. The police quickly moved in, arresting demonstrators and dragging them away. It was a fierce clash, reflecting sharply divided public opinion. Forrest Place provided the public arena for these differing views to be played out. Some in the community thought it a legitimate expression of democratic disagreement; others objected to such direct action, particularly when it concerned the sensitive issue of war service.

Forrest Place had become the most favoured of venues for political party campaign meetings. The parties met there with police permission from 1927 until 1976, the police overseeing rosters during campaigning. Many of these meetings were lively and sometimes disrupted by protesters and hecklers, but most politicians of the period could handle the exchanges. Prime Minister Menzies described Forrest Place as the 'greatest' of his 1963 election meetings although he faced heckling and a pantomime protest. But business and city council opinion was turning against the use of Forrest Place for politicking, a view reinforced by the size and passion of the Vietnam war demonstrations.

Then came the events of 20 March 1974, reported by the *West Australian* the following day, which surely signalled the end of Forrest Place as a venue for political meetings. Angry farmers attended Prime Minister Whitlam's election rally to protest the federal government's rural policies, and particularly the proposed abolition of the federal superphosphate bounty. 'Gough, the new farm pest,' they insisted. 'Hillbillies', 'hicks' and 'hayseeds', 'People who ask you to subsidise their days off', Whitlam and Minister for Administrative Services Fred Daly responded. If it had stopped there the meeting would have been unexceptional, but it did not. People in the crowd (variously estimated at 7000–8000) threw drink cans, tomatoes and pies at the prime minister, several hitting him. He was jostled and his car thumped as he left. Fights broke out. It was 'mob violence', the *Canberra Times* editorial declared. Whitlam described it as 'very violent … ugly'. A week after the dismissal on 11 November 1975, in an environment of political uproar and with the prospect of a bitter federal election campaign, Premier Court announced that no more political meetings would be held in Forrest Place. It was too dangerous, the government insisted. Instead, the more spacious Esplanade was to be used. Protests against this change to traditional practice were unavailing.

Premier Court was not yet finished with his actions to curtail the right to freedom of public assembly. His ruling banning political meetings in Forrest Place was breached in March 1976 by a rally protesting Indonesia's invasion of East Timor. When a magistrate unexpectedly acquitted the five protesters arrested at the event, the government rushed to amend the *Police Act*. It inserted section 54B, which made it an offence to organise or take part in any 'procession, meeting or assembly in any street, thoroughfare or public place' without police permission. Commissioner of Police Owen Leitch made this judgement and there was no opportunity for appeal to a court. Permissions were denied to radical or progressive organisations or individuals. Section 54B was dictatorial, many Western Australians objected. Indeed, it was the most notorious instance of denial of the democratic right to peaceful assembly seen since the nineteenth century.

The new section first targeted trade unionists. Amalgamated Metal Workers and Shipwrights' Union leaders Laurie Carmichael and Jack Marks were dramatically arrested at Perth airport on 11 June 1979, after returning from an illegal outdoor union meeting in the Pilbara during the Hamersley Iron dispute. The next day four workers and three more union officials were arrested. Opposition grew and, in January 1980, members of the Friends of East Timor Group formed the Civil Liberties Action Committee (CLAC), convened by Howard Smith, to fight all legislation curtailing civil liberties, particularly

Musicians playing on the steps of Perth GPO to raise awareness of the situation in Chile, 11 August 1976

section 54b. Despite being refused a permit, on 3 May 1980 CLAC held a public forum in Forrest Place, which resulted in thirty-three arrests, including that of Aboriginal leader Rob Riley. Although everyone who attended such a rally was liable to arrest, there were approximately 650 people at the second CLAC forum held in Forrest Place on 19 July. A succession of speakers addressed the crowd from the GPO steps, each in turn taken away by police. Only one, who protested in sign language, was left alone. Several pieces of street theatre engaged the crowd – 'You will never be free with 54B', they sang; one speaker was dressed as a *54 bee*, and a street theatre group, *The 54Bs*, staged a mock arrest scene for which they were actually arrested. In all, forty-two protesters were arrested at a totally orderly and tightly run meeting. Howard Smith and others were convicted and, after fine default, were imprisoned for short periods. Another Forrest Place rally, this one in December, organised by CLAC and supported by the Campaign Against Nuclear Energy saw Santa Claus (Reverend Afflick) arrested together with other speakers.

Although on the face of it the government won the struggle, section 54B became infamous and a continuing provocation with most of the charges brought under it resulting from meetings protesting the section itself.

Lawyers took up the legal cases in the cause of civil liberty. Although the Court and O'Connor governments were never prepared to back down, eventually, police prosecutions declined in the face of the time and effort required.

Even so, section 54B was not repealed until the election of the Burke Labor government in 1983. The *Public Meetings and Processions Act 1984* made provision for 'the use of the streets for public meetings and processions'. Such gatherings would be authorised by the police upon notification, with the right of appeal to a magistrate in any contested case. This was a reversal of the previous legislation although the new legislation still stated that permission would not be granted if the proposed gathering was likely to 'occasion serious public disorder; damage to public or private property; create a public nuisance; give rise in any street to an obstruction that is too great or too prolonged in the circumstances; or place the safety of any person in jeopardy'. Nevertheless, this legislative change created the possibility that Forrest Place might again be a key public meeting venue for the city, thereby enabling a diversity of voices to be heard.

At the same time, urban planners were rendering this possibility less likely. Reconfiguration of the space was already underway. Vehicular traffic had been excluded in 1978 and the following ten years saw demolitions, new buildings, and the creation of a series of walkways and overpasses. The results – described as 'modernist brutality' – were not only aesthetically unappealing but also not particularly functional. Even more redevelopments were planned and implemented. Forrest Place was never to be restored to what it had been.

Yet, against the odds, protesters returned to use Forrest Place's central city location to draw public attention to their many causes. The site still had appeal, perhaps enhanced by public memory of its history as a forum for protest. In 1991 the Annual Silent Domestic Violence Memorial March to honour the women, men and children who have lost their lives as a result of domestic homicide in WA assembled there. When Iraq was invaded in 2003, UnionsWA, the Greens and various social action groups organised a big peace rally to protest the war and speakers addressed the crowd assembled below from the Forrest Chase balcony before marching off.

So did those organising the 'Stop the Filter' rally against internet censorship in 2010. Then, as shown by Alexis Vassiley, the Commonwealth Heads of Government Meeting (CHOGM) in Perth in October 2011 drew a great many groups and individuals onto the streets to demand the remedying of an assortment of wrongs. The CHOGM Action Network coordinated them all. There were those protesting against particular Commonwealth governments – Zimbabwe's lack of democracy, Rwanda's President Kagame, Sri Lanka's mistreatment of Tamils, Malaysian government actions, killings in the Congo, deaths in custody in WA, refugee rights, James Price gas hub, women's rights and equal marriage rights – as well as protests against continuing war, racism, homelessness, lack of climate change action, uranium mining and the threat of nuclear energy. They all assembled in Forrest Place for their march. This began the Occupy Perth action. Despite being first told that participants would not be allowed to camp in Forrest Place, in the end approximately eighty people did camp overnight outside the Commonwealth Bank without any disruption.

These recent protests, CHOGM and Occupy actions in particular, illustrate the evolving nature of contemporary social protest. Its discontents at widening income inequality and corporate greed sit alongside the great array of social injustices that offend individuals and social groups. These causes are not fully accommodated or satisfied in long established, traditionally structured political parties and institutions. Instead public actions are quickly coordinated using social media; the results are disseminated also on social media, using often transitory organisational structures. The city's physical spaces, in this case Forrest Place, remain central to these enactments of participatory democracy, creating the spectacle and street theatre of enthusiastic crowds with colourful banners to engage virtual audiences online and spread the protest. Democracy continues to depend on the availability of physical, public space, even in a digital world. Nothing replaces people taking to the streets.

4
Occupy Perth
Alexis Vassiley

As Occupy Wall Street kicked off in September 2011, inspiring activists to camp out in public places in over 2000 cities worldwide, WA authorities were preparing for the 28 October Commonwealth Heads of Government (CHOGM) meeting at the Perth Convention Centre. This biennial summit involves political leaders from the fifty-two Commonwealth countries that formerly belonged to the British empire. The military was brought in as well as three thousand police from interstate. Security guards were given police powers. Whole swathes of Perth's CBD were declared off limits to ordinary people. Snipers were placed on rooves for the days of CHOGM. Dozens of activists, mostly those involved in organising an anti-CHOGM protest, were placed on a special exclusion list and faced twelve months gaol if they walked into particular zones. For one woman, this included parts of the university where she studied. All protestors faced the same penalty if they breached police lines.

Homeless people were removed – a tale made familiar from world sporting events and meetings of the rich and powerful. Occupy and anti-CHOGM posters were taken down at UWA, and roads were closed. Police from a special CHOGM taskforce raided three activists' homes on 12 October and arrested them on suspicion of spray painting the word 'PROTEST' next to a massive flower arrangement spelling out 'CHOGM' on the Esplanade. They were never charged but they did have to spend hours in police custody and had their mobile phones seized. A further two activists were held overnight at Fremantle police station and charged with criminal damage for putting up posters days before the protest.

Sleepy Perth was put on high alert and moulded in the sanitised image of the city that authorities wanted to present to the world: the rabble, the plebs, the great unwashed were locked out. This speaks volumes about the state of capitalist democracy. Our rulers need to meet in a location protected by hundreds of police in order to discuss policies that affect the lives of millions. The barricades and lines of police served as a physical and a metaphorical barrier: physical in that it would prevent rowdy protestors from ruining the red carpet experience, metaphorical because in a neoliberal world, the masses' voices would not be heard, let alone their needs and desires met.

It was in this context that Perth's activists organised the city's Occupy events. New Occupy campaigners, taking their cue from events in New York and elsewhere, merged their meeting with an organising meeting of the CHOGM Action Network (CAN). Together they decided that Occupy Perth would start its campout in Forrest Place immediately after the CAN demonstration for Justice and Climate Action, Not Racism and War, to be held on the morning of 28 October.

The anti-CHOGM protest was organised by refugee rights campaigners, Aboriginal activists, feminists, environmentalists and members of Left groups, including Socialist Alternative and Socialist Alliance. The demonstration also saw large mobilisations of the Tamil and Malaysian communities and activists who originated from Rwanda and the Congo. Around a thousand people marched. Their aim was to get to the Perth Convention Centre to make their voices heard as they called for democracy, justice and human rights. The demand of Tamil protesters – that Sri Lankan President Mahinda Rajapaksa be arrested as a war criminal for atrocities committed against the Tamil population in the 2009 war – received much attention.

Speakers included Deaths in Custody Watch Committee spokesperson Marianne Mackay and Kimberley traditional owner Anne Poelina, who slammed the proposed gas hub at James Price Point (this was a successful campaign – the hub never went ahead). A placard reading 'We are many, they are few' drew on the final stanza of Perce Bysshe Shelley's *The Mask of Anarchy*, an ode to the resistance of ordinary people, penned after the 1819 Peterloo massacre in England:

Rise, like lions after slumber
In unvanquishable number!
Shake your chains to earth like dew
Which in sleep had fallen on you:
Ye are many–they are few!

Other placards included the old favourites, 'Human Need Not Corporate Greed' and 'Shut down the nuclear industry', as well as slogans for refugee rights and against sexism, and Aboriginal and LGBTI flags. Messaging connected with the Occupy movement, referring to the 99 per cent against the 1 per cent.

As did overseas heads of state and corporations, Australian leaders also faced protesters' wrath, and not only for backing regimes such as Rajapaksa's. Protesters voiced their disapproval of the Gillard Labor government's treatment of refugees, which was slammed as torture. That government had maintained indefinite mandatory detention of asylum seekers, including children, arranged for the

Anti-CHOGM marchers carrying banners bearing the slogans that marked the protest: 'We are many; they are few' and 'We are the 99%'

forced deportation of asylum seekers to Afghanistan, and tried to divert them to third countries with the proposed East Timor and Malaysia solutions, the second of which was struck down by the High Court due to Malaysia's lack of legal protections for refugees. Only two months before the CHOGM protests, the government signed off with its Papua New Guinea counterpart to reopen the detention centre on Manus Island. Widespread mental illness, self-harm and suicide were features of the detention regime. When detainees in Australian detention centres resisted these policies with protests, hunger strikes or riots, they faced tear gas and rubber bullets. The

Gillard government was also notorious among Left wing activists and unionists for its maintenance of the Howard government's Northern Territory intervention targeting indigenous people, which required suspending the *Racial Discrimination Act*.

Police prevented protestors getting anywhere near the Perth Convention Centre. They were allowed only as far as the corner of St Georges Terrace and William Street, around 1 kilometre away, and had the threat of gaol hanging over their heads if they literally put a foot wrong. CHOGM Action Network spokespeople contrasted the red carpet treatment given to often brutal heads of state with the virtual lockdown experienced by Perth citizens and the harassment and intimidation of activists.

After a sitdown on St Georges Terrace, rally participants marched back to Forrest Place, where they joined and bolstered the numbers of Occupy Perth, which had commenced a three day campout. Occupy Perth, like Occupy Wall Street, declared: 'We are the 99 per cent.' This slogan underscored unfairness and the absurdity of such a tiny minority controlling so much of the world's wealth and power. Oxfam has calculated that in January 2017 the world's richest eight individuals had the same wealth as the poorest half of the world's population. Occupy's declaration was an understatement.

But it did point to the problem and to who was responsible for it, setting up an us and them narrative. Occupy Perth did not have precise demands to place on the government. This was because its aims were more fundamental than a tweak to the law here, a policy change there. In common with the thousands of other global Occupy encampments, Perth's corporate media criticised what it saw as a vague message. Journalists seemed frustrated that they couldn't get their heads around what the protests were for, or at least couldn't fit it into a short sound bite. Yet what Occupy stood for was clear enough: against wealth inequality, against poverty, for real democracy and against a system that puts the profits of the millionaires ahead of the lives of the millions. Its anti-corporate power agenda was its strength. Miranda Wood, a twenty-three year old nursing assistant and trade unionist who participated in Occupy, argued that

> People supported Occupy's message because Occupy was an explosion of pent-up anger at structural inequality and injustice in the world, at the cruelty and barbarism of capitalism. We were protesting an entire system that foisted all of these injustices on people. For everyday people whose existence is a cycle of paying the bills and wondering where the next pay cheque is going to go, how they're going to put food on the table, and scrimping and saving for even the smallest of pleasures, Occupy's message really rang true.

Three years after the global financial crisis and government bailout packages totalling trillions were given to the banks, many felt that democracy wasn't working and the system was the problem.

WA Liberal Premier Colin Barnett and City of Perth officials told the occupiers that they wouldn't be allowed to camp out. Special signs were erected informing passersby of the city's by-law prohibiting camping. But eighty people successfully did it anyway. The threat to kick out campers was not kept, and the occupiers notched up a small initial victory. The nights brought attempts at sleep, long walks to use the toilet, and political conversations. Evenings passed with meetings, music, workshops and information stalls designed to reach out to passersby. The camp's numbers swelled during the day. One week earlier, on 21 October, Melbourne's Occupy camp was brutally evicted. One hundred and fifty protesters defied police orders to clear the area and battled police for hours. Police made ninety-five arrests

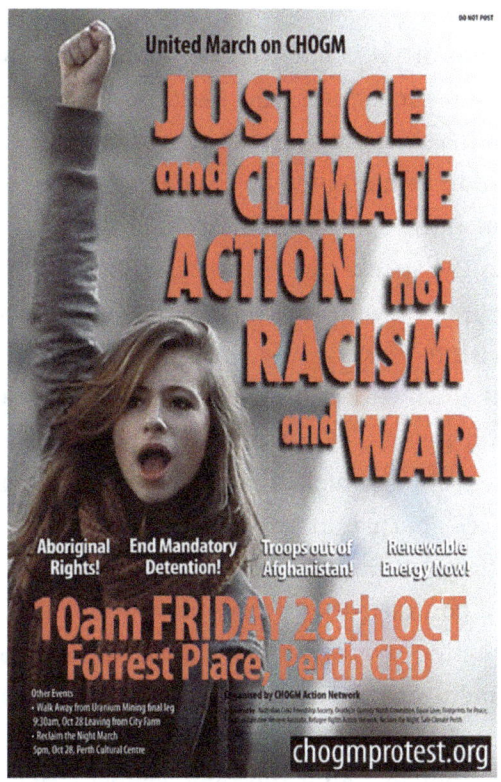

Poster advertising the March on CHOGM

and forty-three reports of police violence were filed.

Occupy Perth first met officially at 1 pm on 15 October in Forrest Place for a general assembly. General assemblies were mass public meetings at which those involved talked through the issues and planned their line of march. At their peak these general assemblies involved thousands of people interstate and hundreds in Perth.

An understanding of the somewhat complicated – and sometimes strange – meeting procedures and hand gestures was required in order to follow these meetings. For example, a speaker's voice would sometimes need to be amplified by others present who repeated out loud the sentence the speaker had just said. People could indicate agreement with the speaker with one hand signal, and suggest they wind up their speech with another. At the eastern states camps, consensus decision making was the norm. This presented huge problems, as it meant that in a meeting that involved hundreds, even a thousand people, only a few could stop a consensus being reached. Debates about which square to move to when police were threatening to clear a camp could take hours, during which the number of participants rapidly dwindled.

In Perth, by contrast, the organised far Left with its traditions of voting dominated over anarchist currents, so disagreements in tactics were usually resolved by a democratic vote. This initial general assembly resolved to commence an occupation of Forrest Place on 28 October, immediately after the rally against CHOGM. And so it came to pass that activists commenced a three day occupation of Forrest Place, which ended on 31 October when they were evicted by police and City of Perth officials. But they resolved to keep their campaigning going.

A few weeks later, on 18–20 November, a weekend occupation took place in Perth Cultural Centre. This featured a march through the city, general assemblies, smaller meetings and even a laughter workshop. After this, the movement petered out. With Sydney and Melbourne Occupy movements having been smashed, Occupy Perth didn't sustain itself. Even though some activists continued to organise forums under the Occupy banner, Occupy Perth had, in reality, wound up. With the overseas and interstate Occupys no more, and demands by the Perth group vague, continuing to occupy public space while declaring 'We are the 99 per cent' seemed pointless.

At its height Occupy Perth was part of a global movement that expressed members' anger at banks and politicians who lined their pockets while they cut jobs. Occupy Perth showed solidarity with the Arab Spring, and it put forward an alternative vision for society. But that couldn't continue indefinitely. Perth was somewhat derivative, reliant for inspiration and sustenance on events in New York, Sydney and Melbourne. Those movements themselves could not overcome brutal attacks by the police.

The heart of Perth's shopping district, Forrest Place, and nearby malls are corporate controlled spaces. Billboards advertise iPhones, designer clothes and mining companies. Freedom of speech in Australia is in reality limited because most people do not possess the vast amount of money required for billboards or mass media advertising, as well as by absurd City of Perth by-laws that ban holding an unauthorised placard. Occupy wanted to challenge those laws and insist that public spaces should be open to … the public. For some newer activists and those whose politics drew from anarchist or autonomist traditions, the Occupy camps were an end in themselves, the prefiguration of a new world. In this view, the camps were a better society in microcosm, a way to 'change the world without taking power', as prominent autonomist John Holloway had put it a decade earlier during a previous anti-corporate movement. By contrast, for the organised Left capitalism could not be dismantled in this way without addressing the question of the state or the wealth of the billionaires. Occupy was more akin to a social issue campaign. Socialist Alternative's Emma Norton argued that

Occupy reflected the disillusionment and anger among masses of people that we live in a world where a tiny minority own and control all of the wealth. Most of the time, this sentiment is not expressed, because parties like Labor and the Greens refuse to mobilise it. But arguments about wealth inequality and capitalism's injustice are the stock in trade of the far Left. We wanted to be there, encourage people to get involved, and push it as far as it would go.

Occupy's 99 per cent versus the 1 per cent may not have been a textbook Marxist definition of social class, which definition sees society divided into two main classes, antagonistically interdependent and defined by their relationship to the means of production. Workers who work for a wage have little control over their labour; the capitalist class owns the call centres, factories and office blocks. It makes huge profits by selling the products of workers' labour. Nonetheless, socialists were not quibbling about definitions, when in fact the slogan brilliantly popularised the notion that we're not all in it together, that there is a small wealthy minority who screw over the rest of us – the vast majority – and who care only about their profits. For the Left, this was a breath of fresh air from the nationalist discourse, which often dominates debate. This includes the racist scapegoating of refugees and celebrations like Australia Day – 'Invasion Day' for many Aboriginal people and radicals – which promote a false sense of unity between workers and bosses: we are all Australians after all. 'We are the 99 per cent', by contrast, pointed to the real divide in society – class – not false divisions fostered by those at the top. This was especially significant for the USA, a country where there is no Labor Party, where unions are marginal and where even workers see themselves as middle class. In Australia, too, Occupy brought the notion of class to the forefront of the public debate, where – with exceptions such as the union movement's campaign against WorkChoices in the mid

2000s – it had been rarely seen for decades.

As with many social movements, new activists and commentators alike pointed to the novelty of Occupy's form. Yet in many ways, the tactic of occupying a public space wasn't new. Occupations have been at times a central tactic of the student movement, with activists occupying university administration buildings, vice-chancellories and other public places in protest against compulsory exams, fee increases, full fee places, the Vietnam war, conscription and other issues every decade from the 1960s through to the early 2000s. The Aboriginal Tent Embassy, established outside Parliament House in Canberra in 1972, and present in some form ever since 1992, is an epic example. As Janis Bailey has shown, twenty years ago in Perth workers pitched tents and occupied an area across the road from WA's Parliament House, named it the Workers' Embassy and later Solidarity Park, in protest against the state Liberal government's third wave industrial relations reforms.

Occupy had an intrinsically radical potential. It asked: How different were Western democracies, in substance, from Middle Eastern dictatorships? In the USA, as in Australia, capital could live with democratic elections, because whoever got elected, the major parties were committed to neoliberalism and the rule of profit, although, as the brutal response to shut down the camps showed, force could still be used. A nerve had been touched. The rich and powerful didn't want people to be discussing, debating, plotting, scheming or thinking – thinking about alternatives for a better world.

Emma Norton has fond memories of Occupy Perth as 'kick starting my smoking habit and making me a communist'. Nicotine and caffeine filled nights spent in flimsy tents in Perth CBD aside, Occupy's moment has passed. Without drawing in broader layers of people, generating new activists and taking actions better able to withstand repression from the state apparatus (such as strikes by workers), no Occupy camp, including Perth, could keep going. But some of its activists, then starting out in politics, are today regular fixtures in Left wing meetings, chairing rallies and rabble rousing on university campuses and in the trade unions. Many are still driven by the kind of anti-capitalist politics that had been so central to Occupy.

5
Katharine Susannah Prichard and the Interwar Peace Movement

Charlie Fox

Katharine Susannah Prichard was, from the 1920s to the 1960s, one of Australia's most prolific authors and probably our best known. She wrote thirteen novels, four collections of short stories, eleven plays and two volumes of poetry, as well as a mountain of pamphlets, articles and speeches. She was also a political activist, a founding member of the Communist Party of Australia (CPA) in 1920 and a member until her death in 1969. In the 1930s there was no more influential radical in Western Australia than Prichard, who seemingly had a hand in organising practically every Left wing organisation in Perth. In 1932, during the depths of the Great Depression, Prichard helped establish a movement for unemployed women and girls, the Movement Against War – later War and Fascism – (MAWF) in 1933, the Workers' Art Guild in 1935, International Women's Day in 1936, the WA Spanish Relief Committee in 1937 and, in 1937, the Modern Women's Club.

Although Prichard gave to all of these bodies her passion and energy, she was most committed to the international peace movement. It was a hard road being a peace activist in the 1930s when fascism and World War 2 loomed. Even so, Prichard was involved in one spectacular victory, the freeing of Czech journalist Egon Kisch from the clutches of the federal government, which will be discussed a little later in this chapter.

Born in Fiji in 1883 and raised in a middle class family in Melbourne and Launceston, Prichard became a reader and a writer at a young age, devouring fiction and philosophy classics, while developing her own writing style. After being exposed to poverty in London before and during World War 1, she returned to Melbourne where she claimed that she discovered communism while walking across Melbourne's Princes Bridge and seeing news of the Russian revolution on a newspaper poster. She threw herself into reading Marxism and Leninism and became a founding member of the CPA.

Prichard arrived in Perth in March 1919 as the newly wed wife of the soldier and Victoria Cross honouree, Western Australian Hugo Throssell. They settled in the hills suburb of Greenmount, where she wrote most of her novels and lived for the rest of her life. Today the house is heritage listed and hosts the Katharine Susannah Prichard Writers' Centre.

Prichard, already a prizewinning novelist, became a celebrity in small, quiet and insular Perth. She also became an educator, setting up Perth's first labour study circle in 1919 for the Social Democratic League, then another for the newly formed but short lived branch of the Australian Communist Party in 1921, where she lectured on Marx and Marxism. The birth of her son Ric in 1922 interrupted her writing, but she did write two more novels later in the decade: *Working Bullocks* in 1926 and *Coonardoo* in 1929. In the Great Depression she subedited *Red Star*, the roneoed newssheet of the WA branch of the CPA, and wrote dozens, maybe hundreds of pamphlets, articles, newspaper stories, letters, introductions and commentaries.

In 1931 Prichard was instrumental in forming a permanent CPA branch. She became one of its most valued and constant speakers and a regular at May Day functions in the 1930s. During the Great Depression, she spoke at Esplanade meetings of the unemployed, one of which, in 1932, was for the famous Frankland River marchers, who she also helped find food and shelter. After her controversial trip to the USSR in 1933, she spoke to many different groups who were interested to hear her thoughts about economic, cultural and social conditions there.

In October 1933, worn down by wartime injuries, debt and worry, Hugo Throssell committed suicide while Susannah was away touring the Soviet Union. It seems she grieved quietly and privately, but, as she said later: 'Only my belief in the need to work for the great ideas of Communism and world peace helped me to survive a grief so shattering.'

So, on her return to Australia, she threw herself into activism but also continued to write. She published *Moon of Desire* in 1941, rewrote the end of *Intimate Strangers* and finished off *The Real Russia*, about her trip to the Soviet Union. She also wrote plays for the actors and activists in the Workers' Art Guild and the Spanish Relief Committee, was active in literary politics and the fight against censorship, and in 1937, became the Australian representative of the International Association of Writers for the Defense of Culture.

Prichard was also a feminist. She helped organise the Working Girls' Club in 1927 and the Unemployed Girls' and Women's Defence League in 1932, but these were transient bodies; organising women and girls in the Great Depression was always difficult. But International Women's Day and the Modern Women's Club, which she also organised, became fixtures of Perth's feminist movement, bringing together contemporary first wave feminist concerns, Labor women's interests in women's work and wages, and her own passions for peace and anti-fascism. Getting women involved in the public

Katharine Susannah Prichard met and supported many activists who visited Perth including Egon Kisch, shown (above) speaking at the Esplanade in 1934, and American singer Paul Robeson who visited Australia in 1960.

sphere was one of her major ambitions.

What was she like? Of course she was widely disliked and derided by the political Right, but she was respected and admired by the Left and had many friends in the local, national and international labour, literary, theatrical, peace and feminist worlds. UWA professor and columnist Walter Murdoch once said of her: 'In the parliament of the world, she is the member for Australia.' Another iconic communist, Paddy Troy, once remarked: 'If ever there was a saintly woman in the world it was she.' Her passions were her family, writing, Australian literature and communism. Urbane, well read and, some say, somewhat remote, she was an immensely hard worker with an

unassailable belief in her causes. She was very well connected in Perth, nationally and internationally. She was an indefatigable organiser, a deft chair of meetings and an inveterate public speaker. Yet, fearful of forgetting her text, she hated public speaking. Her son Ric once described her speaking style on an occasion she was speaking at a Spanish Relief Committee meeting on the Esplanade.

> She looked frail and alone there on the platform, her hands clasped tightly behind her, her head thrown back and tilted a little to one side with the defenceless defiance of a bird with a broken wing ... That gentle voice, so full of conviction, passion.

Speaking often in the face of hostility, abuse and sometimes thrown bottles, Prichard was courage personified.

In Western Australia, alongside small groups of pacifists, three organisations were at the forefront of the peace movement. The first comprised liberal internationalists, who set up a branch of the League of Nations Union (LNU) in Perth in 1932, to support disarmament, collective security and the creation of mechanisms through the League for ending disputes. In Perth the LNU developed from the Women's Service Guild, the first wave feminist body that established the Women's Peace Movement in 1928. Headed by Walter Murdoch and Fred Alexander, another high profile UWA professor, the LNU remained strong in Perth until, later in the decade, it proved unable to deal with the growing aggression of fascist Germany, Italy and Japan. Its appeal fell away and by the beginning of the war it had all but collapsed.

The second body was the ALP's Peace Council, set up in 1928. This body combined one of Labor's traditional concerns, opposition to conscription, with new concerns about the rise of fascism and the causes of war, but it struggled against the isolationist ALP State Executive, which vetoed much that it tried to do and kept it parked on the sidelines of the peace movement. By the mid 1930s the ALP's Peace Council was composed largely of Labor women; its leader, Eden Greville, became the chairman of the Spanish Relief Committee when it was formed in 1937. Clearly, the council still had considerable prestige.

The third was the Movement Against War (MAW), the Perth branch of the national movement. This body, established in 1933, was a Communist Party fraternal with its roots in the Communist International (the Comintern), the Soviet Union's vehicle for managing the international communist movement. It was set up towards the end of the Comintern's third period line of postwar capitalism. From the beginning, the MAW argued that war was a result of capitalism and imperialist rivalries, and that antiwar activists should defend the non-capitalist Soviet Union, the only truly peace loving nation. The MAW changed its name to the Movement against War and Fascism (MAWF) in 1934, when the Comintern, confronted by the rise of fascism in Europe, sought a united front with the labour movement and later a popular front with all parties.

In Perth, Prichard set up the MAW after organising a statewide antiwar meeting in 1933. There, she linked war with capitalism and imperialism and demanded the meeting support the USSR, arguing with Fred Alexander who claimed that her aim was not to stop war but to stop war against the Soviet Union. She spoke regularly at such meetings alongside fellow communists and progressive UWA professors such as Murdoch, Fox and Beasley, and feminists including Irene Greenwood, arguing with and usually winning votes against League of Nations and pacifist speakers.

Prichard had been a pacifist since 1917 when her brother Alan was killed on the Western Front, so there can be no doubt about the sincerity of her antiwar beliefs. But how could she justify defending the Soviet Union? As she wrote in a letter to the *West Australian* on 22 June 1934:

> The Soviet Government has consistently and persistently maintained its opposition to war, and reiterated its demand for international disarmament. But to a world in arms and apprehensive of its economic triumph, it does not turn the other cheek. It is prepared to defend Socialism in the (USSR) because it is a system of social administration, which makes for peace between nations, while the systems of capitalism, based on exploitation, economic rivalry and colonial conquest breed war.

By 1934, then, her guiding principles – as her son Ric described them – were the defence of socialism in Russia and the defeat of fascism. No longer a pacifist Prichard became fervent, fighting fascism wherever she found it: Germany, Italy, Spain and Australia as Joe Lyons' federal United Australia Party (UAP) government tried to suppress Left wing politics. Also in Perth, where black shirted fascists supported by the Catholic church and conservative politicians strutted the streets and a Nazi party raised its ugly head.

In her position at the head of the MAWF, Prichard joined deputations to the government to protest against the glorification of war in school textbooks and the production of warlike toys. She became a patron of a National Women's Peace Conference in 1938. She often spoke to and on behalf of women in her speeches: the Women's Committee of the MAWF in many ways matched both the League of Nations Union and the ALP Peace Council – all three were preponderantly women. In 1938 she was a member of the MAWF National Council before it changed its name to the League for Peace and Democracy.

Prichard was also active in the Spanish Relief Committee, set up in 1937 to raise funds for the Republican government in the bloody and brutal Spanish Civil War. She wrote the one act play, *Women of Spain*, for the committee; it was staged several times by the WAG and others. She insisted that the war was not a war between communists and Christians, as General Franco's Spanish rebels and Australia's Catholic hierarchy claimed, but between democracy and fascism and she argued the case at many meetings of the Committee in Perth. She also spoke at meetings welcoming and farewelling members of the International Brigades – the organisation of foreign soldiers and nurses who fought with the Republicans in Spain – who were traveling to and from the front, praising them for risking their lives in defence of democracy.

The Soviet Union's signing of a non-aggression pact with Nazi Germany in August 1939 must have come as a shock to her anti-fascism but she dutifully followed the new Soviet Union line, which abandoned anti-fascism and now argued that the war was an imperialist one that communists should not support. She once again became antiwar. She condemned the British government for not confronting Japan when it invaded Manchuria, Italy when it invaded Abyssinia and Germany when it seized Austria. It is not known whether she had doubts about the Pact but when Germany invaded Russia in June 1941 it may have been with some relief that she returned to her passionate anti-fascism.

The antiwar movement in Australia was overwhelmed by international events in Europe, as it was everywhere, but if it had one success it was in the strange case of Czech author, journalist and anti-fascist Egon Kisch. Kisch was in Australia as guest of honour for the All Australian Conference Against War and Fascism. Fremantle was the beginning and the end point of his Australian adventure but Prichard wasn't in Perth to see it begin. She was already in Melbourne as part of the WA delegation to the conference. Kisch was declared a prohibited immigrant and prevented from landing when his ship, the *Strathaird*, arrived in Fremantle on 10 October 1934. When the *Strathaird* docked in Melbourne, knowing that if he could somehow land, his case would have to go before the Australian courts, Kisch leapt onto the wharf. In doing so, one of his legs was badly broken; he was taken back on board and the ship headed to Sydney. In the meantime, his legal team successfully appealed to the High Court and Kisch was set free, but in November 1934, police rearrested him and gave him a dictation test under the *Immigration Restriction Act*, which could be set in any 'living

European language'. The test was designed to be given to anybody the government didn't want to enter Australia. Knowing Kisch spoke eleven European languages, authorities gave him the test in Scottish Gaelic. He failed and was promptly charged with being a prohibited immigrant, convicted and sentenced to gaol. Once again, his lawyers appealed to the High Court, which threw the out case on the grounds that Gaelic was not a living European language under the terms of the Act. Once again, Kisch was released.

He began his speaking tour in the eastern states, where he addressed huge crowds. In January 1935 he was again arrested and convicted, but while on bail he continued his tour. Ultimately, the government gave up, offered to drop the charges and pay all costs if he would leave, which he finally did in March 1935. The case was a public relations disaster for the government, especially Attorney-General Robert Menzies. Kisch became a celebrity.

While Kisch's ship sailed to Melbourne, Prichard and others formed the Kisch Defence Committee, which was charged with organising the campaign to free him. On the day he arrived in Melbourne, she was one of a party allowed on board to identify him, then stayed, acting as a bodyguard in case he was seized and put on board a nearby German gunboat. Indeed, she stayed with him the next day, leaving just before his leap to his 'Australian landfall'. Later she joined him and the New Zealand peace activist Gerald Griffen on speakers' platforms. Having failed a language test in Dutch, Griffen had been deported before the conference, but he sneaked back to Australia under a false name and wearing a disguise – apparently, a pair of smoky horn rimmed glasses – and played cat and mouse with the police for weeks.

Late in 1934, Prichard was on the platform with Kisch, who was on bail, at 'Free Kisch' meeting at Festival Hall in West Melbourne attended by a large crowd; Griffen was advertised to appear. At the mid point of the meeting the chairman called Griffen to the stage. A young man stood up in the middle of crowd, the lights were turned off – except two that illuminated him – and he began to speak. He said:

> I was determined, despite the ban placed on me by the government of this Commonwealth to come to Melbourne to deliver the message with which I was charged by the antiwar movement of New Zealand. I am glad to say that despite the order for my exclusion I effected an entrance.

Then, at the conclusion of his speech, a car started up outside, and there was a rush from the building. Police, under the impression Griffen was in the car, chased it and arrested the occupants, but Griffen wasn't there. He'd remained seated in the stadium while Prichard and several others addressed the crowd and left quietly after the meeting with everybody else.

Prichard was on the wharf with the Women's Committee of the MAWF when Kisch's ship, the *Orford*, berthed in Fremantle on 12 March 1935 on its way back to Britain. She took him to the Esplanade for his final meeting where, surrounded by banners reading 'Long Live the International Committee Against War and Fascism' and 'Welcome to Kisch. Keep on Fighting', he wittily observed that 'it had taken him four weeks to come to Fremantle from Europe but four months to get from Fremantle to Perth'. After the meeting Prichard took him off to her house in Greenmount for the afternoon until he left on the *Orford* that evening.

Prichard continued her activism during the war, even after the federal government outlawed the CPA, speaking often in support of the Soviet Union's war effort. After the war she turned to a new peace movement, this time in the context of the Cold War: the threat of nuclear annihilation and a great deal of hostile opposition to communists in Perth. Then, in the last few years of her life, she campaigned against the Vietnam war.

Through it all, though, her support for the Soviet Union never wavered, so she supported the invasion of Hungary in 1956 and the crushing of the Prague Spring in 1968. Ironically, in the end, it wasn't Prichard who moved away from Moscow, it was her Party, which condemned the invasion. As her son wrote in 1975:

> Katharine's mind clung to old truths. She sought reassurance of the worth of existence on her own terms and became intolerant of new ways and ideas; impatient of the concessions to change made by others.

But her friend, Justina (Joan) Williams later wrote that perhaps 'this was steel beneath the gentle manner' at work, the steel that made her who she was.

6
Banners of Hope and Apron Parades
Lenore Layman

> *We women who give life regard it as our duty to protest against the continued manufacture and 'testing' of these [atomic] weapons, as it menaces the future of the children of the whole world.*
>
> **Mary Lester, secretary UAW,** *West Australian,* **14 December 1953**

The year is 1957. A small group of women, five or six in all, walk quietly along central Perth's busy pavements as shoppers and city workers on their lunch break surge around them. Neatly and conservatively dressed, these housewives and mothers are noticed not because of any noise they make or antics they get up to. Carefully observing the traffic rules, they stay off the crowded roads where rattling trams, buses, cars and scurrying pedestrians compete for space. They do not march or stop to make speeches or shake collection tins or hand out pamphlets; they wave no banners or placards and do not shout or chant. But their message is plain for their passing audience to read:

Stop Nuclear Tests

Ban All Bombs

Atomic Tests Murder Children

These words are neatly printed in bold capital letters on the homemade calico aprons and scarves the women wear. Their lunchtime parade takes them from the headquarters of the Union of Australian Women (UAW) in Northbridge across the railway bridge at Barrack Street and into the city centre, where they move through the busiest sections of Hay and Murray Streets before retracing their route as the lunch hour ends.

As active members of the UAW, these women were committed to the postwar peace movement's campaign for an end to atomic and nuclear testing and the arms race. The Cold War must cease, they insisted, if humankind was to survive. Their apron parades targeted Britain's atomic testing in Australia and the Australian government's continuing support for it. Between 1952 and 1958, Britain conducted twenty-one atmospheric tests at Monte Bello Island and Christmas Island off the Western Australian coast and at Emu Plains and Maralinga in South Australia. The Australian public now knows of the damage caused by this testing – to local Aboriginal people, allied servicemen and the environment. At the time, however, only those in the peace movement and political radicals objected to the tests, so the women's protests were not popular (sometimes even within their own families); it took considerable courage to set off on their parades. Madge Cope, one of the marchers, wrote in a short story that they 'all felt rather nervous'.

> But when that old man on the corner said, 'Good on yer' as they passed they began to feel better.
>
> Then Joy heard a woman say, 'I wish I had the courage', and here and there they got a friendly smile.
>
> So a few looks of amazement, and comments like 'What will they think of next?' didn't worry them too much.

Helen hadn't bumped into her son, Jim, in any of the five lunch hours that they had gone out, for which she was duly thankful.

She hadn't told them at home about this venture.

Perhaps the low key protests defused more aggressive responses from those who thought peace was a dirty word because of its association with communist rhetoric in the polarised politics of the Cold War. Even so, Perth police were not willing to overlook the women's actions and in September of that year plain clothed officers stopped the group, confiscated their aprons and scarves, and charged them under the *Traffic Act* with carrying a 'print, picture, board, placard or notice ... in any road, street or public place' without permission. The women had decided to wear aprons and scarves in order to avoid the fate of earlier peace protesters who had carried placards and fallen foul of the repressive regulations, but now they, too, faced court. Barrister Lloyd Davies, acting pro bono, defended them, initially unsuccessfully, but an appeal to the Supreme Court overturned the magistrate's decision. The superior court agreed with police that the aprons and scarves did constitute a notice and that they were carried, but went on to rule that the regulation was beyond the powers of the *Traffic Act* because it did not regulate traffic. Roma Gilchrist reclaimed their confiscated aprons and scarves. In her history, of the UAW, she recalled:

> After some delaying tactics the police handed them back – the expression on his face inferred that he couldn't see why we wanted them. To our members they were banners of hope for a peaceful world for our children in the future.

The women resumed their weekly protests, carrying paper shopping bags covered in peace slogans, until mid 1958 when their campaign culminated in a commemoration of Hiroshima Day on 6 August.

Mercia Barker, Madge Cope, Mary Lester and Joyce Payne at a Union of Australian Women Apron Parade, 1957

The police kept extremely tight control of Perth streets, making spontaneous protests impossible and hemming all demonstrations with multiple restrictions. The power to prohibit or regulate processions on roads had passed into police hands from local government in the *Traffic Act 1919* and had been used to sharp effect against protesters, especially the unemployed, during the Depression. In the postwar period the pressure of containment fell on the progressive Left, and particularly the communists. The postwar peace movement was viewed with deep suspicion because it was seen as a communist front prepared to take direct action and therefore to threaten social disorder.

The actions of the UAW women challenged dominant understandings of the virtuous and the dangerous. It was easy enough to sweep the desperate unemployed, confrontational male trade unionists and radical young students into the official net, harder to see conservatively dressed, mature women who announced themselves as housewives and mothers and behaved circumspectly as a threat to good order. Like the women of the Black Sash protesting apartheid in South Africa and the mothers of Save Our Sons during the Vietnam war protests who organised and demonstrated later, the women of the UAW manipulated these gendered expectations quite deliberately and successfully. Two years before, they had harnessed maternal power to achieve the rapid installation of air coolers at the King Edward Memorial Hospital for Women (KEMH) by selecting 'five large mothers to be' to make up a deputation to the head office of the Public Works Department. In the hot, overcrowded conditions of the old Treasury Building anxious staff assembled chairs for the women and paid them solicitous attention as they presented their concerns. Air coolers were quickly installed at the hospital. The apron parades followed the same imaginative strategy, making the feminine and the maternal into opportunities for radicalism.

The UAW, approximately 100 strong in membership at most times, was active between 1950 and 1973, succeeding the New Housewives' Association and the Modern Women's Club and taking over their struggles to promote peace, rights and opportunities for women and children, and Aboriginal rights. Many of these politically radical women were members of the CPA, devoting their time and energies to Left causes. The UAW was part of a network of women's organisations with the Women's International Democratic Federation (WIDF) at its apex. Until 1962 one room in an old house at 79 Stirling Street in Northbridge served as UAW headquarters, on a site now occupied by an undistinguished office building. At the time the old house, fronted by a lawn with two palms trees, was one of many of its kind in the area: a little rundown and worn by earlier usages with rooms available at modest rent. In the 1960s the UAW moved just around the corner to 36 James Street where the rented premises were larger. These headquarters were 'very busy beehives … where hundreds of ideas and plans were formulated', former president Roma Gilchrist recalled.

The Beaufort Street–Stirling Street area of Northbridge was the organisational centre of Perth's political radicalism in the 1950s and 1960s, housing the headquarters of the CPA and the Pioneer Bookshop, Perth Trades Hall and numerous trade union offices, and the many radical activist organisations of which the UAW was one. The UAW initially shared a room with the WA Peace Council, while the Eureka Youth League was along the street.

Northbridge was a distinctive Perth locality. The official containment of prostitution made Roe Street, running alongside the rail line, the red light district. West of William Street ethnically diverse communities nestled close to the central railway station from where new immigrants constantly replenished the transient population. Boarding houses and cheap hotels provided temporary accommodation. In succession Chinese, Jewish, Greek, Polish, Italian, Slav and Vietnamese people found in Northbridge a place to begin their Australian lives. Cafes, shops, wine saloons and hotels catered to these customers, making it a lively area.

The UAW women enlivened their Northbridge locality with constant activity. Cake and craft stalls were held under the palm trees on the front lawn to raise funds. Members and supporters came from all over Perth to morning and afternoon teas, weekly luncheons and monthly talks on many and varied subjects – everything from reports of the international peace and women's congresses that leaders had attended to the dangers of poliomyelitis, treatment of unmarried mothers, better housing for Aboriginal people, 'A Green Heart for Perth', Alcoholics Anonymous meetings, abortion law reform and student protest. Sometimes there was music. Members catered for each event and brought flowers to decorate the tables. Children played around the premises during school holidays and summer picnics on the river were organised with games, swimming and watermelon provided. The UAW felt that no woman needed to be lonely, although members knew that many in the postwar suburbs were. Suburban UAW groups were formed; their members were as active as their central Perth sisters. The Tuart Hill group, for instance, campaigned successfully for more footpaths and the first kindergartens to be built in that new suburb. 'We were activists for community needs, spearheading things like libraries, schools, canteens,' Noelene Hartley recalled.

Funds raised from the cake and craft stalls, fetes, jumble sales, raffles, quiz nights and luncheons were donated to good welfare causes, such as bushfire relief and helping trade union families during strike actions, to support the progressive campaigns of others and to pay for the interstate and overseas travel of UAW leaders to enable them to attend women's and peace conferences and national meetings. Assistance was provided for immediate local needs, for instance, used baby clothes were collected for the KEMH nursery and money provided to fund several Aboriginal children's education. Other assistance followed the UAW's international perspective. In 1970, for instance, a donation was made to the defence expenses of the American radical activist and civil rights campaigner Angela Davis when she was put on trial in California for conspiring in the violent struggle for the release from prison of the Soledad brothers.

Monthly business meetings were used to plan the organisation's busy timetable, roneo leaflets to advertise all the campaigns and produce a newssheet. *News for Everywoman* grew in length and became a monthly publication costing three pence. The national journal *Our Women* was launched in 1953. Three issues a year were produced with Perth members regularly contributing content and selling copies for the next twenty years. Sales drives occurred at Perth factories, union gatherings and by door to door approaches. The women encouraged one another to overcome their fear of approaching strangers by arranging a meal at a member's home after the sales drive was completed for the day. Some of the canvassers came away with bags heavy with plant cuttings and flowers, and spent the next day busy in their own gardens. An all time record was reached in 1961 when 951 copies of *Our Women* were sold. A lending library was also built up for members' use at a charge of from three to five pence per week. *Good Cooking*, published in 1968, provided a collection of members' economical recipes to help housewives manage their family budgets.

Lazywoman's Joint

Pot roast beef, wipe with oil, cover with dried soup powder (1 packet). Cover with foil. Bake in oven about 300° till cooked.

Each year the office was strewn with placards and decorations in preparation for the UAW's part in the Labour Day or May Day marches. Each year they commemorated International Women's Day.

The UAW kept up a flood of public meetings, deputations, petitions and letters to government ministers and agencies, local governments and businesses as well as letters to newspaper editors to demand action on a wide range of social issues. First was the continuous lobbying to improve the conditions of life for the many families struggling to cope in these postwar years – demands for controls on the rapidly rising cost of living (rents, bread prices, water rates) and for action on the housing shortage; opposition to the building of high rise flats as public housing; and demands for more amenities in the new suburbs (better bus services for shoppers and hospital visitors, more public toilets and immediate attention to dangerous road crossings). No issue was too local for a UAW action.

They lobbied equally on social welfare issues affecting women and children – the need for greater welfare spending, the inadequacy of the maternity allowance, the dangers of violence on children's television and the overwhelming American content in television programs, the need for abortion law reform and family planning, the dangers of cigarette advertising, the damage done by deceptive advertising and pyramid selling, and the rising threat of urban pollution. They campaigned for equal pay as a woman's right and as a significant material benefit to families battling inadequate incomes. Very few issues affecting families in an increasingly consumerist society escaped their attention.

The UAW's peace protests were also continuous – the dangerous influence of war toys for children, the dire circumstances of political prisoners around the world, the wrong headedness of the Vietnam war, opposition to the Springbok rugby tour, and warnings of the dangers of ongoing atmospheric atomic and nuclear testing, including French atomic bomb testing in the Pacific in the 1960s. Aerogram letters were sent to the US government in 1968 to protest the prosecution of famous child rearing adviser and political radical Dr Benjamin Spock for conspiring to aid American Vietnam draft resisters. Spock wrote in thanks, saying that 'It makes me feel good', reinforcing the women's feeling of international camaraderie with progressives everywhere.

The cause of peace was a constant in the life of the UAW and direct action always remained an option. In 1960 members staged another walk through Perth, this time to protest at American U-2 spy flights. 'U-2 Flights Menace Peace' their placards read. The nine marchers did not reach the US consul's office; detectives seized their placards, took their names and addresses, and warned them of prosecution if they persisted. At election times lists of questions relevant to women and to peace were submitted to parliamentary candidates to focus attention on the matters the UAW believed to be most important but were too frequently neglected by all political parties. Women's participation in political discussion was encouraged, as was the education of women to use their vote independently and thoughtfully.

Members made a point of working for the campaigns of others, in many instances helping to establish these groups as organisations: the consumer action movement, civilian widows, those campaigning for kindergartens, childcare and homes for the aged, the pensioners' action group, family planning and abortion law repeal, the moratorium movement as well as environmental campaigns to protect nature reserves. In the mid 1950s they joined the chorus of opposition to the building of a swimming pool in Kings Park: 'Let us keep its straggly, sage-green beauty so close to our city, and hold it against all-comers, for ourselves, our children and their children' they appealed in a letter to the editor of the *West Australian* on 27 November 1954. As a result of this campaign by the UAW and other organisations the pool was never built.

Throughout its life, the UAW strongly supported trade union

campaigns for worker rights and better working conditions, particularly the campaigns of the more radical and militant unions. But the women were also always prepared to take direct action themselves. When, in 1965, a Perth dry cleaning firm denied a pregnant woman her pro-rata long service leave payments, the UAW staged a public protest, and then a boycott of the business.

These mid century radical women were a generational bridge between early twentieth century feminism and its second wave in the 1970s. They campaigned to help mothers and families but added to it a powerful Left political radicalism and internationalism, combining non-confrontational protest strategies (letter writing, deputations, probing questionnaires and such like) with direct action on the streets and assistance to others who were also in militant confrontation with authorities. In 1973, given their ageing membership and the emergence of new, dynamic women's groups, the women decided that the time of their useful existence had passed. As had happened with an earlier generation of radical women, they passed the mantle to younger women in those new organisations: the Women's Electoral Lobby and the Women's Liberation Movement.

The UAW's organisational existence left no lasting mark on the physical fabric of Northbridge, inner urban rebuilding attracting more businesses and government agencies to change the locality, although cheap accommodation has continued to be available into the twenty-first century. The UAW has survived in generational memory and in history but – as the women themselves would fiercely insist – most importantly, in the contribution it made to social and political change through two decades of unceasing radical activism.

7
Solidarity with the Pilbara Aboriginal Station Hands Strike

Nick Everett

On Sunday 19 May 1946, the Perth Esplanade was the site of a 200 strong demonstration in solidarity with a strike launched three weeks earlier by Pilbara Aboriginal station hands. The protest demanded the immediate release of Clancy McKenna and Dooley Bin Bin, two of the strike leaders who were arrested at the strike's commencement on the charge of enticement to strike. Those gathered not only backed the strikers' demands, but were also outraged by the gaoling and cruel treatment of strike leaders under a Labor state government. The audience was informed that Dooley had been chained by the neck for six days while held in remand in Marble Bar gaol. A resolution unanimously adopted by the meeting declared:

> We consider the imprisonment for 3 months with hard labor [sic] of the native strike leaders Clancy McKenna and Dooley to be victimisation of the most brutal kind, incompatible with Australian Democracy. That the sentences were carried out under the administration of the State Labor Government is, we consider, a slur on the Labor movement.

Participants called on the justice minister to 'revoke the sentences and free the imprisoned strike leaders' and 'to secure the withdrawal of charges' laid against Don McLeod, the strikers' representative. Recognising whose interests the laws really served, their resolution stated: 'We consider that the Native Administration Act is administered, not for the benefit of the natives, but for the squatters to provide them with a supply of cheap labour.'

Officially launched on May Day 1946, the Pilbara Strike was the longest recorded strike in Australian history. The strikers' demands were straightforward: a 30 shillings per week minimum wage, the right to elect their own representatives and freedom of movement. Their actions directly challenged Western Australia's *Aborigines Act 1905* and the *Native Administration Act 1936*, which together controlled every aspect of Aboriginal people's lives. The Pilbara's Aboriginal workforce thus defied not only the pastoral station owners by demanding better wages and conditions, but also sought to win independence from a regime of servitude. Though the strike officially ended in 1949, much of the workforce never returned, instead building self-sufficient communities through cooperative mining and other ventures. Their struggle inspired a national campaign for Aboriginal rights, spearheaded in Perth by the Committee for the Defence of Native Rights (CDNR). This chapter will explore how the CDNR built a powerful, broad-based solidarity campaign.

Two days after the Esplanade gathering, a small group met at the offices of the Society of Friends (Quakers) at Chancery House in Howard Street to form the provisional committee of the CDNR. A leaflet authored by Katharine Susannah Prichard urged 'members of trade unions, women's organisations, religious and other bodies, to prevent the continuation of glaring injustice which strikes at the principles of living in which Australia stands' by attending a public meeting at Perth Town Hall on the following Tuesday, 28 May.

The night of 28 May 1946 was stormy. Despite heavy downpours and blackouts that caused havoc with tram services, 300 people turned

S.O.S.

YOUR HELP is requested by members of trade unions, women's organisations, religious and other bodies, to prevent the continuation of glaring injustice which strikes at the principles of living on which Australia stands!

Attend A PUBLIC MEETING

Perth Town Hall

Tuesday, May 28 at 8 o'clock

"Are aboriginal workers slaves?"

"Australian Governments have recognised the right of workers to organise for improvement of their living and working conditions. Should native Australians be deprived of this right?"

"In connection with the recent attempt of aboriginal workers on north-west stations to improve their shameful conditions, Clancy McKenna, a half-caste, and Dooley, a full-blood, native leaders, have been charged under Article 47 of the Native Affairs Act with enticing natives from service, and sentenced to three months imprisonment with hard labor.

"Such an abuse of democratic principles calls for indignation and protest; and for vigorous support of the aborigines making a stand for their right to be workers, not merely as cattle, but has human beings.

"Mr. D. McLeod, who has been associated with the native workers in their efforts to organise has been arrested and will be tried on a similar charge.

"The Press has suppressed or distorted many facts in relation to this matter.

"Come and hear representative speakers next Tuesday night (May 28) and help to prevent a further outrage being committed against the native race."

—Katherine Susannah Pritchard.

Issued by the Rev. P. Hodge, Secretary, Provisional Committee for the Defence of the Native Rights.

Leaflet advertising public meeting of the Committee to Defend Native Rights out to launch the CDNR in the town hall. Present at the meeting were Noongars, trade unionists, students and other supporters of Aboriginal rights. Speakers included Katharine Susannah Prichard (Modern Women's Club), Mrs Vallance (Women's Christian Temperance Union), Mr Payne (Tramways Union), Mr Foxcraft (Quakers) and Communist Party organiser Graham Alcorn. The most enthusiastic welcome was reserved for Noongar elder and activist Tommy Bropho, who was greeted with a standing ovation. Bropho told the meeting: 'Today we are demanding at least similar privileges to the white man and our freedom. These concessions have been too long delayed.'

Following the speeches, the meeting resolved to endorse the strikers' demands, condemn the imprisonment of strikers McKenna and Dooley and

> contact for support all trade unions and people's organisations and societies in Australia, and international organisations which stand for the defence of native peoples, including, if necessary, UNO [the United Nations Organisation].

The meeting elected a committee that included Anglican minister Peter Hodge (secretary), medical doctor and communist Alex Jolly (president), Mr Foxcroft and Don McLeod (vice-presidents), broadcaster and peace and women's rights campaigner Irene Greenwood, and Aboriginal activists Tommy Bropho and Mary Morden. Despite the broad base of the committee, Commissioner for Native Affairs Francis Bray, in correspondence with State Premier Frank Wise dated 29 and 30 May 1946, dismissed the event as 'staged' by the Communist Party. The meeting achieved little, he claimed, 'except that the Communists enlist[ed] some dupes or marionettes for the purpose of Communist propaganda'. However, the pressure brought to bear on the justice minister by trade unions and the Metropolitan District Council of the ALP to release the strike leaders, forced the minister's hand. On 24 June 1946, five weeks into Clancy and Dooley's three month sentence, Minister Nulsen ordered their immediate release. But the reprieve was short lived. Over the following three years, other strikers were frequently detained in the Port Hedland lockup.

The Communist Party, which did play a prominent role in the CDNR, was uniquely placed to build solidarity with the Pilbara strike. First, because the CPA was at the time the only political party in Australia to actively campaign for Aboriginal rights. From the early 1920s, the party's national newspaper, *Workers' Weekly*, accused pastoral industry employers of 'chattel slavery', demanded equal wages for Aboriginal workers and vehemently opposed the North Australian Workers Union (NAWU)'s exclusion of Aboriginal workers from its membership. In 1939, leading communist Tom Wright, federal president of the Sheet Metal Workers' Union and vice-president of the NSW Labor Council, outlined the party's policy on Aboriginal rights in the pamphlet, *New Deal for Aborigines*. The party called for land rights for 'full blood' Aboriginal people, including rights to minerals, water and timber, as well as special courts for 'native offences', the abolition of police acting as Aboriginal protectors and full citizenship rights for all Aboriginal people.

Second, the Communist Party held strategic leadership positions in two important trade unions. In 1948, communist Paddy Troy was elected secretary of the Fremantle branch of the Coastal Dock, Rivers and Harbour Works Union of Workers. That same year, Ron Hurd, also a communist and a veteran of the International Brigades in the Spanish civil war, became secretary of the Fremantle branch of the Seamen's Union. In 1949, at a critical juncture in the dispute, Troy and Hurd were instrumental in imposing a black ban on union crews handling wool bales awaiting export on Port Hedland wharf.

In 1936, following accusations of child slavery, abuse and mistreatment at the Moore River Native settlement, the state Labor government established the Moseley Royal Commission. In the pages of the Perth Communist Party's weekly tabloid, *Workers' Star*, Katharine Susannah Prichard condemned the state Labor government's adoption of Chief Protector A. O. Neville's recommendations, which included increased powers to remove 'mixed descent' Aboriginal children from their families to church missions and state-run native settlements, where they were groomed for low paid rural and domestic work. Prichard described a ban on cohabitation between Aboriginal and non-Aboriginal people as an 'intolerable interference in the domestic lives of both races'. In 1943, Communist Party branches in Perth's working class eastern suburbs campaigned for housing for the Aboriginal fringe dweller community following their eviction from the South Guildford reserve by the Australian army. By the time of the commencement of the Pilbara strike, the Party had established a strong reputation for championing Aboriginal rights, in Perth and nationally.

Local Noongar people also played an important role in the committee, alongside Quakers, Labor Party members and prominent members of the Women's Christian Temperance Union and the Methodist Ladies' Guild. During the strike, Tommy Bropho toured Noongar communities in the southwest in an effort to revive the work of the Native Union, which, during the Great Depression, campaigned for equality for Noongars of mixed descent. Elders such as Bropho, Bertha Isaacs and Bill Bodney, as well as younger activists such as Helene Clarke and Jack Poland, rallied alongside members of the Modern Women's Club and the Communist Party on the Esplanade on several occasions to demand the release of imprisoned strikers. In 1947, Perth Noongars formed the Coolbaroo League, an Aboriginal run organisation that began hosting dances each Friday night in East Perth and soon began agitating for Aboriginal civil rights. In the 1950s, the League rented an office in Beaufort Street from the Carpenters' Union, and published a newspaper, the *West Australian Aborigine*, giving voice to Aboriginal people across the state.

Critical to the success of the CDNR was Don McLeod, the Port Hedland-based trade union militant who represented the strikers in their dealings with the Department of Native Affairs. Throughout the strike, McLeod maintained close ties with the CDNR and Perth-based members of the Communist Party, which he joined in 1944. *Workers' Star* reporter Joan Williams recalled in her autobiography that McLeod attended a Perth Party school in April 1945 and told those present of 'the Aborigines' poor pay, the squalid camps on the stations [and] the plundering of issue rations by some station owners'. McLeod returned to Perth in March 1946, where he reported on preparations for the strike at the Communist Party's WA state conference and addressed a rally held on the Esplanade. Williams recalled that

> By the time the strike was planned, we had recognised that the Aborigines had to produce their own leaders, so we were elated to hear from McLeod that the people's own councils would debate every move, and that outstanding Aboriginal leaders like Clancy McKenna and Dooley had already appeared.

At this point Graham Alcorn took responsibility for communicating with McLeod regarding strategy and tactics, while Williams and author and playwright Dorothy Hewett reported on the strike for *Workers' Star* and for *Tribune*, the Communist Party's national newspaper. Hewett's husband Lloyd Davies, a recent law graduate, and Perth barrister Fred

Curran provided pro bono legal representation for the gaoled strikers. Addressing the CDNR launch on 27 May, Alcorn recognised that the strike provided the CDNR with an 'agitational focal point around which a movement can grow from all parts of Australia to bring about a new deal for Aborigines under Federal control'.

At the time of the strike, not only were town centres off limits to Aboriginal people, but non-Aboriginal people were also barred from entering Aboriginal camps, which were invariably on the outskirts of towns. This enforced segregation presented significant challenges to the Pilbara strikers and their supporters. At the commencement of the strike, McLeod was arrested for entering the Twelve Mile Camp outside Port Hedland. During the course of the dispute he was arrested another six times: three times for 'being within five chains [100 metres] of a congregation of natives' and three times for 'inciting natives to leave their lawful employment.' In August, Peter Hodge travelled to Port Hedland to visit the Twelve Mile Camp and, much to his surprise, was arrested alongside McLeod. Hodge was fined £10, while McLeod was sentenced to three months imprisonment.

With the strong arm of the law bearing down on the strikers and rations being withheld by station owners the CDNR adopted several strategies as part of its solidarity campaign. First, it mounted a legal defence of those gaoled. Second, it used all available avenues to publicise the strike. Third, it raised funds to sustain the strike. Finally, and perhaps most significantly, the Communist Party's influence in the labour movement enabled the creation of industrial bans on wool exports aimed at forcing the station owners to concede.

When, in October 1946, the WA Court of Criminal Appeal rejected appeals by Clancy, Dooley, McLeod and Hodge against their convictions, according to Lloyd Davies the decision 'arouse[d] public indignation throughout the land and much support both material and moral poured into the CDNR from everywhere'. The British Anti-Slavery Society raised funds and sent messages of support and protest. The CDNR appealed to the High Court and to the United Nations, alleging that the strike leaders' arrests amounted to 'feudal treatment of Aborigines in Northern Australia'. The High Court upheld the appeal on the grounds that the intent of the statute was 'better protection of natives' and not criminalisation of McLeod and Hodge's contact with them. While this victory boosted the strikers' morale and secured publicity for their cause, it did not end punitive legal action against them. In January 1947, McKenna and twelve others were gaoled after allegedly preventing several Warragine station hands from working. In August 1947, twelve more Aboriginal men were charged with abduction and gaoled for attempting to rescue children suffering abuse on a station.

While mainstream media largely ignored the strike, *Workers' Star* consistently championed the strikers' cause. Alcorn, Williams and Hewett worked on the paper from the Communist Party's third floor office in London Court, a Tudor-style arcade in Perth's city centre. According to Davies, 'the [daily newspapers] in the other States were forced to rely upon [*Workers' Star*] for sources of information and often quoted from its articles'. Williams recalls that when the *Workers' Star* published a photo of Aboriginal people chained by the neck it caused a public uproar in Australia and overseas.

As news of the strike spread, support poured in. Students at The University of Western Australia marched in support of the strikers. Messages of support and donations came in from a dozen Western Australian union branches, the Australian Labor Party, women's organisations and interstate from the Queensland, New South

Wales and Victorian unions and the South Australian Council for Advancement of Aboriginal Women. Additionally, the CDNR appealed to the World Federation of Trade Unions, the Australian Council of Trade Unions and federal ministers. With the donations it received, the CDNR was able to print and distribute 20 000 copies of a four page leaflet that outlined the history of the strike and the committee's policy on Aboriginal rights.

In March 1947, less than a year into the strike, the Liberal–Country Party coalition defeated Labor to form government. The following year, Stanley Middleton, fresh from administering the natives in colonial Papua New Guinea, was appointed the state's new Commissioner for Native Affairs. Applying what he had learnt in PNG, Middleton advocated the assimilation of the state's Aboriginal population.

At two strike camps – Twelve-Mile Camp, 20 kilometres outside of Port Hedland, and Moolyella, near Marble Bar – hundreds of Aboriginal families were sustaining themselves by collecting pearl shell, kangaroo and goatskins to sell; they later turned their hand to yandying for alluvial tin. The Liberal state government attempted to thwart these efforts by denying the strikers permits to use hunting rifles. Eviction orders were issued on the pretext that the camps were unfit for habitation. Middleton hoped that the strikers could be coaxed into abandoning their self-managed camps in favour of accepting the charity of the White Springs Mission, recently established with a generous land grant from the state government. The strikers refused to move.

Ultimately, it was trade union support, coordinated closely with the CDNR in Perth, that helped break the deadlock and secure a partial victory for the strikers. When in April 1949 forty-three strikers were gaoled for enticing natives to strike, the Seamen's Union called for the prisoners immediate release and threatened a ban on the shipment of wool from stations where 'slave conditions' applied. Their intention was to hit squarely at the hip pockets of Pilbara's woolgrowers. By mid June 1949, all but one of the forty-three convicted strikers had served out their sentences. The state government was hopeful that further strike action could be averted. But when, on 20 June, police arrested another ten strikers at Nullagine, the scene was set for a showdown.

Ron Hurd convinced his members to implement the wool ban. Bails of wool now sat idle on Port Hedland wharf. By mid July, gaoled strikers had all been released. McLeod had little doubt that the strike had precipitated their release. On 15 July, he told *Workers' Star*: 'Intervention of Mr Elliot Smith, Northern Administrator of Native Affairs, secured the dismissal of the charges and the release of the accused natives.' The Seamen's Union declared victory when Smith promised agreements for wages and conditions that matched those of Mount Edgar and Limestone stations, which had already agreed to the strikers' demands. Once the bans were lifted, though, Native Affairs Minister Ross McDonald told state parliament that no such agreement had been made. This setback led McLeod to later conclude that the strike had been defeated, despite many station owners having now conceded to strikers' demands. McLeod observes that despite the 'ringleaders' having 'been in and out of jail like clockwork … the Blackfellows never wilted. Nothing that either the State or police did could shake their solidarity.' Alcorn said of the strike:

> When the Pilbara station hands struck, here was a rallying point for all Aboriginal people, a rallying point for all those white people throughout Australia who wanted to do something; a chance to isolate and defeat the reactionary squatters and the government policies they dictated.

The CDNR played no small part in the struggle for Aboriginal rights. Alcorn observed that while it was the use of the 'strike weapon' and the strength of organisation among the Pilbara workers themselves that was most decisive, the CNDR's national campaign 'held the government's hand and enabled [the workers] to continue their campaign'. There were at times sharp debates within the CDNR. Liberals within the committee expressed unease about its close association with communist-led trade unions. In mid 1947, the CDNR changed its name to the Native Rights League, then in 1949 to the Native Rights and Welfare League, signalling a greater focus on welfare support for local Noongars. By the early 1950s, the League began to adopt the assimilationist approach to Aboriginal affairs now advocated by Middleton. Nonetheless, Alcorn concluded, had the CDNR not built a powerful solidarity campaign with the Pilbara strikers, 'there is little doubt that Don and the native leaders would have been jailed indefinitely, their organisation smashed and the rank and file terrorised back to work'.

8
Yugoslavs and Interwar Radicalism
Charlie Fox

There is a grainy old photo, held in a private collection, taken in 1945 on the Western Australian goldfield that shows a group of about twenty Yugoslav men, two women and a couple of kids gathered together in front of a flag and a banner somewhere on the Gwalia mine woodline rail service. The banner reads:

>Long Live the Federation People's Republic of Yugoslavia.
>Long Live Marshal Tito.
>Long Live Australia.
>Long Live all People.

It's a joyous and infinitely inclusive moment out there in the bush, a world away from Yugoslavia, the newly communist nation in the Balkans. It was a dream come true among Yugoslav migrant workers in Western Australia, who had worked long and hard for this moment. And they celebrated in Perth with the same fervour as they did in the Gwalia bush.

Between 1901 and 1918 about 2000 Croatians immigrated to Western Australia. Most were single men who may have come as sojourners, intending to work, save money, then go home. Most went to the goldfields and worked in the mines or on the woodlines, chopping down trees that were used to fire the goldmines' furnaces.

Yugoslavs on Sons of Gwalia mine woodline rail service celebrating the November 1945 creation of the Yugoslav Republic

Most were interned during World War 1 because Croatia being a part of the Austro-Hungarian empire, they were, formally, Austrians and therefore enemy aliens. After the war and the empire's collapse, Croatia became a part of the new Kingdom of Serbs, Croats and Slovenes, which in 1929 became the Kingdom of Yugoslavia, comprising six nationalities: Serbs, Croats, Slovenes, Macedonians, Montenegrins and Bosnians.

Democratic at first, in 1929 the kingdom lurched into dictatorship. All political parties, trade unions, rallies and protests were banned and a wave of violence was unleashed against them. The kingdom increasingly fell into the orbit of Italian and German fascism, so in

1941 it signed a non-aggression pact with Germany. Overthrown by the military, which wanted no part of an Axis alliance, the kingdom was then invaded by Germany, which set up a puppet fascist government in Croatia that quickly earned itself a reputation for genocide. The rest of the kingdom was partitioned between the Axis nations. Two new movements began, a Serbian nationalist movement loyal to the monarch and the communist partisans headed by Josep Broz Tito.

After World War 1 most Yugoslav immigrants to Western Australia continued to come from Croatia, most of them at this point intending to stay. They were mostly men but a growing number of women came too. While many moved on to the goldfields, this generation was more likely to remain in the city in suburbs such as Spearwood, Osborne Park and Fremantle, moving out to other suburbs and the Swan Valley as time passed. Most came from the Dalmatian coast, sponsored, like the Croatian memoirist Bart Srhoy, by family already here, and most came after 1924 when their favoured destination, the USA, shut the doors on southern European immigration. In Perth they worked mainly as labourers in quarries, market gardens and lime kilns, although some made good in commerce. Many became naturalised Australians but many more did not and remained, in the language of the time, as 'aliens'. By 1935 there were 7000 Yugoslavs in WA.

Many, perhaps most, immigrants left their homeland partly or wholly for political reasons. Traditions of Left wing politics in Croatia, the postwar turbulence in Europe, the inspiration of the Bolshevik revolution, the repression of and violence against trade unionists and communists (the Communist Party was formed in 1919 and banned the next year) led many to seek new pastures, bringing their politics with them to their new homes.

By the 1930s the Yugoslav community in Perth was well established.

Like many immigrant communities it looked outwards to its homeland and inwards for support against a largely hostile Western Australia. Yugoslavs, indeed all non-British immigrants, were despised by Britishers, including those in the labour movement. Sometimes they were hated, sometimes, as in the 1919 and 1934 Kalgoorlie riots, they were the victims of extreme violence.

Unsurprisingly then, Yugoslav politics on the goldfields, in other parts of the bush and in Perth was almost entirely Left wing. In his 1998 autobiography, Bart Srhoy remembers: 'Their [Croatian] left-leanings developed spontaneously, a product of many causes, including the poor living conditions in their former homeland and the difficulties most of them experienced in Australia.' Some, like Srhoy, joined the nascent WA branch of the CPA; indeed, it was often said that the Party's Spearwood branch was the biggest in Perth. At the 1935 May Day celebration, Gus Marusich, perhaps the leading figure in Yugoslav political life, expressed the optimism (and certainty) of Yugoslav radicals and Western Australian communists when, first in what the Party called 'Jugoslav language', then in English, he proclaimed that 'The workers would secure victory in their march against capitalism precisely because they were members of a revolutionary class and history was on their side'. There were large numbers of Yugoslavs at these celebrations.

Judging by the number of stories about Yugoslav issues in the local CPA paper *Red Star*, the early CPA clearly recognised the importance of its Yugoslav comrades. There were many stories about the dire situation of radicals and workers in Yugoslavia and on their often dire circumstances in WA. Indeed, in 1935 *Red Star* introduced a column written in Yugoslav to help build support for a national Yugoslav language newspaper in Australia. Once established, *Napredak* became the national paper for Yugoslavs in Australia.

The community established many political, musical and social clubs. Most if not all of these were associated with the Left wing national Yugoslav Immigrants' Association, headquartered in Sydney; in Perth they frequently combined to advocate for their members' interests and hold cultural events and picnics. The best known was the Oreski Club, named in honour of Mijo Oreski, a young Croatian communist and a member of the Communist Youth League of Yugoslavia who was killed in 1929 by police during an uprising by the Yugoslav Communist Party against the dictatorship.

Oreski was a cultural and educational club but its shining light was its band, the Oreski String Band. It was a thirty-two member *tamburitsa* band, the *tamburitsas* being eleven different kinds of stringed instruments typical of Balkans musical groups, but only about a dozen musicians played at any one time. The band played all over Perth before, during and after World War 2, at Yugoslav weddings and other Yugoslav occasions, but they also spread their talents far and wide. They performed at Communist Party May Day celebrations, at meetings in support of the WA Anti-Fascist League and Spanish Relief. They played for Labour Day celebrations, and regularly at concerts for the Allied war effort and soldiers' charities during World War 2. When the war was over, they played at the VE Day celebrations and again on Victory Day 1946. They were so well known and so good that they even had a session on Perth radio station 6WF. Their repertoire was mainly classical and Balkan folk music but they also played well-known leftist songs. At one CPA May Day celebration, for instance, they performed 'May Day', 'Lenin's March' (perhaps his funeral march), the Italian communist anthem 'Bandiera Rossa', 'The Internationale', the Croatian 'National Revolutionary March' and many others.

From the 1920s to the 1940s, Perth's Left wing Yugoslavs fought battles on three fronts: politics back home, international politics and politics in Western Australia. The local radicals were always Yugoslav patriots; they were not Croatian nationalists. Their anger towards the Yugoslav government was largely directed at its ruthless repression of communist, socialist and trade union activists, and its ongoing flirtation with fascist Italy and – as the war approached – Nazi Germany. They aligned themselves with the international communist movement and the European democracies and demanded in 1939 that the Yugoslav government do the same. In addition they wanted it to settle all the national questions in Yugoslavia.

They personalised their hostility to the kingdom by attacking the local representative of the Yugoslav government, Perth's vice-consul, regularly confronting him and accusing him of being pro fascist. Of course he responded in kind, accusing the clubs of subversion and of being communists. When he called a meeting to collect funds to memorialise the assassinated Yugoslav king in 1935, he was shouted down. In 1937, after a particularly tense meeting, he refused to see them again. He did, however, and in late 1941, when he proclaimed his support for the treaty between the Yugoslav government and the Nazis, he was again called out by the Leftist groups in a big 350-strong meeting at Unity Hall. The radicals continued campaigning against him throughout the war.

The second front for the clubs was the common international Left wing causes of the 1930s. Perhaps the most prominent was the antiwar and anti-fascist movements, which began in Western Australia in the mid 1930s, particularly the Communist Party fraternal, the WA Council Against War and Fascism, which was established in 1934. It was well organised by Katharine Susannah Prichard; its president (for a time) was Keith George, the director of the Workers' Art Guild, and many academic, feminist and religious luminaries took part and spoke at its meetings.

At the forefront of the movement were the antiwar and antifascist men and women from Perth's Yugoslav community whose clubs marched at peace rallies, their bands played at fundraisers and their leaders spoke at anti-fascist meetings. In 1935, for example, the clubs marched behind banners proclaiming 'Yugoslav Emigrant Workers Unite with Australian Workers against War and Fascism'. At the subsequent meeting on the Esplanade the Oreski band had pride of place on the podium while Yugoslav children paraded in national costumes. They were very prominent in the activities around the Spanish civil war in the later 1930s. In 1938, the Oreski Club protested against any official welcome being given to an Italian warship visiting Fremantle on a 'good will' visit.

How important Yugoslav radicals were to the League can be seen when Gus Marusich was selected to be one of the delegates to the 1934 national antiwar and fascism conference in Melbourne, accompanying Prichard and Mrs Leighton from Kalgoorlie and taking pride of place on podiums when the delegates returned home and reported on the meetings.

Two problems confronted the Yugoslav radicals in the early years of World War 2. The first was the federal United Australia Party government's banning of the CPA and two associated organisations, the League for Peace and Democracy and the Minority Movement. The Yugoslav clubs were never banned and apparently not harassed by police; if the newspaper reports of arrests contained the names of all of those arrested, then no Yugoslavs were arrested either. Members of the CPA met clandestinely (Bart Srhoy remembered meeting Paddy

Troy at these secret meetings) and carried on as normally as they could until John Curtin repealed the ban in 1942.

It is difficult to know what the Yugoslav radicals did with the other problem when Germany and the Soviet Union signed their non-aggression treaty in 1939. The CPA dutifully obeyed the Comintern's instruction to abandon its antiwar and fascism campaign and oppose Australia's involvement in the war. It is possible that the clubs did as well; the Yugoslav vice-consul certainly thought so, as he said in 1939. If he was right, perhaps like the CPA, they believed that it was crucial to defend the Soviet Union against what they regarded as the duplicity of the European imperialist powers. Bart Srhoy thought otherwise, that the local Yugoslavs were always fighting on the side of the Allies; indeed, many Yugoslav men joined the Australian army. Then, when Germany invaded Russia in June 1941, the Comintern, the CPA and the clubs threw their wholehearted support behind the war effort. From then until the end of the war, the clubs remained steadfast, even mortgaging one of their properties to invest £500 in a government austerity loan.

The third front concerned issues that directly affected local Yugoslavs. These were mostly related to work and unemployment. The majority of the action in the 1920s was on the goldfields woodlines where Yugoslav and Italian workers took part in two major strikes, one organised by the AWU against employers, the other against the AWU that was organised by radical One Big Union Wobblies, who believed that the AWU was in the pockets of those same employers. Unrest continued into the 1930s and right through the war.

Like workers everywhere in WA Yugoslav workers were hit hard by the Depression. In 1932 fully half were unemployed, so naturally they became involved in the campaigns of the unemployed. Joe

Micholvitch, one of the eleven men arrested at the Treasury riot in 1931, was a Yugoslav. That September, a large group of unemployed Yugoslav and Italian men declared the Marquis Street unemployed relief depot in West Perth black after the government abolished the sleeping allowance for unemployed aliens. They continued their protest at the Italian anti-fascist club, *La Fratellanza*, and later at a larger demonstration on the Esplanade.

The Yugoslav clubs also turned their attention to the infamous 1934 Kalgoorlie race riots. Gus Marusich had addressed the issue on his way home from the 1934 Melbourne Peace Congress, at which the riots had been discussed. The riots, he proclaimed, were

> the outcome of excessive nationalism, and the congress has warned the people of Australia against indulging in such outbursts, as they were only a reflex on fascism and paved the way to militarism.

The clubs no doubt gave their countrymen and women support in kind and money. They also criticised what they regarded as the woefully inadequate compensation paid by the WA Labor government to Yugoslav and Italian immigrant workers who had lost property. They attacked Premier Phillip Collier, who dismissed their claims and accused them of being communists. Then they criticised the Yugoslav vice-consul, claiming that he was hampering efforts to get better compensation deal. They also fought to be recognised by the wider working class movement. By 1937, the CPA's united front policy had replaced its earlier sectarianism, so the Yugoslav clubs began to call for closer relationships with working class organisations (joining the Labour Day marches was a sign of this). They criticised those in and outside the labour movement who called them inferior by expressing pride in their radical and anti-fascist heritage. They declared:

We, the emigrants [*sic*] from Yugoslavia, protest against such weak arguments. We, racially and nationally, are not inferior to any other race. Does not the fight of our brothers and sisters in our native land against bestial fascism prove that as well as all our history? Our history is one of fighting against those who are responsible for our economic and cultural backwardness.

When the war was over, most in the Yugoslav community celebrated the Allied victory and the seizure of power by Tito's communist partisans. Perhaps a thousand of them returned to help build the new nation of Yugoslavia. An unintended consequence of this exodus was the decline and disappearance of many of the clubs. One of these may have been the Oreski Club. When, after the war, new generations of immigrants from Croatia arrived, many were displaced persons; many more were fleeing communist Yugoslavia. In contrast to the prewar immigrants these were Right wing, anti-communist Croatian nationalists, well suited to Bob Menzies' Cold War Australia. Life for the prewar radicals had always been difficult, but it was about to become more so, this time in part at the hands of their own countrymen.

9
Monty Miller and other Early Perth Radicals

Charlie Fox

In January 1897, when Monty Miller arrived in Perth from Victoria, he already had a forty year history of radical politics, beginning at the Eureka Stockade in 1854 where, when just a boy, he tended the wounded and buried the dead. He was a trade unionist, rationalist, free thinker, anarchist and propagandist, already a veteran of the Yarra Bank, Melbourne's open air speakers' corner. In Perth he soon found his way to the Esplanade, Perth's own speakers' corner, where he addressed a meeting on 7 February about a building trades industrial dispute. It was, wrote a journalist from the *West Australian* the next day, 'a highly interesting address', delivered with 'much attractiveness and grace of style'. The journalist was writing about Monty Miller, already an eloquent, spirited and learned orator.

Miller quickly made himself known in other circles, too. Within a month he was elected president of the Theosophical Society, giving talks on such topics as 'Thought and its uses and abuses', 'Charles Darwin' and 'Principles of good and evil'. In 1897 he helped form and quickly became president of the Labour Church. He was an early member and later vice president of the Single Tax League, then, in 1901, was instrumental in forming and became president of the Social Democratic Federation, WA's first truly socialist organisation.

Montague 'Monty' Miller, as a young man

In Melbourne in 1907, he joined the Wobblies, reportedly saying, 'This is the organisation I have been waiting for all of my life'. Monty's favourite speech was entitled 'Why I am a Socialist'. Truly, he was the father of Western Australian radicalism and the patron of Perth's small radical subculture.

Monty arrived to a booming and bustling Perth, still small with about 65 000 people but filled with gold fever exuberance. The city's working class – largely composed of refugees from the misery of Depression Melbourne, many of them miners who had given up and gone on to Perth – was growing and organising: by 1900 there were about thirty trade unions in Perth and Fremantle, often led by British immigrant unionists or unionists from the east. Oddly, until 1900, unions were illegal and striking was forbidden under the *Master and Servant Act 1842*, yet working with middle class liberals, unions were able to win the eight hour day in 1892.

The coastal unions were largely craft bodies with trade related concerns and restricted visions, committed to respectability, happy to work with the status quo. But mixed in were occasional militant unions such as the Fremantle Lumpers (waterside workers), who in 1899 struck for a closed shop. After a false start, several unions set up a coastal Trades and Labor Council (TLC) in 1892. Then in 1899 it joined the goldfields TLC to form a colonywide body that quickly turned its attention to politics. In 1900 unions won an arbitration and conciliation system through a deal with the conservative but artful premier, John Forrest, which also required that they be legalised, promoted union membership and drew them into the system. Of course they had the awful example of the defeat of the big strikes in the east to prod them towards arbitration and politics, so in 1899 they also set up the Political Labor Party, forerunner of the Australian Labor Party (ALP), which stood candidates for the federal and state parliaments in the newly federated commonwealth. And did well. The Labor Party had been launched.

Perth's radical culture was tiny and located mainly in the CBD. Today, it is hard to find any trace of many of the places where it was nurtured: Green's Building on the corner of Hay and William Streets was an earlier favourite for meetings; indeed, the early TLC and several unions found homes there. Others were the YWCA Leisure Hour Club in Hay Street, the Oddfellows' Hall on William Street, the old and new Mechanics Institutes, both in Hay Street, the latter a splendid baroque building designed by the same architect who designed His Majesty's Theatre, and the Hibernian Hall in Murray Street. Then of course there was the Esplanade. Indeed, it was Perth's small radical movement that did as much as anybody to claim the Esplanade for a public meeting place. Only the Hibernian Hall remains today.

What might Monty Miller have told the Labour Church at its first meeting at the Oddfellows' Hall in William Street? He might have pointed out that it was the first real radical labour organisation in Perth; that from small beginnings in Manchester, England, it had spread rapidly around the English-speaking world. He might have said that it was an attempt by non-conformist Protestants in England to engage with the labour movement. Then he might have become theological, showing how the church rejected evangelicalism, theological abstraction and biblical literalism for a belief that the divine was immanent in every human and human society. But most likely he would have said that the Labour Church was about the brotherhood of man and it was on this ethical grounding that a Christian socialism could be built.

The Labour Church must have seemed a strange beast to regular churchgoers. There were no church buildings, priests, services, bibles or pulpits, just a chairman, speakers and a crowd. Initially, it met weekly but soon set up a discussion evening on Wednesdays, and then a library, lending books to members. Its early leaders were all trade unionists: William Mellor was secretary of the Builders' Labourers' Federation (BLF) and a former president of Sydney's Australian Labour Federation (ALF), Fred Davis was the secretary of the Coastal TLC, H. Gibson was an officer of the Federated Engine Drivers' and Firemen's Association (FEDFA) and, of course, Miller was everywhere.

Despite that, the Labour Church was short lived. In February 1898, it handed over its fortnightly meeting to the new Single Tax League (STL); then, in March, it ceased meeting altogether. Perhaps it fell apart. William Mellor was killed at work in 1897 and Miller moved on. In 1901 he was arguing against any relationship between Christianity and socialism. Or, perhaps as was the case in England, the church became uncertain about its purpose. Was it educational or activist? In goldrush Western Australia, could the ideal of the brotherhood of man cut it? Whatever, the novelty and millenarian promise of the single tax simply took its members away.

The STL began in Perth in February 1898 at a twenty-strong meeting, with some carryover members from the Labour Church. It grew quickly and was bigger, longer lasting and more influential than the Labour Church, but it arrived in WA well after it had lost its radical credentials in the east. It seems to have lasted here until 1908. Percy Meggy, chairman of the first meeting, introduced the concept of the single tax to a small audience. The earth, he argued, which belonged to humanity in common and was hence the source of all wealth, had been monopolised by the few, the consequence being the poverty of the many. How to return the earth (or land) to the people? The answer was given by US economist and visionary Henry George. It was the single tax, a tax on the unimproved value of all land, a tax that by its universality would make all other taxes unnecessary. From the land seized from those who sat on undeveloped land and from a fund created by this tax, all this now-socialised rent would be returned to the community to create jobs, raise wages, end poverty, and reduce rents and prices.

The attraction of the single tax lay in its simplicity, its appeal to traditional radical values and to Henry George's brilliantly persuasive writing. In Perth it appealed to the same people as it had in the east: sympathisers with the labour movement and supporters among a wider progressive middle class. But in 1903 it ran into trouble. To single taxers, tariffs were just another burdensome tax to be abolished but tariff protection of Australian manufacturing had become an article of faith in the early labour movement. Who then should the STL support: its labour movement supporters or free traders, who were concentrated in conservative politics? It went with the conservatives. To Perth's labour and radical movements who railed against exploitation, the single tax then became just one plank in their political platform.

Perth's first avowedly socialist organisation was established in 1901, when Perth's radicals met at the Leisure Hour Club to found the Social Democratic Federation (SDF). Mirroring similarly named bodies in the eastern states, it was both socialist and democratic. As it stated in its first article in the workers' paper, the *Westralian Worker*, on August 23, 'Democracy without socialism is futile and socialism without democracy is tyranny'. It had come, the article continued, to 'broaden the spirit of the labour movement, to give it purpose', and this meant turning the movement to socialism. Its socialism was 'the socialisation of the means and instruments of production, distribution and exchange'. But the message in the article was broader, for it was also antiwar, arguing that 'the interests of labour is everywhere peace', and that 'all wars are capitalist wars'. At the time Australia was sending troops to the Boer War. Its socialism, the SDF said, was ordained by history, its pacifism by the build-up of armaments already going on in Europe.

Sadly, it too quickly disappeared. After apparently going into recess in 1903, it returned briefly the next year before disappearing altogether from the Perth scene. A branch of the SDF remained in Kalgoorlie, at least until World War 1, where it acted as ginger group in the ALP's Eastern Goldfields District Council.

Each of these bodies was educational (the SDF called its method 'propaganda by tongue and pen'). They each rented a clubroom in the Perth CBD where they held their executive meetings, discussion groups and public meetings. The former dealt with the run of the mill business requisite of any small organisation: plan strategies, get the message out, arrange speakers who could draw a crowd, or debates that would raise their profile and prove their virtue. They advertised their meetings in Perth's daily newspaper or on printed handbills, or simply around the streets. Depending on the speaker (and the weather) a small band of supporters or a larger body of the curious would file in, find a seat and sit down. They were mostly men, with a sprinkling of women, for these movements were largely masculine affairs. Mostly workers, there may also have been a good turnout of middle class followers. Like many union leaders, the leaders were most likely to have come to WA from the United Kingdom or the eastern colonies and brought labour, trade union and radical ideas with them. They were usually busy people, working in their trades for long hours, some also working for their unions and political bodies, others simply doing the rounds of whatever was on.

The chairman opened the meeting, then there was often music, singing or poetry, for these were musical times; singing and recitation were traditional forms of family and public entertainment. So one night in the Labour Church, it was the English parlour song 'Children's Home', on another, a recitation of Wordsworth's 1799 poem *The Ruined Cottage*, or Henry Lawson's book *In The Days When The World Was Wide* (1900), performances that would entertain and make people think. Then would come the speakers, sometimes famous visitors such as the English socialist Tom Mann, who spoke to an overflowing SDF meeting in the Hibernian Hall in 1904. In 1901, John Lane, brother of William Lane, founder with others of the Paraguayan utopian settlements, New Australia and Cosme, spoke to a meeting in the new Mechanics Institute. Sometimes vigorous debates would spill over to a next meeting, such as when, also in 1901, Monty Miller debated a fellow member of the SDF, the Reverend G. D. Buchanan, on the relationship between socialism and Christianity.

More often, though, speakers would be veterans of Perth's public speaking roundabout or committee members, who addressed an astonishing range of topics: politics, philosophy, history, biology, economics and theology. Among Monty Miller's lectures were 'The future of labour', 'The curse of drink' (he was a fervent temperance advocate), 'Human physiology', 'Social progress', 'Woman's position as a worker', 'The difference between socialism and anarchy', 'Bi-metalism' (a doctrine that advocated gold and silver as the basis for national currencies) and, of course, socialism. While some speakers were from the radical middle class, most were self-educated members of the working class, voracious seekers of knowledge and wisdom, learning all that they were never taught at school and would never learn at university.

They also loved books. The SDF was fond of quoting Ralph Waldo Emerson's dictum: 'Fellow workers, begin now. Read, think, act and be free.' Although, by the end of the nineteenth century, Perth had a state and a travelling library and there was also a library in the Mechanics Institute, none it seems purchased radical political tracts, so radicals set up their own libraries and bought books such as Marx's *Capital* (1867), Robert Blatchford's *Merrie England* (1893), Henry George's *Poverty and Progress* (1879), Edward Bellamy's *Looking Backward* (1888), William Morris' *News From Nowhere* (1890) and many more. There were also Australian and overseas labour and radical newspapers and, from 1901, WA's new labour paper, the *Westralian Worker*.

These bodies also took their messages outdoors. Having played their part in establishing the Esplanade as Perth's speakers' corner, they would set up their stands on Sunday afternoons. They became regulars, indeed once or twice they joined forces, for instance, celebrating Henry George's birthday in August 1901. Monty Miller was the standout performer. The *Westralian Worker* wrote of his 'sonorous eloquence and white hot earnestness', the *Daily News* praised his 'fine gift of speech, [and his] flow of eloquence that never fails to impress'. But Monty was at his best on May Day, the day that became Perth's radicals' most important day.

Perth's first May Day was in 1897, when a small crowd organised by the Democratic Reform League and the Labour Church called a meeting on the Esplanade to deliver motions, which, in one form or another, became staples of May Day meetings for years: sending fraternal greetings to radical groups everywhere, demanding universal peace, and setting out a program for a new world order. In 1897 – reflecting the ideology of the Labour Church – the meeting called for a society based on 'mutual cooperation and universal brotherhood'. Two years later Monty Miller moved a motion calling for the abolition of monopolies.

Then, in 1902, the SDF took charge of May Day and socialism became the banner motion. According to the *Westralian Worker*, the SDF resolved that

> This meeting declares that the wage slavery of the workers, and the poverty, misery, and degradation attendant on modern civilisation, arise from the private ownership of the sources of wealth, and the capitalistic organisation of industry, that political freedom without economic freedom is a delusion and a sham and that the economic freedom of the workers can be achieved only by the socialisation of the means and instruments of production, distribution and exchange and by the fraternal organisation of industry.

These bodies didn't restrict themselves solely to propaganda; they also worked inside the Labor Party and the trade unions, trying to draw them to a commitment to the single tax, socialism and peace. And it worked. You can find the STL's tax on unimproved land values in early ALP platforms. The SDF proclaimed that the true position of Labor and of trade unions was socialism, and it worked hard to persuade them to believe it too. Again with some success. In 1901 the SDF persuaded the third Trade Union and Labour Congress, held in Kalgoorlie, to adopt a socialist declaration, for the establishment of an 'industrial commonwealth, founded upon the collective ownership and use of land and capital and upon popular control of legislation and administration'. But there were contradictions in the SDF's work too. It claimed success in turning the Labor Party towards socialism and so urged workers to support it in elections, but it also hammered the Party relentlessly for adopting 'palliatives' to deal with injustice and poverty and for not being socialist enough.

Monty Miller's journey in WA radicalism continued until he died. He became a stalwart of the IWW locals and the Esplanade. Wobblies vehemently opposed the war and, after being tried for sedition in early 1917 and given a good behaviour bond, Miller went to Sydney to continue the fight. He was sent off by a large and admiring party. John Curtin remarked in his farewell speech that he 'knew of no man in Australia who had done more for the labour movement than Monty Miller'. Miller was sent to prison again for breaking his good behaviour bond and after his release, having been stripped of his old age pension, was forced to travel the country making a living by public speaking. He returned to Perth after the war and flung himself once again into politics. In 1918 he was propagandising in Fremantle and the goldfields for the Wobbly successor, the One Big Union. In December 1919, at the age of eighty-eight, he spoke at Trades Hall. For a man of his age, his energy and stamina were extraordinary, but it couldn't last. A year later he was dead, buried in Karrakatta Cemetery with red flags flying, a hero of the labour movement. In December 1920, a new party emerged that would carry on the radical tradition – the Communist Party of Australia.

10
The Red Dean and Rock Masses in the Long 1960s
Charlie Fox

As cathedrals go, St George's Anglican Cathedral in Perth's central business district is rather small, smaller than Perth's Catholic cathedral and tiny compared to the grand cathedrals in Europe. Like all churches it is a place of prayer, solemnity, meditation and peace. A more unlikely place for bringing together heavy rock music and Christian masses would be hard to find. Yet in 1970 and 1971, a rebel priest, a progressive rock band and a jazz band, gathered thousands of Perth's young together in the cathedral for five rock masses to celebrate love, peace and freedom. This was the 1960s, that great romantic era, which, in Australia, we suggest, began in 1960 with first staging of Alan Seymour's seditious play, *The One Day of the Year*, and ended with the dismissal of the Whitlam government in 1975. It was a time of cultural revolution, when change was in the air and anything seemed possible. In Australia the rock masses took place in its high 1960s. There was no year of rage as there had been in Europe and the USA, and no Paris 1968 in Australia. It was the early 1970s when Australia's youth was at its most radical: Australia's anti-Vietnam war marches reached their peak and the anti-Springbok demonstrations disrupted matches. Germaine Greer's *The Female Eunuch* was published in 1970, the Aboriginal Tent Embassy was established in Canberra in

1972 and the Nimbin countercultural festival was held in 1973. If the 1960s was more a spirit of the times than a decade, then the 1960s kept on keeping on in Perth in the 1970s and the rock masses were prime moments in it.

St George's Cathedral, opened in 1888, was home to Perth's Anglicans. It was built in the English Victorian gothic revival style, with its historical traditions and conservative overtones. As a cathedral it is home to Perth's Anglican bishop and therefore to the administrative and hierarchical life of Perth's Anglican diocese. One might expect, therefore, some opposition among the Anglican establishment to the upheavals the rock masses seemed to promise. There was, but not much. After the first one, they took on a life of their own and some twenty-eight were staged in all, in the cathedral and in other Anglican churches around the state.

There were five original rock masses: the rock mass for peace held in December 1970, and the rock masses against pollution, for freedom, love and life, all held from March to July 1971. They were the brainchild of the Dean of Perth, the Very Reverend John Hazlewood, who arrived in 1968 to take charge of St George's Cathedral. Hazlewood was tall, good looking, fashionably dressed and with it. He was popular with Perth's youth because of the interest he took in them. He was also a bundle of contradictions, sometimes radical, sometimes conservative. One moment he could defend young people against the hypocrisy of their elders, the next he could lambast them for not respecting 'discipline, pride in work, loyalty, patriotism and the honouring of parents'. He was opposed to Australia's involvement in the Vietnam war and the conscription of young men to fight in it. He supported homosexual law reform (homosexual acts were punished with prison terms at that time) and the decriminalisation of marijuana, and criticised police and the courts for the way they enforced these laws. On the other hand, he opposed the anti-Springbok demonstrations and later opposed the ordination of women. Most importantly for this story, though, was his belief that the church was out of touch with young people.

The second party to the rock masses was Perth's leading progressive rock band, Bakery. Bakery had met the Dean at the Bindoon Rock Festival – he used to hang out at concerts and nightclubs – in early 1970 and, remarking on the presence of the Dean at a rock festival, laughingly suggested taking rock music to church. Religion at a rock festival, rock music in a cathedral. The Dean liked the idea and began the planning. The members of Bakery who played the rock masses were Peter Walker on guitar, Hank Davis on drums, Eddie McDonald on bass and Rex Bullen on keyboards; Tom Davidson was lead vocalist. Progressive or prog rock was existential rock, expressing the tropes of that love, peace and freedom ethic that stood at the centre of the 1960s counterculture. Prog rock bands played serious music and were more likely to be heard at music festivals than on Top 20 radio, on long playing records rather than singles. Unlike pop and its guitar, drums and verse:chorus format, this music was innovative, creative and experimental. It was music best listened to rather than danced to, high on dope rather than cold. Its lyrics were intelligent and committed, a far cry from the boy meets girl theme of pop. The themes of prog rock – love, peace, freedom, life – were also the themes of rock masses.

The third party was the Jazz Ensemble led by drummer Bruce Devenish, with Lionel Davis on baritone and tenor saxes, flute and clarinet, Tony Ashford on soprano and alto saxes, Des Kirk on trumpet and Bill Gumbleton on electric piano. Devenish was a jazz-loving hippie and atheist. He took the gig because he wanted to be a part of something that promised to bring new ideas to Perth's youth. In Perth, jazz was a small part of the music scene; perhaps it was outsiders' music, as it once was in early twentieth century USA. Black jazz and white radicals had a long relationship in the USA. In the 1950s, black jazz musos and white beatnik authors such Jack Kerouac and Allen Ginsberg worked up a relationship out of their shared exclusion and alienation. The beat writers loved jazz and wrote jazz beats into their writing – think of Kerouac's *On the Road* and Ginsberg's *Howl*. Devenish was a fan of Miles Davis so brought a little bit of Miles' musical journey to the masses.

Between 4000 and 6000 people turned up to each of the rock masses, half finding their way into the cathedral, the rest watching on closed circuit TV and listening to loudspeakers on the steps and the grass outside. The masses made quite a picture. Inside, the pews had been removed to make way for as many people as possible. Two thousand young people crammed in, sitting on the floor or leaning against the walls. They listened quietly to the Dean but laughed at his jokes, applauded the music, sometimes politely, sometimes raucously. The Dean, Bakery and the Jazz Ensemble did their thing, sometimes in a smoky haze of incense, dope and tobacco. A video from the time shows a very hairy Bakery standing behind the altar with their microphones, instruments and amplifiers, surrounded by psychedelic posters proclaiming love and peace, religious iconography and the paraphernalia of the mass: candelabras, crucifixes and the rest. Strobe lights lit the scene. Tom Davidson, bare chested under a Native American jacket, moved like an early Peter Garrett. The Dean looked serious one moment, grooved the next; his assistants, the archdeacon, sacristan, verger and sidemen in their religious vestments, clapped

Poster advertising the Rock Mass for Peace

Bakery setting up, St Georges Cathedral, The Rock Mass for Love, 1971

and swayed to the beat.

The crowd was mixed, young men in hippie gear, barefoot, long haired young women in minis, maxis and jeans. Some doubtless came for the mass, others for the novelty, others just for the music, but to come for the music meant coming for Bakery and a journey into the underground.

The masses took a traditional form: prayers, readings from the Bible, blessings, and addresses from the Dean, who welcomed people to the cathedral and delivered the theme of the day. Hundreds of people took Holy Communion from a row of six priests, to background music played by the bands. Anglican masses are musical so in the rock masses, Bakery and the Jazz Ensemble took the place of the traditional organ and choir. Devenish wrote the liturgical music, giving it a jazz treatment and the Jazz Ensemble played it. For the Mass for Love he composed music for the prayer *Kyrie Eleison*, the backing for several other prayers, words and music for *Song of the Creed* and the backing music for holy communion. Indeed, listen to the long playing record *A Rock Mass for Love* and you will hear as much of Devenish as of the Dean and Bakery.

Bakery performed four of their own songs, two of them – 'Do You Really Care?' and 'Trust in the Lord' – written especially for the masses, plus several covers from the 1960s songbook: Deep Purple's 'Child in Time' in the Rock Mass for Peace, Healing Force's 'Golden Miles' in the Rock Mass for Freedom, John Mayall's 'Nature's Disappearing' in the Rock Mass Against Pollution, and The Hollies' 'He Ain't Heavy, He's My Brother' in the Rock Mass for Love being some of the better known. The band had great songs to choose from. Think, for example, of the Beatles' 'All You Need Is Love', the antiwar songs of Country Joe and the Fish, John and Yoko's 'Give Peace a Chance', Joni Mitchell's

'Big Yellow Taxi' and Ritchie Havens singing 'Freedom' at Woodstock. The 1960s protest songbook is large and magnificent.

The Dean presented the Rock Mass themes from Anglican doctrine, in which God was the source of all things that are good, where peace, love and freedom were gifts from God; doubtless the religious tones resonated with many of the young. To others, peace, love and freedom were secular beliefs. To some they were fully articulated in political programs. It was these people who formed the counterculture, the hippie communes, the intentional communities, where peace, love and freedom would be nurtured. For those unwilling to make such a commitment, it was hard to invent a political program that would deliver such inchoate ideas; for every hippie activist there were a hundred fellow travellers who just looked for a better world free of prejudice, violence, hate, war and oppression.

Yet, the love–peace–free ethic came from well-articulated intellectual sources: mystic religions from India, New Left philosophers, indigenous metaphysics and Christian doctrines. The committed were opposed to all wars, although Vietnam acted as a catalyst for all antiwar sentiment at the time. They were opponents of capitalism and communism, critics of Australian racism, nationalism, imperial subservience, orthodox politics and political parties. They condemned big institutions such as prisons, hospitals for the insane, the military, universities, schools and bureaucracies for propping up the system. They sought new human relationships unmediated by the alienating tendencies of rationalism, technocracy and the market; instead they believed in the emotional life of love, beauty and imagination. Freedom, they believed, lay less in the acquisition of political rights and more in freedom from the repressive social world and the repressed self, from freeing up sexuality to rebelling against parents, from wearing what you wanted to, listening to the music you wanted to, to exploring the unconscious through dope and LSD, freeing yourself from inhibitions to allow the full play of self-expression and imagination. Herbert Marcuse, the revisionist Marxist and guiding light of the young revolutionaries, described it best in his book *An Essay on Liberation*, in which he wrote that the New Society 'will be one where the hatred of the young bursts into laughter and song, mixing the barricades and the dance floor, love, play and heroism'.

By the middle of 1973 the rock masses were over. In 1975, the Dean observed that young people now found pop music shallow and without depth. And, as historians of Australian rock music will say, it was. Ominously for prog rock, while Bakery was playing in the cathedral, Daddy Cool's anthem to fun, 'Eagle Rock', was number one on the Australian charts, signifying the beginning of the end for the serious lyrics and sonorous chords of the great underground bands. By 1973, too, the protest movements had faded, the future looked brighter, Australian troops had left Vietnam and Gough Whitlam's Labor government offered the possibility of real change. But a year later Skyhooks wrote their lament for lost opportunities, 'Whatever Happened to the Revolution? / We all got stoned and it drifted away'. The rock masses disappeared and the love–peace–free ethic was on its way to becoming a golden age set in the stone of the past.

11
The 1931 Treasury Building Riot
Alex Salmon

It is the early afternoon of 6 March 1931 and thousands of unemployed workers have gathered on the Perth Esplanade to protest the continued inaction of James Mitchell's National–Country Party government and its inability to provide employment or adequate relief for the unemployed and their families. After attending a protest meeting, the men will march from the Esplanade to the Treasury Building at the intersection of St Georges Terrace and Barrack Street to await the results of a deputation carrying a list of demands to Mitchell for the government to address. Among the protestors is a young communist named Sid Foxley, who emigrated to Western Australia from England in the early 1920s. Having seen the worsening unemployment situation leading up to the Great Depression in Western Australia Foxley joined the Communist Party of Australia in 1931. Foxley will be one of the key participants in the events that will become known as the Treasury Riot.

Built in 1874 in a late Victorian style by architects R. R. Jewell and G. T. Poole, the Treasury served as the main building in the city for government business; the premier and the opposition leader had their offices there. For unemployed protesters, the Treasury Building was conveniently located near the Esplanade, which unemployed men had long used for demonstrations and where many unemployed men were forced to sleep. Not far from there was the Perth Labour Bureau where the unemployed went to apply for relief work and sustenance. On Beaufort Street in Northbridge was the Trades Hall, where the unemployed went to collect meal and bed tickets and hold organising meetings. Its location made the Treasury Building a perfect target for protest. On that March day, it was the site of the biggest protest in Western Australia during the Great Depression, when up to 3000 unemployed protestors demonstrated against the government's lack of action in regard to the growing unemployment and fought back after being attacked by the police. Up to 7000 people looked on, no doubt amazed by the size and fury of the protest.

By 1931 the unemployed had plenty of reasons to feel unhappy at the inaction of the Mitchell government, which had come to power the previous year promising to provide work for all, but had failed so far to do anything for the unemployed. At an earlier protest in February 1931, unemployed activists had managed to get James Scaddan, a former ALP member turned conservative politician who was responsible for unemployment relief, to promise that if they would wait for Mitchell's return from a premiers' conference in Canberra he would see if anything could be done for them. Upon Mitchell's return on 5 March, nothing was done so activists decided to organise a protest meeting on the Esplanade. The meeting would march up to the Treasury to wait while a deputation presented its demands to Mitchell. To advertise the protest, some of the unemployed chalked up a notice – 'Unemployed Demonstration, 1.30pm Friday, March 6, Police cordially invited' – on the base of the Alexander Forrest statue outside Government Gardens (now Stirling Gardens). Handbills headed 'Solidarity or Starvation' were distributed, calling for the unemployed to 'Parade their poverty, parade it on the Esplanade and to those who are responsible'.

Although times had been tough for the unemployed in the 1920s, as evidenced by the unemployed protest movement, the Wall Street crash of October 1929 signalled the beginning of the Great Depression. By June 1930 it was reported in the *West Australian* that an estimated 3250 men were out of work in the Perth metropolitan area between Midland Junction and Fremantle, but this number would have represented only a fraction of those out of work. To gain any relief or sustenance, a married man had to report to the State Labour Bureau on Pier Street, and then wait seven days before reporting to the Bureau's Bennett Street office in West Perth to fill out a form and attach a declaration stating how many children he had. After that he would be given 7 shillings a day for himself, his wife and up to five children. The most a family would receive was 49 shillings a week, meaning the family was expected to survive on 1 shilling or less a day for each family member.

For single men the situation was even tougher. According to Sid Foxley, there was no proper sustenance or relief for single unemployed men before 1930, so they were forced to rely on private charity. In 1930 the lord mayor of Perth set up a relief fund that allowed for a number of single men to get two 6 penny meal tickets and a 1 shilling bed ticket a day, which could be used at a Salvation Army hostel. Until 1931 this fund was privately administered but subsidised by the government. Afterwards the government was forced to take it over.

It had become clear that Australian governments, whether Labor or conservative, were unable to deal adequately with the growing economic crisis. By early 1932 unemployment peaked in Western Australia at around 30 per cent. It was the growing frustration at government inaction that led to unemployed demonstrations taking

Three thousand unemployed men march to the Treasury Buildings to confront Premier Sir James Mitchell 6 March 1931

on a militant edge in the early 1930s. In late 1930 the CPA's national leadership sent over Jack Stevens to lead the party's intervention into the unemployed movement in Western Australia. The CPA leadership believed that, by carrying out disciplined and organised protest, the unemployed would win better conditions and sustenance.

On 6 March, the unemployed gathered on the Esplanade for the demonstration. All the leaders of the demonstration emphasised that they didn't want trouble with the police. Between 2000 and 3000 people marched from the Esplanade to the Treasury Building to await the outcome of the deputation to the premier. The deputation presented the following demands:

1. Three 1/- meals a day, instead of two sixpenny ones.
2. Unemployed single men should have the choice of sleeping accommodation and men who did not have homes should receive bed tickets and rations.
3. Unemployed people coming to Perth should not have to wait seven days for sustenance.
4. Entrance to Blackboy camp should be made voluntary.
5. No unemployed should be forced to work for sustenance.
6. In cases of necessity, the government should provide books and clothing.
7. School children of unemployed should be given free schoolbooks.
8. Unemployed should be able to earn 30/- a week and still retain sustenance.
9. Marquis Street (Unemployed and rations depot) should be improved so men didn't have to stand in the rain.
10. Civil Servants and others in employment should be debarred from taking weekend jobs.
11. Unemployed married men should be given their equivalent in rent and sustenance.
12. A woman should be appointed to assist in issue of relief to expectant mothers.

When the protesters reached their destination they found their way blocked by the police. Foxley and another protestor were holding a banner when Police Inspector James Douglas told them to move back off the road. Foxley said he couldn't because of the crowds behind him and that they were backed up against a bus. It is unclear what happened next but very soon the police and the protestors were fighting running battles, surging backwards and forwards along St Georges Terrace. Police witness Alexander Berkeley, assistant secretary to the premier, claimed that it was Foxley who struck first and that when the crowd started getting unruly the police had to baton charge the protestors. Other witnesses said that it was Douglas who was the first to strike and that police wielded their batons with force. When the fighting started, the unemployed protestors gave the police as good as they got, fighting back with whatever they could find, including stones and pickets from fences from the nearby Government Gardens. According to one report these stones and pickets could be seen flying through the air. Reports in the press claimed that just nine people were injured, but it would surely have been more, as police also attacked some in the watching crowds. Eight demonstrators, including Foxley and Stevens, were arrested.

Then began predictable attempts to attribute blame and justify police violence. The *West Australian* disapprovingly reported that all the speakers at the Esplanade meeting before the march began had 'foreign accents' and a communist banner was carried on the march. The communist bogey was also used by WA Police Commissioner Robert Connell to justify the conduct of the police that day. Writing to John Scaddan, who held the portfolio of police minister, Connell claimed that the 6 March protest was all part of a communist plot to incite disorder by exploiting the discontent of the unemployed, who would be receptive to their ideas. The police had to act to stop this from happening. Scaddan undoubtedly agreed with commissioner's anti-communist beliefs and was only too happy to blame the CPA for the Treasury Riot. Despite CPA involvement in the protest, it is clear that the unemployed were protesting because of their own grievances.

Although in the past the ALP hadn't been sympathetic to the radical unemployed movement – and relations between the unemployed and the labour movement had been strained – the ALP used the protest to attack the record of its conservative opponents. In its 13 March issue, the *Westralian Worker* wrote a damning attack in an article entitled 'Give them a dose of the baton':

> The men are hungry men, disappointed men who have realised that the Mitchell promises were mere election cries and not to be fulfilled; men who are becoming desperate; men who took the only course to impress upon the smug and well fed men the condition they were in. And men who were informed in the most convincing manner that for every head who harbours thoughts of resentment there is a baton in the hand of a hefty, well-conditioned policeman.

Other elements of the working class movement also protested. Some 200 people attended a meeting at the Midland Junction Trades Hall to complain about the police treatment of protestors. The meeting called on the ALP to organise mass stop work meetings of unionists throughout Western Australia. The Fremantle Lumpers Union (FLU), the Society of Operative Plasterers and the mining branch of the AWU all passed resolutions of protest. The FLU also called for the dismissal of the police inspector responsible for attacking the protestors. The CPA's national paper, *Workers Weekly*, denounced the police as hirelings of capitalism and reported on a march later that day outside the GPO in the city that called for the dismissal of Inspector Johnstone, the officer with overall responsibility for police tactics. In this, they were supported by an unlikely source. That scandal sheet, the *Mirror*, also called for his removal. An anonymous leaflet entitled

'Black Friday', probably produced by the CPA, accused the police of acting like Cossacks in tsarist Russia.

Some police later expressed sympathy for the unemployed. After he retired, H. E. Graves, one of the officers involved in policing the 6 March protest, wrote in his memoir:

> Now rioting is all wrong and cannot be tolerated. I am all for stopping it quickly; but at the same time men do not rampage up and down the street waving the hammer and sickle, demanding food and relief, for no reason at all.

Later that month, the eight defendants, along with three people who were arrested at the protest outside the GPO on the night of 6 March, appeared in court. In relation to whether Sid Foxley started the riot by striking at Inspector Johnston or was defending himself, all the police witnesses and Alexander Berkley agreed with Johnston's account. Many other witnesses, including an Anglican minister, claimed that Foxley was defending himself and that the police unjustly and violently attacked the protestors. The magistrate ruled that, while some young police had indeed used excessive force, they were justified because the protestors outnumbered them. After one of the defendants pleaded guilty, seven (including Foxley) were found guilty, five were sent to prison, two were fined and four were acquitted.

As for the demands that the deputation of unemployed men presented to Premier Mitchell, he dismissed the three 1/- meals a day demand as 'hopeless' and took no action on the other demands. Later in its period in office, the government did institute relief projects, including at Frankland River in the state's southwest. This would see another protest in September 1932, when relief workers stopped work and marched to Mount Barker, where they boarded a train to Perth to campaign for better conditions. Katharine Susannah Prichard eloquently described the misery on this march in a pamphlet she called *The March from Frankland River*.

This protest helped to seal the fate of the Mitchell government, which was trounced at the polls in 1933 by the ALP. Fortunately, the Collier Labor government was slightly better in dealing with mass unemployment. The unemployed would continue to organise throughout the 1930s, but the government refused to tolerate the existence of any organisations of the unemployed, actively crushing the Relief and Sustenance Workers Union in 1933–34. Still, the unemployed persisted, a Council Against Unemployment being formed as late as 1938. But no other protest matched the scale of the so-called Treasury Riot of 6 March 1931.

The Treasury Building ceased to be used for government offices in 1996 and stood empty for many years. Recent renovations that transformed the building into a five star hotel are a far cry from the bitter days of the Depression for this backdrop of the Treasury Riot. But it is worth reflecting on the history of this magnificent edifice on the corner of St Georges Terrace and Barrack Street and remembering the hungry men of 1931 who were desperate enough to fight back against the police batons.

12
Art as a Weapon: The Workers' Art Guild

Charlie Fox

> Believing that the commercial theatre, if it has any relation to reality, concerns itself in only a small part of life, the Workers' Theatre has set itself the aim of showing Perth a drama which is nearer the interests of the ordinary man and particularly a drama dealing with the social structure from the point of view of the working man or woman.
>
> **Maurie Lachberg,** *Daily News,* **6 June 1936**

This was how one of its founders, Maurie Lachberg, launched the Workers' Art Guild (WAG) theatre program in Perth in 1936, with a clarion call for a new form of theatre, with new perspectives, styles and topics. What followed for the next five years was a succession of stunning plays, the likes of which Perth had never seen. An international movement, emanating from Europe, the USA and the Soviet Union in the 1920s and 1930s, had arrived in Perth – a movement of radical, working class theatre with politicised plots, avant-garde methods, sets and artwork. Yet there was much more to the WAG than its presence in Perth's theatrical world.

Although stories about its beginnings differ, it is definitely known that the Guild was formed in 1935 after meetings between Katharine Susannah Prichard, carpenter Maurie Lachberg, theatre director

Keith George and others, the intention being to set up an organisation to not only foster all the arts, but also to give them a radical, even revolutionary, twist and a more democratic form. The Guild formed different sections: literary, dance, plastic and graphic arts, drama, and music. For radicals it also acted as a point of entry into wider philosophical and political debates.

By 1934 the worst of the Great Depression was over, but unemployment was still sky high, misery and poverty endemic, wages low and working hours long. Perth was still in the grip of Depression politics as it cautiously edged its way out of the gloom. After three years of conservative government, there was now a Labor government, and the local branch of the CPA was growing, but there were still demonstrations of unemployed workers in the streets and John Harcourt had just published *Upsurge*. Economic recovery was slow and grinding. By 1937, unemployment had nearly receded to pre-Depression levels, but it didn't disappear until war began. Yet, as a measure of recovery appeared, dances, the cinema, variety shows and other entertainments reopened for those who had the money to pay.

The Great Depression and an accompanying entertainment tax effectively killed off Perth's professional theatre and many of Perth's live theatres were recreated as picture theatres. By the mid 1930s, a vibrant amateur theatre had blossomed. The Repertory Club, the WAG, several smaller groups such as the Shakespeare, Marlowe and Garrick Clubs, all ran their productions in small – sometimes makeshift – halls, venturing forth on occasions to the grand old 'Maj', His Majesty's Theatre.

Although it had staged some small plays the year before, the Guild's first major play was in 1936. *Till the Day I Die*, written by the young American playwright, Clifford Odets, was a blistering attack on German fascism. It was then followed by Irwin Shaw's famous antiwar play, *Bury the Dead*. Perth was gobsmacked. The reviews were sensational. The *Daily News* reviewer described *Bury the Dead* thus: 'In these days when the theatre is occupied by emasculated plays of escape, it is refreshing and even thrilling to see drama, which attacks current great problems with skill and courage.'

Over the years the reviews were excellent, although reviewers – particularly Paul Hasluck, who wrote a theatre column for the *West Australian* under the name Polygon and was a big supporter of the Guild – were quick to point out slipups in production, criticise some underwhelming acting (Guild actors were after all mostly amateurs) and some of the plays chosen. 'Backseat', the theatre critic for the CPA's *Workers' Star*, probably surprised the Guild when he criticised it for staging too many plays remote from 'things that touch [workers] here and now'.

The Guild was nothing if not versatile. It staged public performances of antiwar plays such as *Bury the Dead*, anti-Nazi plays such as *Till the Day I Die* and *Blood on the Moon*, socialist realist dramas about the class struggle such as Odets' *Waiting for Lefty*, Albert Maltz's *Private Hicks*, the German play *Floridsorf* about the 1934 socialist riots in Vienna and the theatrical adaptation of Walter Greenwood's famous novel, *Love on the Dole*. It also produced satires such as *Where's That Bomb?* and *Cannibal Carnival*, an attack on Western imperialism. It put on feminist plays such as Clare Booth's *The Women* and Olive Popplewell's *The Bondage*. The performance of *The Women* was a first for Perth. The cast was, of course, all women but so was the crew. It staged plays from the USA, Britain, Germany, Australia (Betty Roland's *Are You Ready Comrade?*) and the Soviet Union, as well as Western Australian plays such as Prichard's *Women of Spain* and

A scene from the Workers' Art Guild productions of *Latitude 40* (actors and date unknown)

Penalty Clause and Phyl Hartnett's *I Am Angry*. It played the classics, too, staging Ibsen's *Ghosts* in 1937. It even had a children's theatre and, in 1937, produced *Tommy Tucker*, a play by kids for kids.

In 1937 the Guild produced its first plays for competition at the drama festival at His Majesty's Theatre, organised in part by Paul Hasluck. It was immediately successful. In the competition for new play scripts, Phyl Hartnett won with *I Am Angry*. For full length plays it won third prize for the performance of the German antiwar play *Hinkemann*, but it went two better in the competition for one act plays when *Private Hicks* won first prize. The Guild staged plays for the festival each year until 1940.

Keith George was the creative genius of the dramatic section. He chose and directed most of the plays up to 1937 and sporadically thereafter. He was later described as the man responsible for introducing avant-garde theatre to Western Australia. His directing was out of the box, unique for its time. He had – as one of the WAG actors, Poole Johnson, recalled in a 1976 interview – a 'genius for production'. He is credited with introducing method acting to Perth, inspired in part by Konstantin Stanislavski, one of whose books was in his bookshelves. As Poole Johnson remembered:

> He invoked a performance, he didn't instruct, you see, because acting is purely mental … it comes from within. People worry about the face, why should you worry about the face, why should you worry about expression, because if the thoughts are there the expression will follow.

George also had an eye for talent. He might see somebody on the street whom he thought could fill a particular role and he would sign them up, so turning what was already an amateur troupe into a more amateur one. He also introduced new forms of set design. Paul Hasluck remarked on the 'adventurous' methods of set design in both of the Guild's first two plays, *Till the Day I Die* and *Bury the Dead*, observing that the WAG had adopted the style introduced by the constructivists in the postwar years of the Soviet Union. Ernst Toller's play, *Hinkemann*, had no set at all, just the bare stage, so as, the director said, to avoid distracting the audience from the play and the players.

George was expelled from – or left – the Guild in late 1937. It seems that other members grew tired of his autocratic ways and his refusal to accept suggestions. Although he continued to direct through 1938, he finally left in 1939 and other WAG members gradually took over. Old stalwarts Mary Berry and Phyl Harnett produced some plays and Vic Arnold, a member of the CPA and former director of Sydney's New

Theatre League, did others.

The Guild was to an extent the artistic voice of the WA branch of the CPA, one of a number of Communist Party fraternals or, more pejoratively, fronts, set up in WA in the period when the CPA was advocating a united front with like-minded but non-communist groups. The Guild was never subject to close control by the CPA as some of its equivalents in the eastern states apparently were. Bill Mountjoy, the CPA state secretary, once said he knew nothing about theatre so how could he try to control the Guild, although Prichard did keep watch over it. Like all fraternals the Guild comprised people from a range of backgrounds: George, for example, was never a member of the CPA. The Guild was both intellectual and activist and its members – many of them famous or later to become famous – brought along many skills. Prichard was there. Well-known photographer Axel Poignant did the photography. Architect John Oldham built sets and created art. Maurie Lachberg, a carpenter and union activist, also acted in the plays. Harold Vike was a well-known artist who built sets and drew programs and posters.

The Guild's plays weren't just for the paying public; they were also staged to raise funds for Left wing causes and organisations. In 1936, a performance of *Till the Day I Die* in the Unity Hall of the Trades Hall building in Beaufort Street raised funds for the Labor Women's Organisation. In 1937 and 1938, the Guild staged several plays for the Spanish Relief Fund, which supported the Republicans in the Spanish Civil War. In 1937 the play was *Private Hicks*. In February 1938 *The Secret* was performed at a big public meeting at which Walter Murdoch, Irene Greenwood and other Perth notables spoke. In August 1938, the WAG staged *Women of Spain* and in December its musical section held a cabaret and dance.

The WAG supported other causes, too. Early in 1939 it exchanged its theatres for the backs of trucks to stage street dramatisations on topics such as the housing problem and unemployment, which it did for the ALP at the 1939 state election. Phyl Hartnett wrote *I Am Angry* for the Modern Women's Fair at the Perth Town Hall. It also presented a play to celebrate the anniversary of socialism in the Soviet Union and wrote and produced *Workers Beware* for the fiftieth anniversary of the founding of the Fremantle Lumpers Union. In the late 1930s its plastic and graphic arts section designed floats and trade union banners for Perth's annual Labour Day procession, in which Maurie Lachberg starred as the chief marshal, leading the parade mounted on a white horse.

The WAG's musical section was busy, too. It ran lectures on music appreciation and performance and staged public and community concerts, musicales and entertainments at its clubrooms and in local halls. It ran cabarets for good causes at which its performers read poetry and its choir sang. At a 1937 recital to raise funds for Spanish relief the audience heard Phyl Hartnett read *The Chant for the Mothers of the Slain Militia,* written just a year earlier by the Chilean poet Pablo Neruda, and a chorus of children reciting Australian poet Frank Wilmot's anti-conscription poem *Nursery Rhyme*, which he wrote under the pseudonym Furnley Maurice.

The WAG also took part in debates in Perth's intellectual circles. In 1938 it hosted meetings on civil liberties and the Spanish Civil War at which Professor F. R. Beasley from UWA spoke. In 1939, its literary section hosted a visit by Hartley Grattan, the Left wing American journalist and writer whose interest in Australia was well known. In the same year it staged a talk by another UWA academic, Professor N. F. Bayliss, entitled 'Science and Life', and a discussion on the causes of war. And there were many more.

One of its biggest ventures was a 1939 exhibition of modern art and an accompanying series of lectures, co-sponsored by the Adult Education Board of UWA. It was a sign of Perth's conservative art world, who refused to countenance modern art, that the exhibition could find only reproductions of modern European art to exhibit, although it was able to show original works of modern artists from Melbourne and Perth. The three Perth artists featured were Harold Vike, Max Ebert and Max Lunghi, all members of the Guild. The first talk was on the 'Origins of Modern Art', the second on Revolutionary and Surrealist Art. At each, the three speakers, Phyl Hartnett, E. Hamill and Max Ebert, were all Guild members. Then followed 'The Problem of Appearance', 'The Social Significance of Art' and 'Imagination in Art'. Big crowds attended.

Who were the audiences for the Guild's theatrical performances? At the plays and events for particular Left wing groups it was most likely to have been members and supporters of the CPA and Left wingers in the wider labour movement and middle class supporters of the particular campaigns. At the truck tray plays it was likely to have been workers with an interest in elections or on the streets seeking diversions. Of its public plays, it's very hard to tell. One source says audiences were mainly middle class theatregoers, perhaps progressively minded or radical. Indeed 'Backseat', from the *Worker's Star* observed that the numbers of workers would need to be 'multiplied ten-fold before the theatre could be regarded as an essential part of working class life'.

Yet prices were set to attract as wide an audience as possible. Although the best seats at the June 1936 performance of *Till the Day I Die* at His Maj were 4/- each, there were seats priced as low as 1/-, and the *Westralian Worker* tried to encourage workers to go by pointing out that the cheaper seats were both affordable and equally as good as the seats the silvertails would sit in. There were 1/- tickets for other performances that compared well with vaudeville shows where seats would sell for 2/4d and 1/6d, or films that could cost as little as sixpence at some suburban cinemas and 1/- at cinemas in the city. The Western Australian basic male wage in 1936 was £3/13/9; for women it was just above half that. It might have been possible then, for workers to spend a shilling to go to a play but many jobs were still part time and intermittent. The economy improved as time went on and unemployment, although still high in 1936, didn't return to pre-Depression levels till the war began.

Although the WAG flourished in 1939 and even in 1940, the war and the Menzies government killed it off. In April 1940, it staged *The Women*. Then in August it performed *Love on the Dole* and *Penalty Clause*. In December it was *This Bondage*. But 1940 was its last full year; it seemed to go into a hiatus in 1941 until *Till the Day I Die* was reprised in October, but this play, with which it began in 1936, was its last performance.

Poole Johnson thought that the Guild's disappearance could be explained by the fact that all the little theatre groups closed during as wartime austerity hit, but it's more likely that wartime repression played the major part. In 1940, after a year of war, the Menzies government began censoring communist publications, and then banned them. Then in June 1940 it outlawed the Communist Party altogether. Several leaders were gaoled, police harassed many more, and the Party went underground. Many members put their heads down, moved to the eastern states or joined the military. Some sources suggest that the WAG lost its spark as members became more bourgeois, at which time it began to produce bourgeois plays, but the list of plays staged in 1940 doesn't support this assertion.

So this most impressive moment in Perth's cultural life came and went. It wasn't the end for radical theatre though. A decade later, over a six year period, New Theatre, again with the help of radical connections, staged a new generation of this time mostly Australian plays.

13

Fighting for the Foreshore
Lenore Layman

In an archetypal image, the protester stands defiantly, seemingly alone in the face of a gigantic and relentless machine, mounting a challenge to the overwhelming power of opposing forces. In Perth this symbolic confrontation calls to mind an oft reproduced photograph of an old woman – eighty-nine years of age at the time – warmly dressed against the drizzling rain in coat, hat, gloves and wielding an umbrella, standing bare-footed at the water's edge in the face of a looming Bell Brothers tip truck which is depositing infill into the Swan River at Mounts Bay. This roadwork is creating the Narrows interchange linking the Kwinana and Mitchell Freeways and, in that process, Mounts Bay is disappearing altogether. It is April 1964 and the protester is Bessie Rischbieth.

Bessie was already renowned as a leader of the women's movement, her community activism beginning around 1906 and continuing until her death sixty years later. She led the early twentieth century fight for women's rights and social reform to raise the status and improve the welfare of women and children, particularly through the Women's Service Guilds and the Australian Federation of Women Voters. She was a crusading First Wave feminist and a well-known public figure, who did not retire from public conflict as she aged. Rather, she threw

Bessie Rischbieth at age 89 facing the bulldozers in a protest against the land filling of Mounts Bay on the Swan River

herself into two early nature conservation struggles – the preservation of Kings Park bushland and the survival of Mounts Bay.

These were Perth's first major nature conservation campaigns in which a conservative defence of nature's *status quo* became a cause for protest activism. While Western Australians' belief in the necessity for economic development and improved amenity continued strong, limits to development's acceptability were becoming evident. Not everything needed improvement and not all unused bushland was wasteland; aesthetic, scientific and historical values could on occasion override the promise of material progress. A new language of ecology and conservation was in its beginnings and these campaigns saw a merging of old and new discourse and action. Old activists such as Bessie Rischbieth joined young conservationists such as Vincent Serventy to fight for the park and the foreshore.

A series of proposals to build an Olympic-sized swimming pool on bushland in Kings Park led to immediate opposition and the establishment in 1956 of a Citizens' Committee for the Preservation of Kings Park with Bessie as chairman. 'Hands Off Kings Park' was the message. The Women's Service Guilds had been active from the 1920s in its opposition to any further excisions of Kings Park bushland for development and so they initiated this resistance. The scientific, naturalist and historical groups who joined with the guilds in the fight were all seeking to conserve what they especially valued: a metropolitan A Class Reserve, the last city remnants of native flora and fauna, the lungs of the city, the character of Perth or the wishes of the forefathers. Together they made effective appeal to Western Australians' pride in and respect for the park, waging sustained resistance to the determination of Lord Mayor Howard and the Perth City Council to situate their planned pool with its attendant large car park in the Park.

The Citizens' Committee deluged politicians, government and the media with protest letters and proposed alternative sites. At a public meeting in 1957 they won the media battle by unfurling a large banner from a balcony proclaiming 'Burswood, not Kings Park'. They organised to ensure that two parliamentary votes on the proposal, in 1957 and 1959, were lost, the latter despite the blandishments of new and influential Minister Charles Court. 'Kings Park Remains the People's Park', their celebratory sign read.

While this campaign was an important nature conservation victory, the looming battle to save river frontage from an entirely new type of road was an altogether tougher one. Town planning and road experts advised that the USA's express highways and Germany's *Autobahnen* were civilisation's future. The state government determined in 1953 that Perth would have its version – a six lane controlled access highway with a speed limit of 60 miles (97 km) per hour from the developing industrial area at Kwinana to Spearwood and on to Perth via either the Causeway or a new bridge over the Narrows. The Stephenson–Hepburn Plan for the Metropolitan Region (1955) mapped that highway along the length of the Como foreshore, crossing the river at the Narrows, proceeding north through an interchange covering Mounts Bay and cutting a swathe through West Perth to reach the northern suburbs. Large areas of the river were slated for reclamation and foreshores sacrificed for high speed roads and their feeders.

Reclamation of Perth's foreshores had been ongoing since the 1880s – first the Esplanade, and then Langley Park, Heirisson Island and Point Belches – the aim of successive public works projects being to eliminate backwaters, straighten shorelines and build up swampy flats. In 1908 Chief Justice Parker wrote to Perth City Council regretting that 'the naturally picturesque appearance of the north shore of Perth Water had been destroyed by the perfectly straight line formed by the reclaiming wall' and asked for the Council's intervention to stop government dredging then threatening to straighten the curved shoreline of Mounts Bay.

> The beauty of the river is enhanced by the irregularities in the contour of its shores, and the many little bays and points which Nature has created … The Public Works Department apparently is under the impression that Nature should be corrected.

The Department's engineers insisted they were not 'a pack of Goths and Vandals' and the curved sweep of Mounts Bay and its reflection pool survived for another five decades to be much admired and photographed from Mount Eliza and appreciated by those travelling Mounts Bay Road.

Nonetheless, reclamation of Perth waters continued. In the 1930s South Perth foreshore was infilled behind a retaining wall built to enable the construction of Riverside Drive. A few disgruntled residents wrote letters to the editor: 'A beautiful natural beach has been converted into an eyesore.' Infills had left 'a dreadful wilderness of sand', 'a glorified rubbish tip'. The only organisational opposition to the reclamation came from the WA Historical Society in 1937 when Millers Inlet at Mill Point was infilled, preventing future interpretation of the workings of the Old Mill. Protesting alone and to no avail, the Society proposed instead cleaning and improving the natural feature. At this time Perth residents seemed mostly torn between the promise of clean-ups of unsightly and smelly neglected areas and the threat of wholesale destruction of river frontages.

The end for Mounts Bay came in 1954 when the government resolved to begin construction of the long-anticipated bridge across the Narrows. According to planner Gordon Stephenson, who was commissioned to produce an ambitious new plan for the entire metropolitan region, a bridge with adequate approaches to the north and south was urgently needed; dredging and reclamation began in October. In the next five years as the bridge was built, 70 acres (29 hectares) were reclaimed from the river. Protest continued to be muted and minor: a few letters to the editor. The WA Historical Society, led by the convenor of its Monuments Committee, Joe Sewell, waged a successful campaign of letter writing and persistent lobbying to save South Perth's Old Mill from the bulldozer but, beyond that, no organised opposition emerged. Many viewed the developments sadly as the cost of progress. Vincent Serventy recalled that 'The planners were determined to let cars devour Perth'.

More opposition was generated over the size and route of the northern interchange that would link the new bridge to the city and the northern suburbs. Minister for Works John Tonkin explained that a network of roads surrounded by landscaped gardens would replace the 'odorous and stagnant' Mounts Bay. But Mounts Bay with its small boats, water reflections and sweeping avenue of mature flame trees was a pleasing element of the river landscape familiar to Perth residents. A spaghetti pie of feeder radial roads was not an appealing replacement. To make matters worse, following advice from American engineers, the size and spread of this interchange were increased.

In December 1963, the Brand government, without notice and on the last day of the parliamentary sitting, authorised 8 hectares of river infill to begin the project. Protest followed immediately, although those opposing the development were caught unprepared by the sudden announcement. The newly renamed Citizens' Committee for the Protection of Kings Park and the Swan River was reinvigorated, springing into action in January 1964 with similar campaign tactics to those it had used previously with success – a blitz of letters to politicians, deputations, newsletters to rally support, press releases, public meetings and leaflets. A petition containing 3500 signatures was presented to parliament. The committee set out the conservation case, pointing to the future problems that increased car usage would bring, the better alternative being improved public transport and rail's extension. Planning, it was argued, involved more than road engineering solutions. Not surprisingly, overseas experts and road engineers ruled supreme; they were the planning experts with an enticing vision of Perth's future modernity.

The protesters came from diverse backgrounds to coalesce around a conservationist ethic. The Women's Service Guilds and other women's organisations (for instance, the Housewives' Association, Business and Professional Women's Club, Country Women's Association and Labor Women) provided the core. They used Bessie Rischbieth's maxim:

> There are women on the warpath
> And we mean to make it plain
> That dictatorial parties
> Won't get our vote again.

Environmental groups, such as the Naturalists' Club, and young conservationists, notably Dom and Vincent Serventy, were also strong supporters. Mabel Talbot from the Tree Society was active, as was architect John Oldham. The cause attracted several well-known public figures – Harold Boas, Sir Charles Latham and Mervyn Forrest. The list of committee members indicates the community spread of those who rallied to fight.

In April 1964 a public meeting drew 300 people and heard

Councillor Florence Hummerston report that the city council opposed the reclamation. Full public debate was needed before work proceeded, the meeting resolved. A few days later Bessie Rischbieth staged her one-woman river protest for the camera, Vince Serventy later commenting admiringly that, 'Today she would have 10 000 companions but in those days conservationists were more timid than they are today'. While the photograph became iconic it did not change the course of things.

The reclamation had become a party political issue, with Labor opposing it (although its own record in the area was no better than the government's). But this divide did not assist the Citizens' Committee for it had to remain assuredly non-partisan or lose supporters. Despite a growing flurry of letters to the editor and another large public protest meeting the government was unmoved. Developmentalist ideology drove its agenda and, at this stage of its political life, determination to achieve economic change made it uncompromising. As well, cars were king, unsurprisingly when they were becoming available to the average family for the first time. Transport development planning was seen at this time as value free and there was widespread naivety about the coming congestion, especially as public transport was neglected.

The campaign to save Mounts Bay had failed; in Bessie Rischbieth's words, 'The rape of the river' proceeded. Despite their losses, those seeking to preserve Mounts Bay learnt from their campaign. In 1965 they formed a permanent organisation, the Society for the Preservation of Kings Park and the Swan River, claiming 1000 members, to replace the *ad hoc* Citizens' Committee. Bessie retired as president and became patron, a position she held until her death in 1967. Preservation-minded architects and planners joined, bringing needed professional knowledge. The Society also formed alliances with new community groups, for instance, the Southern Foreshores Protection Society and the Nedlands–Crawley Residents Association. Inaugural Perth city planner Paul Ritter persuaded the council to oppose the inner ring road scheme thus saving Perth from another riverside freeway. These were signs of change and were followed in 1967 by the formation of the Nature Conservation Council (later the Conservation Council of WA), which signalled the emergence of a conservation identity. Conservationists realised that effective resistance to dominant developmentalism required stronger and more coordinated responses than they could deliver as individuals or through a multiplicity of organisations. They needed one voice and one plan of action. At the same time residents' groups began to form at the local level to fight for local places threatened with destruction. Conservationists increased in numbers, creating an intertwining network of people and organisations.

The Kings Park and Mounts Bay campaigns were significant steps in this shift to a conservationist identity and to widespread activism. Interest in the natural environment and its protection became no longer the province of scientists and naturalists alone. Bessie's pioneering protest against the earthmovers was repeated many times as direct action was increasingly utilised in the 1970s as a weapon, particularly in struggles to protect native forests against wood chipping and bauxite mining. As for preserving Perth's foreshores, never again have conservationists faced a threat of the dimensions Bessie and her fellows confronted in the mid 1960s.

Eliza Tracey, second from left, outside her house

14
Annie Westbrook, Wobbly, Eliza Tracey, Stirrer

Charlie Fox

Green, open spaces are a treasure in cities, refuges from the hustle and bustle, car fumes, concrete and bitumen, noise and the ever-upward climb of skyscrapers. Green spaces are also places where cities renew themselves and their people, where great events in their histories take place, where civic ceremonies jostle with demonstrations and rallies, where speakers corners jangle with the sound and fury of competing visions of the past and the future. Perth's great green space was the Esplanade, on the Swan River foreshore at the edge of the city. It was Perth's version of the Domain in Sydney, Hyde Park in London and Central Park in New York.

Over the years, hundreds of demonstrations took place on the Perth Esplanade. Protests by striking shop assistants in 1904, meetings of the unemployed in the 1890s and Great Depression, mass rallies against the Vietnam and Gulf wars in the 1970s, 1990s and 2000s, even protests by the Billionaire's Liberation Front against the Commonwealth government's mining tax in 2011. Practically every cause and campaign found a home on the Esplanade. So, too, did hundreds of Esplanade orators, men and women who set up their blackboards, tables and chairs or stood on a box, to harangue onlookers with fierce rhetoric or reasoned argument, jousting with the cynical, the amused or nonbelieving. Among them were fiery evangelical Christians, scientific and utopian socialists, temperance advocates and others with a grudge against the powers that be. Some spoke while in physical danger, others attracted a crowd who came for a laugh. Annie Westbrook was one of the former, Eliza Tracey the latter.

Annie Westbrook was a Wobbly, a member of the revolutionary Industrial Workers of the World (IWW), which was born in the USA in 1905 and arrived in Australia in 1907. Two types of Wobblyism arrived in Australia: one, originating in Detroit, envisaged industrial and political class struggle, while the other, from Chicago, wanted no truck with politics (think of the Aussie Wobbly song 'Bump Me Into Parliament'). It was the latter and its vision of revolutionary action that became the dominant brand in Australia. Wobblies wanted to organise workers into big industrial unions, which would take control of their industries by direct and revolutionary action. Their mission was to overthrow the wages system and bury capitalism.

Australia's Wobblies were fierce. They despised the ALP, exclusive craft unions and other socialist parties for their reformism, moderation, insularity, bureaucracy and betrayals, and, it must be said, they were feared and loathed in return. Wobblies were itinerant workers who gloried in the image of the hobo, and inner city workers who urged fellow workers to slow down ('Fast workers die young' was one of their most famous slogans). They were rank and file democrats, anti-racists, organisers, confrontationists, public speakers, singers ('Hallelujah, I'm a Bum', 'Solidarity Forever' and 'Joe Hill' are Wobbly classics), satirists (conscientious workers were called slaves) and wits. With 1500 members in Sydney, 500 elsewhere in Australia, and a reputed 20 000 circulation of *Direct Action*, it was the biggest revolutionary organisation in Australia before the arrival of communism in the 1920s.

The Wobblies arrived in Western Australia in 1914, when two organisers from Broken Hill set up the first local in Fremantle, then a second in the eastern goldfields town of Boulder. The third, in Perth, with Annie Westbrook as secretary–treasurer, was established shortly afterwards. The IWW was never very big in WA. In 1916, Monty Miller called it our 'little rebel band' and its leaders often described its difficulties in the 'somnolent west'. But they were busy. The Fremantle local rented headquarters first at a hall in Phillimore Street, then at the Rechabites Hall in Parry Street, where they held Wednesday night lectures, Friday night economics classes and Saturday night business meetings. In Perth the local met at the Literary Institute, but their most important rendezvous was the Esplanade, which by then had a twenty year history of radical and working class meetings.

There, IWW speakers included the local worker-intellectual Mick Sawtell and the charismatic J. B. King and Charlie Reeve, who had been sent west from Sydney to help consolidate and expand the locals. Reeve went to Fremantle where he got a casual job on the wharves and, for a time, bedded down in the Victoria Coffee Palace on Pakenham Street just around the corner from one of their meeting places. He returned to Sydney in May 1916, only to be arrested and gaoled as one of the Sydney Twelve, IWW members framed for various serious offences in 1916 and sentenced to long prison terms. After they had moved back east, they were organising in the country or simply looking for work (they were blacklisted everywhere they were known); the Wobblies relied on the grandfather of WA radical politics, Monty Miller, and the 'rebel girl' Annie Westbrook.

For a largely masculine organisation, the Wobblies were more open to equal partnerships between women and men members than were other socialist bodies and never denied women members the right to

Victoria Coffee Palace, Pakenham St, Fremantle. Wobbly stalwart, Charlie Reeve, roomed here in 1916. Now offices

speak in public spaces. Annie was a great speaker for them, although she often bemoaned how few women were in the group. Miller wrote in the Wobbly newspaper *Direct Action* in 1916 of one meeting, describing Annie as 'in full swing with one of her glowing diatribes against the injustice of capitalism and the sufferings of workers, especially women workers'. Of another meeting, he described how 'She took the platform and held the meeting with a majestic speech that never flagged from start to finish'.

Like her fellow workers, as Wobbly members were called, Annie would speak from a chair or a stand that positioned her above a banner declaring that this was the IWW stand and placards proclaiming Wobbly slogans such as 'Sabotage' and 'Kick like Hell'. There, they would sell copies of *Direct Action*, books and pamphlets. There are no pictures of Annie at the Esplanade, but it is easy to imagine the scene. She would be standing on her chair, surrounded by men in hats, some seated, those at the back standing, some forming a barricade between her and possibly hostile elements, shouting down hecklers and driving them away. Sometimes, Annie was beneficiary of conservative chivalry. Political scientist Verity Burgmann quoted Annie as saying, 'Women can get in where a man cannot'. She would speak on a range of subjects, including the IWW program, free speech, women and work, current political issues and, of course, on war and conscription, many times speaking until she could speak no longer.

When the Wobblies arrived in WA, Australia was at war. The Wobblies were internationalists, violently opposed to the war and, in Western Australia – because lust for war was widespread – their stump on the Esplanade was a dangerous place to be. In 1915 and especially 1916, the year of the first great conscription plebiscite in which the Wobblies vehemently opposed the draft, the Esplanade became crowded with gangs of soldiers and 'loyal Australian Britishers', as civilian supporters of the war called themselves, who regarded any speeches against the war and conscription as treason. They seized the Wobblies' rostrums and threw them in the Swan, dragged speakers from their podiums, beating some and chasing away others. Some speakers had to be rescued by the police; others fled and took refuge wherever they could, one well-known labour identity, Don Cameron, ironically, in the aristocratic Weld Club.

In November 1916, as described by Eric Fry, twelve members of the IWW, including Monty Miller and Mick Sawtell, were arrested and charged with seditious conspiracy. In the arcane language of the law, they were charged with plotting to carry into execution an enterprise, having for its object to raise discontent and dissatisfaction amongst the subjects of our Lord the King, to promote feelings of ill-will and enmity between different classes of the subjects of our said Lord the King.

Three were discharged at the Magistrate's Court, but the other nine were sent to trial. There, they used the court to set out their beliefs and await the verdict, doubtless filled with trepidation after the savage sentences handed down some months earlier to the twelve Wobblies in Sydney. All were found guilty, but far from suffering the same fate as the Sydney Twelve they were given suspended two year sentences, bound over to keep the peace, and then released.

The sentences notwithstanding, their arrest and trial were a devastating blow to the Wobblies because it took away most of their spruikers, and possibly their city members, leaving Annie Westbrook as their most important speaker. Anxious to protect other speakers from prison, she 'kept very quiet', as she wrote to *Direct Action*. In addition, speakers now required a permit from the Perth City Council, so for her to spruik without one – council would never have given her one – meant prosecution. Also, after the trial, Mick Sawtell was sentenced to six months gaol on another charge, after which he went to NSW and was gaoled again in Parramatta, and then Broken Hill. In January 1917, Annie left too, farewelled on Victoria Quay on Fremantle harbour by Monty's rendition of 'Keep the Red Flying'. Then, Monty was stripped of his pension and also had to leave for the east, surviving there on speaking engagements until he was banned from public speaking altogether. Without speakers, funds or literature, was this the end of the Perth Wobblies?

It seems so. The anti-conscription movement continued to work up to the second plebiscite in December 1917, but it was now more mainstream labour as the anti-conscriptionists in the movement took on Prime Minister Billy Hughes and the WA government; the old IWW speakers seemed not to be there. Then, in late 1917, police rounded up nine alleged Wobblies, four of them from Perth, the rest from the Goldfields or the southwest, and charged them with the same offence as the 1916 trials. If the first trial was a threat, the second was a farce, and all but one was acquitted. None of the men named seemed to have links to an organised Wobbly group or at least never boasted of it, as those in the earlier group had.

In 1917, Billy Hughes' government, supported by the Labor Opposition, outlawed the IWW and banned *Direct Action* being sent through the post. By the end of the war the organisation had all but disappeared from Australia, its leaders and many rank and file members in gaol, deported or spread out across the country looking for work. Back in WA, the old IWW was revived in 1919 in the form of the One Big Union movement, active in Perth but mostly on the goldfields. As might be expected, Alfred Callanan and Mick Sawtell were at the forefront of the revival. But it was short lived, smashed by an unholy alliance between the AWU, the ALP and employers.

Meanwhile, Annie Westbrook kept active, joining the campaign to release the Sydney 12 from prison. In 1920 she helped disrupt a conservative women's meeting that was protesting against the Twelve's early release. In 1928 she was selling a new version of *Direct Action* for a revived IWW. Then, in 1948, when she was nearly eighty, she was part of another revival, always hopeful of new revolution.

In contrast, Eliza Tracey was never at risk of gaol. The worst that happened to her was the occasional visit from city larrikins, who once flicked lighted matches at her. She was more than a match for them for she had an irascible temper, red-hot rhetoric and was ablaze with indignation at the wrongs done to her. Mrs Tracey, as she was known, was a little Irish woman who, when she first stood on the stump at the Esplanade in 1897, was probably in her late fifties. She gave her last address probably in 1915, and died two years later, as well known, said the *Sunday Times* obituary of 25 February 1917, as John Forrest.

Mrs Tracey, who gave her occupation as a ladies' nurse, would stride down Barrack Street to her place on the Esplanade every Sunday, arriving at 3pm. She would set up her chair or stool, two baskets, one wrapped in the Australian flag, and a piece of tin with the inscription:

Mrs Tracey
Robbed by the Malice and
Corruption of the Judges and Lawyers of Western Australia.
Authoress of 'Legal Robbery in Western Australia'

Her speeches would last as long as she was able to draw breath – which was sometimes for three hours. Passers-by stopped to listen and regulars settled in for the afternoon. In her early speeches she would reserve seats in her front row for Sir John and Lady Forrest, more to remind her audience the politicians were at one with the lawyers more than any expectation she or her audience might have that they would attend. At the end of each day she would pass around the hat, for she was poor and needed money. She would finish with the hymn 'Abide with me'.

Mrs Tracey's speeches were all essentially about the one thing: how she had been swindled out of land by two of Perth's leading lawyers, and how the legal profession, courts and judges had conspired to protect the swindlers. Although she haunted the courts, took her case as far as the High Court and had it inquired into by two parliamentary committees, she received no satisfaction whatsoever. 'The first thing we do, let's kill all the lawyers,' says Dick in Shakespeare's *Henry the Sixth*, Part 2. Mrs Tracey would have heartily agreed. Thus the subjects of her regular Sunday speeches had titles such as 'The plague-stricken justices of Western Australia', 'Three lying thieves in Western Australia' or, in a title dripping with irony, 'The Honest Judges of Western Australia and the Truthful Members of the King's Bench'. Another was a warning to all stirrers: 'Speak not the truth in Western Australia; if you do a strait jacket awaits you'. Another was entitled 'The Fallen Men of Perth and their Unwanted Offspring'. A clever *Sunday Times* journalist observed in May 1907 that

> Mrs Tracey evidently forgot to announce that if all the fallen men attend the lecture, in case the Esplanade won't hold the crowd, Kings Park has also been hired for the overflow oration.

Mrs Tracey was very skilful at making her speeches relevant to contemporary circumstances and current issues. In 1901 as the Labor Party was entering state parliament, she addressed her followers on the rights of the working man and keeping lawyers out of parliament, the latter she described as those 'sixpenny and eight penny blokes'. In 1899, as the WA government was considering extending the franchise to women, she spoke on women's suffrage and her belief that the vote would prevent what happened to her happening to women generally. A much later retrospective in the *Sunday Times* described her slogan 'Up with the petticoats and down with the trousers'. Like Monty Miller, Mrs Tracey was an opponent of federation. About her address 'Poverty, Crime and Cure', a *Sunday Times* journalist wrote: 'Hers was the "poverty", the Supreme Court's was the "crime" and the "cure" was the proceeds of the collection.'

She addressed her audiences in a rich Irish brogue. She was full of vitriol and enjoyed the badinage with her audience, but only so far. Of the three great thieves of her discourse she said, 'They are as full of lies as a dog is of fleas'. She told one young interjector, 'Bejabers, if yez don't shut up I'll get down and give yez one'. Of another grand eminence she observed, 'I know him. He's always talking about morality and being saved but he's playing with another man's wife.'

Mrs Tracey died in 1917. During her lifetime she was treated with a mixture of affection, amusement and bemusement by the press that ran many a story about her, once or twice even trying to unravel the arcane byways of her original grievance. She was always funny, said one journalist; the Esplanade was a dreary place once she'd gone, said another. She seemed not to present a coherent ideology. None of her diatribes was about socialism but they were all damning critiques of Western Australia's unequal society and how the corruption and greed of the powerful kept it that way.

The Esplanade has gone. It is now Elizabeth Quay, Perth's Darling Harbour, a glossy tourist spot that ultimately will be surrounded by highrise buildings. Barring a few posters, all signs of its history have been obliterated. Governments won't mourn its passing. It was always a nuisance to them because they viewed its rallies and demonstrations as a threat to law and order, peace and harmony. Open spaces in cities attract radicals, dreamers, revolutionaries and protesters. What better way to end their agitations than to take away their platforms?

15
Battle for the Barracks

Jenny Gregory

We associate protest with radical movements in which people fight for extreme political reform or change. Those who fight against change are usually defined as reactionaries, even though they may adopt many of the mechanisms of protest such as petitions, deputations and demonstrations. Such forms of protest were employed in the 1950s and 1960s in Perth in response to proposed changes to the city's natural and built environment. But those who spearheaded these battles were hardly radical in today's sense of the word. They were often well to do, women active in Perth's numerous women's organisations, including feminists, professional women and housewives, men active in the Western Australian Historical Society and the emerging National Trust movement, including architects, naturalists, teachers and clergy. They coalesced to protest against changes imposed by postwar governments bent on transforming society in the image of modernism. These were respectable mature women and men who lived in the midst of the Cold War and feared totalitarianism. They remembered how the Nazis had overthrown parliamentary democracy, were alarmed by the purges and massacres that had occurred under Stalinism; they would be shocked when Soviet tanks rolled into Budapest in 1956 to crush the Hungarian uprising. They were prepared to stand firm against government when, in its pursuit of modernist progress, it ignored the wishes of the people, and would adopt the hallmarks of radicalism to preserve Perth's natural and built environment.

Postwar modernism signalled the advance of science and technology, increasing industrialisation and urbanisation and with these a rejection of the old. Engineers, architects and urban planners were among the experts who would transform society. In his 1933 book *The Radiant City* the influential architect and planner Le Corbusier had proclaimed his vision of the brave new world of the future: 'Authority must step in, patriarchal authority, the authority of a father concerned for his children.' New materials forged in the crucible of war enabled engineers and architects to design buildings that soared to the sky, and new ways of thinking enabled urban planners to draw lines on a map that would transform city living. But it was also a time when individuals – many veterans who had seen the devastation of war – were intent on creating a better society. What that better society would be like was a matter of debate.

The modernist attack on the city of Perth first surfaced in 1954 when the purpose of Kings Park, gazetted as a public park in 1872, began to be questioned. Could a growing city afford the luxury of 1000 acres of bushland in its heart, asked the *West Australian*, suggesting instead that although many would regard this as sacrilegious, town planners could find better use of the area as the site of a public hospital or a recreation ground. Following an intensive protest campaign against the building of an Olympic-sized swimming pool in the park, the *Parks and Reserves Act* was amended to protect the park from such intrusions. Five years later, an attempt to amend the Act again, this time to allow development in Kings Park, was defeated. Nineteen fifty-four also saw the commencement of nearly two decades of protest against the reclamation of Mounts Bay for the approaches to the Narrows Bridge and a freeway interchange. The Old Mill in South Perth that had been slated for demolition for the southern approach the bridge was saved thanks to the activities of the WA Historical Society. But, as related by Lenore Layman, despite a long protest campaign, a total of 85 acres of river – known as the city's reflecting pond – was sacrificed to the needs of the motorist.

The reference to town planners in the press signalled the work being undertaken by Professor Gordon Stephenson. An eminent town planner from the University of Liverpool, Stephenson had worked on planning for the postwar reconstruction of London and was the designer of Stevenage, the first town built under Britain's modernist project New Towns initiative. He was commissioned by the state government to prepare a plan for the metropolitan areas of Perth and Fremantle. Just as it was in Britain, metropolitan planning was part of the *Zeitgeist* of postwar Australia, with five other capital cities developing metropolitan plans in the late 1940s and 1950s. Stephenson's arrival in Perth on 10 January 1953 was heralded by the *West Australian* as 'a red letter day in Perth's history': he was given a lord mayoral reception and treated like a celebrity. Less feted was British born Alastair Hepburn, the new town planning commissioner for Perth and Stephenson's collaborator, who arrived from his previous planning appointment in Sydney a little later.

There were few aspects of metropolitan regional planning that Stephenson did not consider. The centralisation of power within the state government in those years, gave him the ideal opportunity to put his ideas about comprehensive planning into practice. During 1954 he established a team to work on the plan and began extensive surveys.

Understanding the workings of the public service, he held many discussions with key bureaucrats, readily taking on their suggestions when feasible. He also recognised the importance of public relations, happily becoming a commentator on various proposals affecting the city and writing articles for the local press in order to prepare the public for his ultimate plan.

When the plan was published in 1955 it proposed the demolition of Perth's Old Barracks.

> For vital traffic needs and for the general improvement of the City, the Old Barracks, an inadequate and obsolete office building … should be displaced. Although there may be a sentimental attachment to the Old Barracks, which for reasons long since passed was placed in a commanding position, it is not a building of distinction or architectural merit.
>
> Parliament House should be the fitting climax to the finest and most important street in the State.

The barracks also stood in the way of one of the legs of the inner ring road that Stephenson proposed. This later became a complex freeway interchange, designed by US engineering company De Leuw Cather. It was constructed on the site of the reclaimed Mounts Bay and linked to the Mitchell Freeway.

The barracks had been built in 1866 as accommodation for the Pensioner Guards, who had accompanied the convicts to Western Australia and were the colony's main defence force. Converted into offices at the turn of the century, they became the headquarters for the Public Works Department and, from the late 1920s, for the Metropolitan Water Supply, Sewerage and Drainage Department as well. Famed engineer Charles Yelverton O'Connor had his office there. The Goldfields Water Scheme, the Port of Fremantle, the Hills Water

Supply Scheme, the Ord Scheme – all the state's major engineering projects – were planned there, and most of its public buildings were designed there. The barracks grew to accommodate increasing staff numbers. Some of the additions were temporary measures, most of them done on the cheap. But despite its dilapidated rear sections, in the early 1960s the Barracks still managed to impose, and its twin towers and mock Tudor battlements still spoke of the rule of law, as they had done nearly a hundred years before when they looked down on convict Perth.

Best-selling Western Australian novelist Dorothy Sanders expressed the reaction of many to the threat of demolition of the barracks through the voice of one of her heroines, a daughter of one of Perth's old families, in her 1961 novel *Monday in Summer*:

> At the top of the hill she could see the old red brick Barracks with their mock battlements.
>
> A town planner from abroad had advised West Australians to remove that old historical building in order to allow a finer vista down the length of the Terrace from Parliament House. The Barracks were not architecturally beautiful, he had informed the citizens.
>
> This advice had been received in courteous silence. West Australians could not explain to a man from abroad that the Barracks held a beauty for them he would never be able to see with foreign eyes. That building stood for their history, their birth pangs. As a nation they had not come trailing clouds of glory from some other world. Their primordial memory was one of discovery ships, pioneer ships, convict ships, immigrant ships. The Barracks, relic of the birth of a nation, reminded the citizens they were not born of privilege but of hardship, endurance and the will to survive.

Defenders coalesced to form the Barracks Defence Council (BDC) in 1961 with Bishop Tom Riley as president. Membership of the BDC included influential members of Perth society who were active in the Royal Western Australian Historical Society, the National Trust (established in WA in 1959) and other community groups such as the Tree Society, the WA Fellowship of Writers, the Women's Service Guild, the National Council of Women and the Citizens' Committee for the Preservation of Kings Park and the Swan River. The latter was headed by the indomitable feminist and activist Bessie Rischbieth ('Mrs Rich Bitch' as some politicians were reputed to call her). Ranged against them were a determined Premier David Brand and the ruling Liberal–Country Party coalition.

With many of its members already seasoned by campaigns against development in Kings Park, the BDC had considerable organisational skill. They printed pamphlets and stickers depicting the arch in silhouette flying a black banner with the words 'Preserve Democracy' emblazoned on it, and organised a public opinion poll, speakers and media publicity. They arranged for the visiting chairman of the English National Trust to make a well-publicised call on the premier, for visiting Poet Laureate John Betjeman to come out in support of the barracks, and for visiting New South Wales National Trust Chairman Mr Justice McClemens to speak out against demolition. The issue was raised in federal parliament by Senator Agnes Robertson: 'This is almost the last straw ... destroying a beautiful building like the Barracks in order to build a road leading up to Parliament House.' Professor Walter Murdoch, well-known essayist, said he saw red every time the demolition was mentioned. Lord Euston, chairman of the British Society for the Preservation of Ancient Buildings, flew to Perth from the eastern states to see the barracks and was 'charmed' by the building, which he suggested had been designed along the lines of the Gate House at St James Palace in London. Even the *Australian Women's Weekly* featured two articles in its 19 September 1962 issue on the threat to the barracks: a 'romantic and well-loved building ... Its threatened demolition has caused heartburning in Perth.'

The arguments went on and on over the next few years. The BDC held meetings with government planning committees, ideas were batted about, petitions were submitted. The government proposed a compromise: the arch would be retained and only the wings demolished. It was rejected by the BDC. A radio station conducted a public opinion poll, resulting in 2688 votes for retention and only fifty-nine for demolition. The premier tried to minimise the poll, leading Bishop Riley in a 24 March 1966 statement to 'warn the government of the mounting public opinion against the sacrifice of the Barracks on the altar of an engineering Moloch'. Notwithstanding such outrage, the demolition of the wings of the barracks began. Ironically, this was just as Perth residents received copies of the new phone directory carrying a colour photo of the barracks on the cover.

After demolition of the wings was completed in July 1966, leaving the archway in front of the deep scar that marked the freeway works, the *West Australian* took a poll of passers-by to gauge the public's views on its appearance. 'I think the archway looks marvellous. It gives distinct character to this end of the terrace,' said a housewife. A taxi driver thought that 'It looks like a pimple on a pumpkin'. But the majority were on the side of the arch, describing it as striking, mellow, picturesque and elegant, and declaring that 'It is not a public nuisance. Posterity will thank us', and 'It helps hold back the concrete jungle.' The premier, firmly in the grip of modernist urban planning and development, continued to press for complete demolition of the barracks. He believed that people who were against a proposal would always be the most vocal and were best ignored. 'The tendency to be influenced by our emotions' should be put aside for the sake of town planning and the demands of the car.

Continuing pressure against the demolition of the archway forced the government to commission a Gallup Poll on the issue. It showed that most people were against demolition. A panel of experts discussed the results on television. Their opinions were evenly divided, with those in favour of retention speaking of their personal, sentimental and historical attachments to the archway. Controversial City Planner Paul Ritter threatened to jump from the top if they tried to pull it down.

Within days a cartoon by Paul Rigby, one of Australia's most brilliant cartoonists, appeared in Perth's evening newspaper, the *Daily News*. It showed that the forces of modernisation and development would not be easily vanquished. In the cartoon Rigby depicted the barracks archway surrounded by a ring of respectable citizens defiantly facing the bulldozers, a swastika emblazoned on an enormous flag flying over Parliament House in the distance and the armband worn by the bulldozer driver. The deadline to begin demolition is not far off, and the driver waits for a signal from the man in the suit (an engineer) to begin. Meanwhile, on the roof of Parliament House, Rigby's trademark little boy (who appeared, with his dog, as a quirky alter ego in almost all Rigby's cartoons) lifts a sledgehammer to begin the assault. The boy's dog balances precariously on a power line strung on a 'gallup' pole. The allusions set up by Rigby suggest a complexity far beyond the immediate political point made by the caption, in which one protestor says to another: 'I wonder if they'd take any notice of a 49 per cent vote for Labor?' This was a reference to the Gallup poll that showed that 49 per cent of people were against demolition of the Barracks Archway, while only 35 per cent were in favour.

Cartoonist's Paul Rigby's acerbic comment on the government's attitude to public protest over the proposed demolition of the Barracks Arch

The premier decided to put the issue to parliament in a non-party vote. The crowded public gallery broke into applause when, in a historic division (twenty-six to eighteen, with thirteen backbenchers voting with the Opposition), the Legislative Assembly rejected the premier's motion for the removal of the archway.

As the *Daily News* explained in an October 1966 editorial headlined 'Big Brother Rebuffed':

> [T]he Barracks archway became a symbol. People tended to identify its planned destruction with so much of the recent casual scarring of the city in the name of progress – and, in a general sense, with governmental and departmental arrogance. It may be that many people who protested about the planned demolition of the archway would not have felt deeply

about it if they were not already resentful. Whatever the aesthetic value of the archway, it is to be hoped that the successful fight for its survival has taught the Government a lesson – that it cannot consistently act on the basis that Big Brother knows best.

The Battle for the Barracks was a partial success in that the Arch remains. But after that success, the strength of the powerful modernist development ethos in Perth, plus the absence of heritage legislation, inadequate planning regulations, and the power of investors and developers, led to the demolition of many city buildings. This was especially noticeable in St Georges Terrace, home to banks, insurance companies, the stock exchange and major commercial houses. In the 1950s it was a gracious European-style boulevard with few buildings higher than four storeys. By 1990 the Terrace was lined with skyscrapers in imitation of the archetypal modern US city. Only pockets of nineteenth and early twentieth century buildings remained.

Punctuating those years were a number of heritage battles. Until the enactment of heritage legislation in 1990, protection largely depended on the National Trust, which has only moral authority. Although it was successful in protecting a number of city buildings and streetscapes, such as the King St and Murray St precincts, many important historic buildings were demolished. The battle for the retention of the Palace Hotel between 1971 and 1986 was the longest running after the barracks. It attracted the support of the NSW branch of the Builders' Labourers' Federation (BLF), fresh from its successful green ban on development of Sydney's Rocks area, and was largely successful, although extensive reconstruction has compromised the hotel's authenticity. But it was the battle for the barracks that first signified major opposition to the excesses of modern development ideology in Perth and demonstrated the potential strength of people power.

16
The Workers' Embassy at Solidarity Park

Janis Bailey

Who would have thought a purpose-built protest site – the very term appears to be a contradiction – would be officially heritage listed within seven years of its creation and listed precisely because of its protest activities? Solidarity Park, on the corner of Parliament Place and Harvest Terrace, West Perth, was created in 1997 by the union movement to thumb its nose at the WA government regarding new industrial relations (IR) legislation. The embassy was listed by the Heritage Council of Western Australia in 2004. It is a rarity for any historical site to be officially recognised so quickly, but an extraordinary campaign led by the Trades and Labor Council of WA (TLCWA), makes this small piece of ground highly significant.

From May to November 1997 the site was the focus of protest about new IR legislation. The conservative Coalition state government under Premier Richard Court and Minister for Labour Relations Graham Kierath implemented three tranches of counter-progressive IR reform (the word is used ironically). The 1993 and 1995 reforms introduced and reinforced an individualised bargaining regime with the lowest safety net of any IR laws in Australia. The 1997 amendments – colloquially known as the Third Wave – were designed to restrict unions' ability to recruit and organise members. This was all prior

The Workers' Embassy, 1997

to the actions of a conservative federal government that shifted the locus of IR to the federal sphere. Hence in 1997 state IR legislation really mattered: more WA workers were covered by state-based IR legislation than by its federal counterpart.

In response to the Bill, unions began a widespread protest campaign of marches, rallies and industrial action as the parliamentary debate progressed. The Workers' Embassy (as it was initially dubbed) began with a caravan – a kind of protest office – parked outside Parliament House. Asked by the police to move on, unionists towed the caravan to a car park directly opposite parliament. This 500 square metre site was promptly staked out as a prospecting licence under the *Mining Act* by ETU organiser Mike Mitchell, and protestors rallied there for six months. The state government and Perth City Council each owned part of the site, but the latter quickly relinquished its ownership. Unionists occupied the site around the clock and built a compact of solidarity in opposition to the legislation. Tents were erected around the original caravan, then a sandpit, scarecrows bearing the faces of the premier and Minister for Labour Relations Graham Kierath, vegetable gardens, and temporary and later permanent barbecues.

Although unions led by TLCWA provided resourcing and overall organisation of the site, it was very much a people's place. The site was emphatically for all unionists and indeed for anyone opposed to the IR legislation, not just full-time officers and delegates. It grew into a motley and colourful encampment that used performances and installations to create solidarity, which kept protestors, particularly families, coming to the site, even after the Bill became law in late May. As one rank and file unionist described it:

[At first] it was just a tent. It was just a tent and few barbecue things and it was a piece of dirt here, right. And slowly when they developed ideas ... all the ideas come together and then they develop into beautiful barbecues with permanent pergolas and with the memorial for Mark Allen ... Each time I come and see, from a little tent and a few barbecues they transformed it into paving and all this ...The Parliament calls them thugs, [but] they can create! ... To many of them, I say, 'Can I just shake your hand to get some courage from you?'

While the Workers' Embassy was inclusive and open to all, decision making remained the responsibility of TLCWA, which represented thirty-seven affiliated unions, and its campaign committee. TLCWA Secretary Tony Cooke and others on the campaign committee, including liaison officer Tim Kucera, actively sought the views of site participants. Assistant Secretary Stephanie Mayman played a pivotal role in many aspects of the campaign, complementing Cooke's role. Many of the day to day tactics that drew public participation and media attention were generated onsite. A notable figure during the campaign was Electrical Trades Union (ETU) organiser Percy King who lived there for much of the six months, providing continuity and order, and being a fix-it person for any difficulties that arose. Cooke himself, a full-time TLCWA official from 1981 to 2001, the last six years as Secretary, undoubtedly carried the major responsibility for the campaign.

By any measure Cooke was an outstanding transformational union leader: inclusive, consultative, creative and highly gender aware. His time as secretary covered a significant period of development of new organising approaches in unions, and Tony had the foresight to apply the principles of this approach to the campaign. Cooke's tenure also saw the TLC expanding to resource environmental and urban development protests, indigenous issues, Friends of East

TLCWA Secretary Tony Cooke with Janis Bailey's son, Alan (left)

Timor, and the *Southern Initiative on Globalisation and Trade Union Rights (SIGTUR)*. These forays into social, environmental and global justice issues were consistent with the approach of the Third Wave Campaign: engaging with unionists *and* the wider community, and creating dialogue and open fora for input into decision making.

The site erupted in a profusion of activity, particularly in the first few months. Performances – some as part of family fun days – were frequent: drummers, life-size puppet figures of political characters, stilt walkers, singers, poets and musicians. Opportunities for participation were manifold, and went way beyond the usual industrial action, marches, rallies and letter writing (although all

Tony Cooke with his daughter Ella and Janis Bailey's daughter Meaghan (right) at the Workers' Embassy

these strategies were part of the mix). More mundanely, teacher unionists brought their marking to the site after school finished, university lecturers brought students to study the nuances of social and industrial protest and nurses gave participants blood pressure checks under the banner 'Graham [Kierath] Makes My Blood Pressure Rise'. The garden's vegetables were harvested and eaten onsite and new seedlings planted. Amazing meals were cooked. Campfire nights brought people together. A ceremonial handing over of barbecue tongs took place each evening, at the changing of the guard when one union replaced another. 'Defiance via domesticity' was one phrase used. Joanne Pike, a young union organiser, commented on the multiple and fluid possibilities of the site:

> Anybody who comes here can do anything they want. If they want to just come up here and sit and have a look and read a book or something like that, that is fine. If they want to get up and cook on the barbie, then that's really good as well. If they want to get up and plant a tree or build a wall ... whatever they want to do. I don't think people should feel that they've got to come here and do something. If they just want to come and sit and contemplate, think about what it is to be a unionist, or even just sit and think about nothing, then that's fine.

Visitors were many. On one memorable day, to the delight of those present, a frail Don McLeod, who had helped lead the 1946–49 Pilbara strike for the human and industrial rights of Aboriginal pastoral workers, came to site.

As the weeks wore on, members of the construction unions, with help from others, built picnic shelters, brick barbecues, a low People's Wall around the park's perimeter, a memorial wall to dead and injured workers, a fountain for (not of) youth, a large rock with plaques affixed commemorating international visitors to the site and a special monument to building worker and union organiser Mark Allen, killed on a building site in Perth the previous year. But with the legislation passed, the unions could not stay there forever. At this point, the site assumed the name Solidarity Park, and a transition period began. In November 1999, the park was handed over to the people of Western Australia.

Media coverage of the campaign was comprehensive and remarkably benign, and indeed often favourable. This contrasted with other union campaigns that had gone awry, notably the Australian Council of Trade Unions' 1996 Cavalcade to Canberra just a year earlier, which had erupted into violence and attracted negative media attention. The varied and often humorous Third Wave strategies created photo opportunities and fodder for journalists, tapping into the truism that politics is spectacle, not just talk: the medium is the message. The Workers' Embassy provided the platform for such spectacle. From May to August 1997 the campaign rarely failed to feature in the daily *West Australian* (although less frequently thereafter), which kept the legislation and the government's role in creating it in the forefront of the public's mind.

Creating Solidarity Park did not stop the legislation. The government had gained control of the Legislative Council in the 1996 election and used its power to push through the law. However, the sheer longevity of the campaign, and its many eye-catching tactics undoubtedly influenced public opinion. And so, at the next WA election, in February 2001, the ALP (with a platform of repealing the laws) was voted into government by the electorate. Labour Relations Minister Kierath (moved sideways from his portfolio in 1998) suffered a massive swing in the election and lost his seat.

The campaign had less tangible but nevertheless real outcomes, too. Twenty years later many participants cite it as a particularly memorable time in their lives that led them to further activism. One says:

> The campaign was a blast. It was hugely engaging, without necessarily being time-consuming. It was sociable, humorous, kid-friendly if you had a family. It had a kind of safe weirdness about it that took you right outside your normal life. It definitely cemented my identity as a unionist; that will always be part of me, I'll always try to do my bit, whatever that might be – delegate, office-bearer etc. I wouldn't have the same solid union identification, if not for the Third Wave campaign and the Workers' Embassy.

Learning from its successes at Solidarity Park, TLCWA conducted particularly successful activities in the maritime dispute in 1998, a national campaign to defend workers dismissed by shipping company Patrick Stevedores, which likewise used 'peaceful assemblies'. The lessons from the Third Wave – peaceably occupying public space, creating a safe space for protestors and using the presence of older people, women and children to deter police action – informed the union movement in this subsequent dispute (for a full discussion of this dispute see chapter 20, 'War on the Waterfront').

The campaign was noteworthy for three reasons: cultural, geographical and social. First, the campaign used an extraordinarily diverse cultural toolkit. Some tools were traditional union activities, such as rallies, strikes and the display of union banners. Others drew on time honoured working class traditions such as the appropriation of public space for speakers corners and the claiming of the commons (the Embassy itself, and the People's Wall that was later built around it). The construction unions had dubbed Parliament House 'Bullshit Castle' to undermine its legitimacy. Some tactics drew from political protest more broadly. The Workers' Embassy nomenclature referenced the Aboriginal Tent Embassy outside Old Parliament House in Canberra. Australia's suburban culture undoubtedly inspired the ambience of the site with its vegetables and flowers, garden gnomes, sundials, children's toys and makeshift kitchens. Protestors occupied the public gallery of Parliament House while the Bill was being debated and Miscellaneous Workers Union Secretary Helen Creed knitted while the guillotine fell (a parliamentary device to bring the debate to an end). This echoed a character in Dickens' novel of the French Revolution, *A Tale of Two Cities*, in which Madame Defarge knitted while heads rolled. In Karl Marx's words, the protestors borrowed 'names, battle cries and costumes from the past' to invoke 'the sanction of precedent'.

The *Braveheart* protest was a hilarious example of a cultural mash-up. As the Bill was debated, from behind a sandbagged wall, unionists trained cannons (made of plastic piping) on Parliament House. Then male officials and delegates from several blue collar unions who were wearing kilts bared their bottoms – in unison – in the direction of Parliament House. The whole spectacle drew on a scene from *Braveheart*, a popular film starring Mel Gibson playing thirteenth century hero William Wallace leading Scottish troops in the First War of Scottish Independence against England. There were elements of the ribald carnivals of the Middle Ages here, perhaps references to the Celtic origins of some of the unionists, and more than a hint of Australian male larrikin behaviour (the latter problematic in some contexts, of course). The event, like others, operated on a discursive level. Participants were claiming and thus disrupting the power of the term 'union thug', which, as noted in a quote above, was used extensively by conservative politicians and media. None of the newspapers was game to print the resulting photos, although press photographers gave copies to the protestors. One of the line-up later commented:

> Baring bums was an act of defiance, we're baring bums to a political process that really ultimately showed itself up to be an arsehole ... showing a big moon to the government over its treatment of workers. [We were] all dressed up in kilts and painted faces and whatnot ... [But] my bum isn't there, my bum has actually been [cropped from] the photograph ... My mother would be happy about that.

These Celtic warriors did not have a consistent strategy; some still had their underpants on. Tactical confusion or shyness? We'll never know.

Second, the campaign was emphatically a space claiming and

place making one. Staking out the land as a mining lease, for example, echoed ways in which Australian pastoralists and miners have grown rich using public land and resources. Further, the park's far from marginal place contrasts with most workers' monuments that are in working class suburbs and outback towns. The park is the central node in an extensive precinct of public buildings in West Perth: not only Parliament House, but also the National Trust, the Constitution Centre, a large building of government offices including that of the minister for labour relations, and many commercial buildings. The park is thus surrounded by the architectural embodiments of history, the state, capital and the law, yet makes an emphatic statement about the enduring if contested nature of people's power. From a place making perspective, Solidarity Park made an enduring mark, in contrast to early worries by protestors that all the monuments might be bulldozed by the government.

Third, the campaign created a social space for protestors. It was a place to mobilise people, using family ties, friendship networks, work units and other links such as church groups. It was strongly celebratory of common interests, but also recognised difference, particularly differences of class and gender, in the union movement. With its sandpit and toys the site was family friendly; the campaign also provided multiple channels of participation such as 'Wear red on Thursdays', which for the more timid could be socks or underwear. An anecdote recounted by Helen Creed, secretary of the Miscellaneous Workers' Union, illustrates another tactic.

> One group of workers from Sir Charles Gairdner Hospital … came down to the Embassy. They had a bit of an exchange with [Legislative Council President] Clive Griffiths over the legislation. They said, 'Look, we've made our point, we hope you politicians listen, we're regular workers'. Of course,

most of them were middle-aged women in their hospital uniforms. And then they left. They went across the road, and they all had a sausage, and then went back to work.

There were tensions during the campaign. The site was occupied longer than most TLCWA and union leaders thought desirable, largely due to pressure from the construction unions; this caused arguments. Day to day participation and energy fell away from August onwards and media coverage dropped off. There were gender tensions, although reports of outright harassment were few and strongly countered by campaign organisers. So the social fabric of Solidarity Park developed cracks, as happens in any diverse and prolonged protest event.

What of the site now? With Perth's riverside Esplanade having disappeared under a morass of badly designed tourism facilities and high rises, Solidarity Park has become the city's preeminent site of labour protest. But not just labour protest; it is used by many groups rallying for many causes. The Heritage Council's website has this to say about the site:

- The place is highly valued by the union community and contributes to their sense of place as it reflects bonds of solidarity and united union defiance against the Coalition Government policy in 1997;

- The place contains the largest concentration of labour monuments in Western Australia and, together with the Tom Edwards Memorial in Fremantle, is one of only two labour monument sites in Western Australia; and

- The place is valued by parts of the community as a commemorative and protest site.

But the last words quoted should be Percy King's.

I can see myself coming back here in 20 years' time ... Even if [the park's] not here, even if the structures are not the same, they will never take away the memory of what was here and what happened here and the friends that were made ... There is a symbolism to this place. There's a very hard-tied knot to the place, and it will take a long time to undo.

Perhaps Percy was thinking of the Celtic heart knot, a symbol of love of and devotion to a cause as well as to a person. The dust has long settled on this particular campaign, but participants looking back affirm that the hard tied knot will never be undone.

17
Goonininup versus the Old Swan Brewery

Charlie Fox

On 3 January 1989, in probably the first claim of its kind, a group of Aboriginal people made a land rights claim in an Australian city, occupied an area they called Goonininup just 1 kilometre from the CBD on Mounts Bay Road and set up a protest camp. Goonininup was also the site of the old Swan Brewery and was the centre of a bitter fight between local Aboriginal people and the Western Australian Labor government, a government intent on redeveloping the Swan Brewery against the wishes of Perth's Aboriginal people, who believed it was a sacred site. They wanted the buildings demolished and the land on which they stood returned to parkland. As well as the federal government, also involved were the Perth City Council, trade unions with different points of view about the issue, heritage lobby groups, churches, doctors, and others and, of course, big business.

The occupation lasted for nine months until police invaded and broke up the camp. Then came stalemate, as redevelopment plans and court cases came and went. Then, protestors set up a permanent picket line at the site. In 1992, the government signed a secret deal with another Perth developer who had new proposals for development. Once again police intervened and broke the picket line to allow workers on to the site. Effectively, the fight was over, although skirmishes continued and one of the Aboriginal leaders maintained a vigil at the site for years afterwards.

Despite the many naysayers at the time, Perth's Aboriginal people had a long and documented relationship with the site of the struggle. As early as 1836, settlers had described Aboriginal use of the area; a string of similar observations followed into the 1980s as Aboriginal elders, authors, anthropologists and others set out the connections Aboriginal people had to this small piece of land. It was the land of Yellagonga's clan, the river people, whose country extended northward from the river. The site's significance lay in its creation by the *Waugal*, the creator being in the shape of a snake, which constructed it in the Dreamtime as it moved southward from the river's source, using Goonininup as a resting place on its way. As people inhabited the area, they used it for rituals, camping, trade, food gathering, teaching and initiations. Then, when the British arrived, a military company camped at the site until, in 1834, it was transformed into the Mount Eliza Native Institution. In 1838 it was sold off as private property, meaning that Aboriginal people, who had no concept of this, could be charged with trespass if they went there. Later, in the early years of the twentieth century, Aboriginal protection legislation meant that Aboriginal people were excluded from the area by law.

The Swan Brewery Company began brewing beer in Perth in 1857 and moved to the river site in 1880, where it brewed its beer until 1966 when it moved to another river property, the Emu Brewery site, closer to the city. In 1978 it moved again, this time from the city to Canning Vale, an industrial suburb southeast of the city. Henceforth, the Swan River site was used for storage until it was put up for sale in 1978. In 1981 Alan Bond bought the whole Swan brewing business. Bond, who became a local hero when the crew of his syndicate's *Australia II* won the 1983 America's Cup yacht race, was a central figure in the 1980s and 1990s WA Inc. scandals that engulfed the Labor governments of Brian Burke, Peter Dowding and Carmen Lawrence. Almost immediately, Bond sold the brewery to another WA Inc. figure, Yosse Goldberg, who in 1985 sold it to the Western Australian Development Commission in a business deal that would later be investigated by a Royal Commission. From then until 1989, various plans for the development of the Brewery site came and went, all of which involved keeping it for its colonial heritage value and developing it for tourism. Some were rejected by the Perth City Council, all by Perth's Aborigines.

After the 1986 proposal to redevelop the site into a massive tourist precinct, Aboriginal people began to protest and other non-Aboriginal groups joined in: the RAC, doctors, the Kings Park Board, the Foreshores and Waterways Protection Council, The Brewery Action Group – even the Perth City Council. Leading Aboriginal elder Ken Colbung had been arguing for many years for the brewery to be levelled and the creation of riverside parklands. In 1988 the Swan Valley Fringe Dwellers, headed by Robert Bropho, another Aboriginal elder, the Black Action Group headed by Len Culbong and Clarrie Isaacs, and the Uniting Aboriginal and Islander Christian Congress joined the fray.

Then another plan was proposed, with an inducement to protestors. The development would house a large collection of Aboriginal artefacts as a 'gift' to Aboriginal people. The trouble was, Aboriginal people weren't consulted about the plan and anyway the artefacts were from the Northern Territory. Colbung and Bropho, who had become the leaders of the protest, turned down the offer. Then, suddenly, Colbung changed his mind about the redevelopment, after being persuaded that the land on which the brewery was built had been reclaimed from the river and could therefore not be a sacred site, a position vehemently denied by the other protestors. He now decided to support it, a backflip that enabled the government and others to claim that Aboriginal people now supported it or were divided on the matter.

More legal actions followed, with one court announcing, amazingly, that the government was not bound by its own Aboriginal heritage legislation. By then Aborigines had begun direct action. Thus, on 3 January 1989, after a march through Perth to protest the continuing scandal of Aboriginal deaths in custody and as an immediate response to the refusal of the government to discuss the redevelopment with them, a group of Aboriginal people and their non-Aboriginal supporters set up the protest camp opposite the brewery. This was on the narrow strip of land between Mounts Bay Road and the base of the Kings Park scarp, the site of the old brewery stables.

Photos of the early days of the camp show three or four big tents with Aboriginal flags fluttering in the breeze, rented toilets, a car, a van, some people sitting around a campfire, clothes hanging on a clothesline and the ever-present placards placed to catch the attention of passing motorists, of whom there were thousands every day. At the camp the protestors discussed tactics, met visitors, including Native Americans, held concerts (a didgeridoo and guitar together making a striking sound), ate meals and displayed the Aboriginal flag as a sign of Aboriginal sovereignty. They hosted study tours and even church services because the churches, especially the Uniting Church, were always supporters of the protests. The camp even had its own mailbox, where it received letters sent to addresses such as The *Waugal* Sacred Site Vigil Camp and The Rightful Occupants: *Waugal* Sacred Grounds. They held meetings, some among themselves, some with supporters and occasionally with members of the government.

The protesters followed several strategies. First was, of course, the protest camp itself, chosen because of the site's visibility and its proximity to the brewery. Second was to use the courts; here the Aboriginal Legal Service was an essential partner, taking many cases to various Western Australian courts and even to the High Court in Canberra. The Aboriginal and Torres Strait Islander Commission (ATSIC) also gave support. The third strategy was to engage in constant dialogue with government and the people. Increasingly, as protestors and government grew further apart, the protestors turned to the people as allies, a good strategy given that for the entirety of the dispute Western Australians had opposed the redevelopment.

As the WA Inc. scandal gradually surfaced and the government was increasingly regarded as being on the nose, its claims became increasingly desperate and crude (accusing campers of using an underpass under Mounts Bay Road as a toilet was one) while the Aboriginal response was increasingly moderate and reasoned. The government made claims, the protestors riposted. The government asked why Aborigines hadn't used the site for years, the protesters replied that they had been excluded by law from the CBD and the area. At this point the government had few allies. The Brewery Preservation Society was one; Howard Sattler, a Right wing shock jock from radio station 6PR was another.

Dozens of placards set out the protestors' case. 'Go slow your [*sic*] on sacred Ground', 'We appeal to the public to get the government to consult us', 'Always was, always will be our land', 'Black and white together with nature at this sacred place in peace'. This last placard was pointing out that the proposed park would be for all Western Australians, not just Perth Aborigines. In April 1989 they petitioned

The old Swan Brewery today. Once a brewery, now million-dollar apartments and restaurants

the Queen. She didn't bother to reply.

Crucially for the protest, another group intervened: building trade unions, whose members would be working on the site if the developments went ahead. The Builders' Labourers' Federation (BLF) let it be known that it would ban work on the site if police attacked protestors; the Construction, Mining and Energy Union (CMEU) and the Electrical Trades Union (ETU) had already voted to ban work there. Given that no work could proceed without workers, these bans were absolutely crucial to the Aborigines' campaign.

In April 1989, the federal Labor government under Bob Hawke intervened, using 1984 federal legislation on Aboriginal sites to protect the land on the Kings Park side of the site. Shortly afterwards, federal Minister for Aboriginal Affairs Gerry Hand granted protection over the whole site. The campers rejoiced. Victory seemed to be in sight. Yet a few months later, after a back room deal between federal and state Labor, it back flipped, sacrificing the Aboriginal protestors for a commitment by the WA government to legislate to make it subject to its own *Aboriginal Heritage Act*, although why it wouldn't have done this anyway is something of a mystery.

Before dawn on the morning of 9 October 1989, the police surreptitiously closed Mounts Bay Road to traffic, arrived in force at the campsite and arrested the three leaders, Isaacs, Culbong, Bropho (indeed, arrested Bropho twice because he returned to the site after appearing at court) and many others. They then cleared the site of people and their belongings and the artefacts of protest. Crowds quickly arrived, calling workers sent to dismantle the camp scabs, and under the eyes of union officials the workers stopped work. More people gathered that night to protest, but because bail conditions effectively precluded those arrested leaders from returning, the camp had ended.

The protesters kept up the pressure, this time through the courts and by demonstrations and a picket line at the site. In late 1991 the museum's Aboriginal Cultural Materials committee declared against redevelopment, but the government simply ignored it, thus launching another round of legal challenges. Later, the government also ignored a Legislative Assembly vote in favour of demolishing the brewery.

Suspicious of the government's tactics and aware of rumours of new plans, protestors, in trade union style, set up the picket line in late 1990 to prevent workers from entering the brewery site. It was to be permanent, running from 7am to 5pm every day. The protesters called on supporters to visit, join and stay, organise petitions, write letters, bring tucker and refreshments, take messages and phone calls, and bring thoughts, ideas and contacts. At one point a 30 000 signature petition circulated. ATSIC called for the brewery's demolition, but by June 1992, in a blow to the campaign, the brewery was given permanent heritage protection by the new WA Heritage Council.

In July 1992, Labor Premier Carmen Lawrence and Aboriginal Affairs minister Jim McGinty signed a contract with another WA Inc. figure, John Roberts of Multiplex, one of Perth's biggest building companies, to redevelop the brewery site, extraordinarily for several years at a peppercorn rental. Roberts had donated $600 000 to the Labor Party during the WA Inc. years so this was excellent ammunition for the protestors. All of the government's opponents alleged that the brewery development had a stink of WA Inc. about it. One protestors brochure in June 1992 advertising a meeting on the Esplanade, noted:

A park for the people or a palace for the Mates of WA Inc?
Turn out and tell this Government
Demolish xxx Demolish xxx Demolish
This monument to Corruption

Three thousand people protested at the brewery when the announcement was made and protests were held at Parliament House where the Liberal Opposition promised to demolish the brewery if it won the next election.

The protesters continued to have the support of the two crucial trade unions, the ETU and CMEU, the latter having placed a black ban on the building work. However, the BLF had changed its policy and began to support the redevelopment, arguing that it would provide jobs for its members. It also began disrupting Aboriginal protest meetings at the Esplanade and the brewery site, including one addressed by former NSW BLF secretary and champion of the green ban movement in Sydney, Jack Mundey, who was trying to bring something of the Sydney green bans to the conflict.

In August 1990, union support ended. The ETU and CMEU had been under immense pressure from the government, and then the Industrial Relations Commission threatened to deregister them if they didn't lift the ban. The CMEU called a vote of its members, which, by a narrow majority of 278 to 243, resulted in a vote to accept the ruling. If just eighteen more members had stuck fast to the protestors, the brewery would probably have been demolished. At this point the union opposition was over, which meant the Aboriginal people's campaign lost its most important ally. Robert Bropho prophetically described what was to come as 'the last battle for the brewery'.

The coup de grâce came on 26 August 1992. Over 500 people joined the picket line on the day before, but the police arrived in force the next day. Hundreds of picketers arrived and fought running battles with police. Police removed people from gates to allow trucks to enter. Protesters lay down in front of the vehicles and were dragged away. Many were arrested. Bizarrely, Aboriginal people from Kalgoorlie and elsewhere, paid and trucked in by Multiplex and Labor member for Kalgoorlie Graeme Campbell, staged a counter demonstration. Police escorted workers onto the site and the work began.

More blows to the campaign followed. After another appeal by the protesters, the federal government refused to get involved and the Perth City Council approved the development. Protests, rowdy at times, continued at the site, at government offices and Parliament House, but over time they dwindled as courts continued imposing stringent bail conditions. Aboriginal leader Galarrwuy Yunupingu visited one day to offer comfort but there was little comfort to be had.

The protesters had lost the battle.

While the government won the battle, it lost the war. In the February 1993 state election the Lawrence government lost office to Richard Court's Liberals. WA Inc. had come home to roost. The election result turned out to be of little comfort to the protestors. Previous commitments by Liberals to knock down the brewery were thrown out the window and the redevelopment continued. More court cases by Aborigines were brought and lost. Isaacs and Bropho were banned from the Swan Brewery site. The protests faded away.

Perth got a redeveloped brewery, transformed into flash restaurants and million dollar apartments, a standing monument to WA Inc. Aboriginal people got nothing. Probably the only winners were John Roberts and Multiplex, which made buckets of money from the redevelopment.

So what was at stake for the Aboriginal protesters? At one level their struggle was to overturn the historical dispossession of a sacred site. At another, it was a struggle between European and Aboriginal heritage. At a fundamental level, though, it was a struggle between two radically different cultures and the rights of Aboriginal people to the protection of their own culture. If the campaign was the first of its kind in WA, it was not the last: it foreshadowed another campaign that was to come fully twenty-five years later.

I wish to acknowledge Erin Gothard-Fox for her invaluable research assistance on this article.

18
The Single Noongar Claim
Chris Owen

The *Native Title Act 1993* arose out of the historic 1992 High Court's Mabo decision, which overturned the assumption that Australia was *terra nullius* or unoccupied when Europeans arrived and set up a legal process whereby Aboriginal people could claim native title rights over unalienated land. Some thirteen years later years, on 19 September 2006, in a packed Perth courtroom, Justice Murray Wilcox delivered a native title judgement that was of such national significance that commentators described it as a 'bombshell in the centre of Perth'. *Bennell v State of Western Australia* [2006] FCA 1243, more commonly known as the Single Noongar Claim, was a radical bombshell because for the first time in Australian history native title had been established over a capital city. (Noongar is also spelt 'Nyungar', 'Nyoongar', 'Yungar').

The case mounted by the native title representative body, the South West Aboriginal Land and Sea Council (SWALSC), was radical and audacious in that it involved upending many preconceived ideas around Aboriginal history. The Single Noongar Claim case was this. The Noongar people claimed a communal native title to the state's southwest, of which the Perth metropolitan area forms a part. At the date of British sovereignty over the Swan River Colony in 1829, the claim area was occupied and used by Aboriginal peoples who spoke dialects of a common language and who acknowledged and observed a common body of laws and customs. The Noongar people were a part of the broader Aboriginal society but shared a commonality of belief, language, custom and material culture, which distinguished them from neighbouring peoples such as Yamatjis (north of Noongar country in the Murchison Gascoyne region) and Wongis (east of Noongar country in the Goldfields). Subgroups or families exercised responsibility for particular areas of land or water, but the laws and customs under which the subgroups possessed those rights and interests were the laws and customs of the broader Aboriginal society.

The decision led to front page newspaper reports expressing alarm. The *West Australian* declared on 20 September 2006 that 'Aboriginals want native title over 185 000 sq. km of the State'. On the same day the *Australian* reported the 'landmark decision' that Perth was 'hit with native title win' that could open up other capital cities to a native title claim. Radio shock jocks tried to whip up the public into a frenzy by falsely claiming that private freehold property, that is people's backyards, were at risk. The reality that freehold title extinguished native title, that native title in the southwest was over 90 per cent extinguished and that native title generated a limited number of rights held under presovereignty laws and customs was irrelevant to the scaremongering.

The Single Noongar Claim was a remarkable win for many reasons. WA, which has the second largest Aboriginal population after Queensland, relies heavily on mining and pastoral industries. Historically, governments of all persuasions have been unreceptive to notions of Aboriginal rights to land. Formal land rights were finally legislatively raised in the 1980s only to be abandoned under pressure from mining and pastoral interests. WA remains the only state in the country not to have established some sort of Aboriginal land rights legislation.

The earlier Victorian and New South Wales Yorta Yorta case (1994), brought under national native title legislation, meant the bar for claimants gaining a successful determination was set very high. In native title cases, European records are privileged over Aboriginal oral history. In Yorta Yorta, the judge utilising such historical records as evidence remarked: 'The tide of history had indeed washed away any real acknowledgment of their traditional laws and any real observance of their traditional customs.' Following this, the onus was on claimants to prove that despite 200 years of colonisation they had '*for each generation* since sovereignty, acknowledgment and observance of the laws and customs have continued *substantially uninterrupted*' (my emphasis, CO).

Given this background, the Single Noongar Claim was not taken seriously by a great many people. After all, if native title in a well-populated rural area such as the Yorta Yorta claim could be denied, then what chance did a claim over a capital city have? Noongar people were at the scarifying coalface of colonisation in Western Australia and had to deal with Western Australian government policies designed specifically to eliminate their traditions, laws and customs, if indeed, in many cases, not the people themselves.

The primary respondents to the trial proceedings were the state Labor government of Western Australia and the federal Liberal–National Party Coalition. In addition there were sixty-six other respondents (or opposition parties), none of whom offered any evidence. At the state's insistence a trial commenced on 11 October 2005. The state's legal argument was stark and dismissive. It denied the existence of 'an identifiable society or community of Aboriginal people called "Noongar people" [around Perth] who currently acknowledge and observe traditional laws and customs'. It disputed that a system of laws and customs that distinguish the claimant group from other Aboriginal or non-Aboriginal people existed. It argued that the word 'Noongar' was a recent invention that had emerged since 'the breakdown of traditional laws and customs'. The state also claimed that these laws and customs had become 'limited to a few old men, who died without passing on the knowledge in a systematic way'. It asserted that the evidence from Noongar people about their traditions relating to the Perth metropolitan area had been 'reconstructed' from books and stories sourced from areas outside the Perth area.

Most contentiously, the state asserted that a barrage of factors dispossessed the Aboriginal people of Perth: introduced disease, murder by colonists, forcible removal and institutionalisation, starvation through removal of traditional resources and adaption to European ways. Perhaps not realising the implications of its argument, the state inferred that in the formative years of Western Australia the colonists had subjected Noongar people to genocide, defined by the United Nations as acts 'committed with intent to destroy, in whole or in part, a national, ethnical, racial or religious group'.

The Single Noongar Claim was a combination of what initially were over 100 separate family claims lodged more than ten years earlier that were later reduced to six underlying claims that exist to this day: Ballardong, Yued, Whadjuk (Perth), Wagyl Kaip, Gnaala Karla Boodja and South West Boojarah. The Single Noongar Claim group identified ninety-nine originating ancestors from which the Noongar people are descended and over 200 family names in a 2017 population of around 27 000.

Today it is no longer possible for all members of the claimant group to physically access many parts of the land and waters within the boundaries of the metropolitan claim. But, as the SWALSC legal team argued, the continuity of the acknowledgement and observance of traditional laws and customs does not require the claimants to show a continuing physical connection to the land. It is possible for Noongar people to acknowledge and observe traditional laws and customs throughout periods during which, for one reason or another, they have not maintained a physical connection with the claim area.

Where SWALSC was most radical was in shifting the accepted history and anthropology of the people of the claim area. The history of Aboriginal people is often characterised as a negative one that involved loss of country and destruction of people and culture. Books such as Charles Rowley's *The Destruction of Aboriginal Society* and Peter Biskup's *Not Slaves, Not Citizens* told the story and detailed harrowing tales of loss of law and culture. In native title claims, this written material was utilised by opponents to prove that culture, law and custom were not present when applications for native title were made.

The discipline of anthropology has been particularly detrimental. Early anthropologists mirrored contemporary scientific and social thought that Aboriginal people were a doomed race destined to become extinct. Later, professional anthropologists showed little interest in Aboriginal people in settled areas of Australia and did little work in the southwest. Their tendency to work away from settled areas reflected a view that remote Aboriginal society was complete, and traditional, whereas Aboriginal society in urban and settled areas was non-traditional and incomplete. This established a belief that traditional Aboriginal people live in the relatively sparsely settled and unsettled areas of northern Australia, while those in heavily settled southern Australia are non-traditional Aboriginal people. The current generation of anthropologists argues that Noongar culture in heavily settled areas was seen as irretrievably destroyed by European contact and that Europeans considered Noongars to be detribalised, acculturated and remnant, and that their culture was beyond recovery. Their work informed government policies on the assimilation of Aboriginal people into white society.

Government officers in variously named native welfare departments categorised Aboriginal people into racial categories and percentages of blood and caste relative to a white ideal. They were described as half caste (meaning the offspring of an Aboriginal person and a European), quadroons (one-quarter Aboriginal), octoroons (one-eighth Aboriginal), and so on, or full blood. These categories were essentially meaningless, as if a Noongar's skin colour or the way they were described by the government, affected their ability to pass on traditional knowledge, yet these categorisations defined government policies and affected entire generations.

The anthropology of the southwest is perhaps best associated with the work of the self-trained anthropologist Daisy Bates, who was one of the last researchers to have worked with Noongar people born within a decade of European colonisation. Bates used the term 'Bibbulmun nation', which is another name for the Noongar people of the southwest of Western Australia, when she wrote that the 'Bibbulmun Nation ... had but one fundamental language, and possessed similar customs, laws etc'. Bates' materials are regarded as an invaluable account of the first contact period in Western Australia; however, aspects of her work are considered deeply flawed. Daisy Bates was very much a product of her time, adopting contemporary evolutionary thinking on the status of Aboriginal people who she deemed a 'dying race, whose final pillow she had a duty to smooth'. Bates disregarded Aboriginal people of mixed descent and even denied they were members of the Aboriginal community. In opposing the Single Noongar Claim, the state gave enormous emphasis to Bates' genealogies and arguments identifying the 'last natives' from the Perth area. Joobaitch, 'the last' from the Swan and Canning districts who died in 1907, was one.

Bates' claims, however, need to be examined in the context in which they were made. She wrote about a group of people whom she thought was destined to become extinct and whose offspring she deemed to be inauthentic Noongar people. By denying that Aboriginal people of mixed descent were Aboriginal Bates was able to announce the death of one race of people and deny the existence of future generations of Noongar.

After Bates, anthropological studies in Western Australia tended to reflect the contemporary legal and marginal social status of Aboriginal people and focus on issues relating to problems of politics, conflict and assimilation in the urban setting. Accordingly, those investigating Aboriginal people were seeing a problem rather than a people. It was not until the last quarter of the twentieth century that this approach to anthropological enquiry changed. More recent anthropology has concluded that Noongar culture is multifaceted, diverse and maintains a structural integrity of its own.

For the case, SWALSC used expert witness testimony from historian Dr John Host, anthropologist Dr Kingsley Palmer and linguist Dr Nick Theiberger, who all worked extensively with the Noongar claimants before they were cross-examined in court by the state. In the trial proceedings, witness after witness gave evidence that established that colonisation had not broken their connection with their traditions, culture and their country, or boodja. Elder Angus Wallam from the

Nyungar elders at the Native Title Conference, Perth 2008

Wagin area gave evidence about how his people were slowly pushed off the land yet retained their spiritual connection to it: 'It's not ours now but it's still ours in my heart. White fella got it but it's still in my heart this is my country.' Witnesses spoke of how important it was that Noongar language and country were passed onto the next generation and many spoke of spiritually dangerous places (wirrnitj) and the spirits of their dead people (wirrin). Almost all witnesses spoke of the mythical dreamtime snake – Waugal – that created the rivers and mountains of the southwest and is most notably associated with the Old Swan Brewery site at the foot of Kings Park, as discussed in Charlie Fox's chapter. Indeed, colonists had observed this belief in Noongar people as early as 1833. Other witnesses spoke of traditional practices such as hunting for kangaroo in the Perth Hills and turtles in Perth swamps. They spoke of how they would call out for spirits before a hunt by throwing sand in the water to 'let the Waugal know you are there'. This evidence and much more showed that despite being in a heavily urbanised area Noongar people continue to practise traditional ways. It was clearly very persuasive.

When the judgement was to be handed down, the courtroom was packed with Noongar people. Justice Wilcox rejected the state's arguments and found that

> no doubt that Aborigines inhabited Part A, Perth, at date of settlement and that they were members of the single Noongar community which acknowledged and observed the traditional laws and customs.

The courtroom exploded with joy. It was official acknowledgement for Nyungar people of something they had always known: they existed as a community and this was their country.

The state and the Commonwealth immediately jointly appealed the judgement. In an aggressive appeal they argued that Justice Wilcox had wrongly identified a single Noongar society at European settlement. They denied that there was continuity of traditional law and custom and that a firm connection to the Perth metropolitan area was made. Echoing the earlier anthropology, they argued that Justice Wilcox had taken 'a farrago of cultural remnants to be sufficient'. The appeal was heard over three days in April 2007 before three Federal Court judges. On 23 April 2008, to much disappointment, Justice Finn delivered the appeal decision in Perth. The Federal Court judges upheld the state and Commonwealth appeals echoing the Yorta Yorta judgement that there needed to be a physical connection through genealogy and a level of cultural activity showing that 'for each generation since sovereignty acknowledg[e]ment and observance of the laws and customs have continued to be substantially uninterrupted'. The Single Noongar Claim matter was not dismissed but referred to the next Federal Court docket judge for a possible rehearing of the entire proceedings.

In late 2008 a change in state government bought a fresh approach to native title in the southwest, and in 2009 an alternative native title settlement began to be negotiated between the state Liberal government and SWALSC. Called the South West Native Title Settlement it was a genuine attempt at conciliation with the Noongar people and the most comprehensive native title agreement proposed in Australian history. In exchange for the resolution of all native title claims in the Single Nyungar area a range of benefits was to be provided. These included the recognition of the Noongar people as traditional owners, funding, joint management of the conservation estate and processes for the protection of heritage, the transfer of up to 320 000 hectares of Crown land with the land to be transferred to an independent Noongar Boodja Trust, which would also have $50 million deposited into it every year for the next twelve years.

In June 2015, details of the arrangement were mutually agreed. In a series of meetings in the southwest, the Noongar people voted to authorise the agreement and all parties formally signed off negotiations for the alternative Settlement. Before the deal could be registered, those who rejected the proposed agreement were given three months to lodge their objections with the National Native Title Tribunal. A small number of Noongar people did so, accusing the SWLASC of 'selling their country', though these objectors were conflating native title with different issues such as land rights and sovereignty. The reality is that, due to the extent of extinguishment, even in the event of a successful native title claim, the benefits would not be substantial for most Noongar people. In February 2017 the Federal Court delivered a shock decision based on a legal technicality within the *Native Title Act* that had the potential to derail the entire process. The Federal Court found the agreement could not be registered because four Noongar

Nyungar dance, Burswood, WA

representatives refused to sign off on it. Showing a misunderstanding of what the agreement meant, one objector celebrated and claimed, 'Our sovereignty cannot be bought for no amount of money'.

By mid 2019 the entire alternative settlement treaty still remained mired in the Federal Court as dissident Noongars, represented by one of the architects of the Mabo decision, Greg McIntyre, fought the agreement. There remains a real danger that the entire settlement, the biggest in Australian history, could be killed off, the result of which would be a disaster for the great majority of Noongar people seeking a positive outcome. Certainly amendments are being made to the *Native Title Act*, but these are stuck in the Senate. Whatever may come next is just one more episode in the long, winding and tortured road to the recognition of Noongar country. Whether a lot of the old Noongar people, who lived through the hard times before finally being recognised, will still be alive is another story.

PART 2
WALKING MILITANT FREMANTLE

LEGEND
WALKING MILITANT FREMANTLE

1. Victoria Quay, Fremantle Harbour (See chapter 19)
2. Victoria Quay, Fremantle Harbour (See chapter 20)
3. Victoria Coffee Palace, Pakenham St (See chapter 14)
4. Tom Edwards memorial, Kings Square (See chapter 21)
5. John Curtin's statue, Kings Square (See chapter 22)
6. Victoria Hall, High Street (See chapter 23)
7. Fremantle Prison (See chapter 24)
8. Fremantle Esplanade (See chapter 25)
9. Old Fremantle Trades Hall, Collie St (See chapter 26)

FREMANTLE

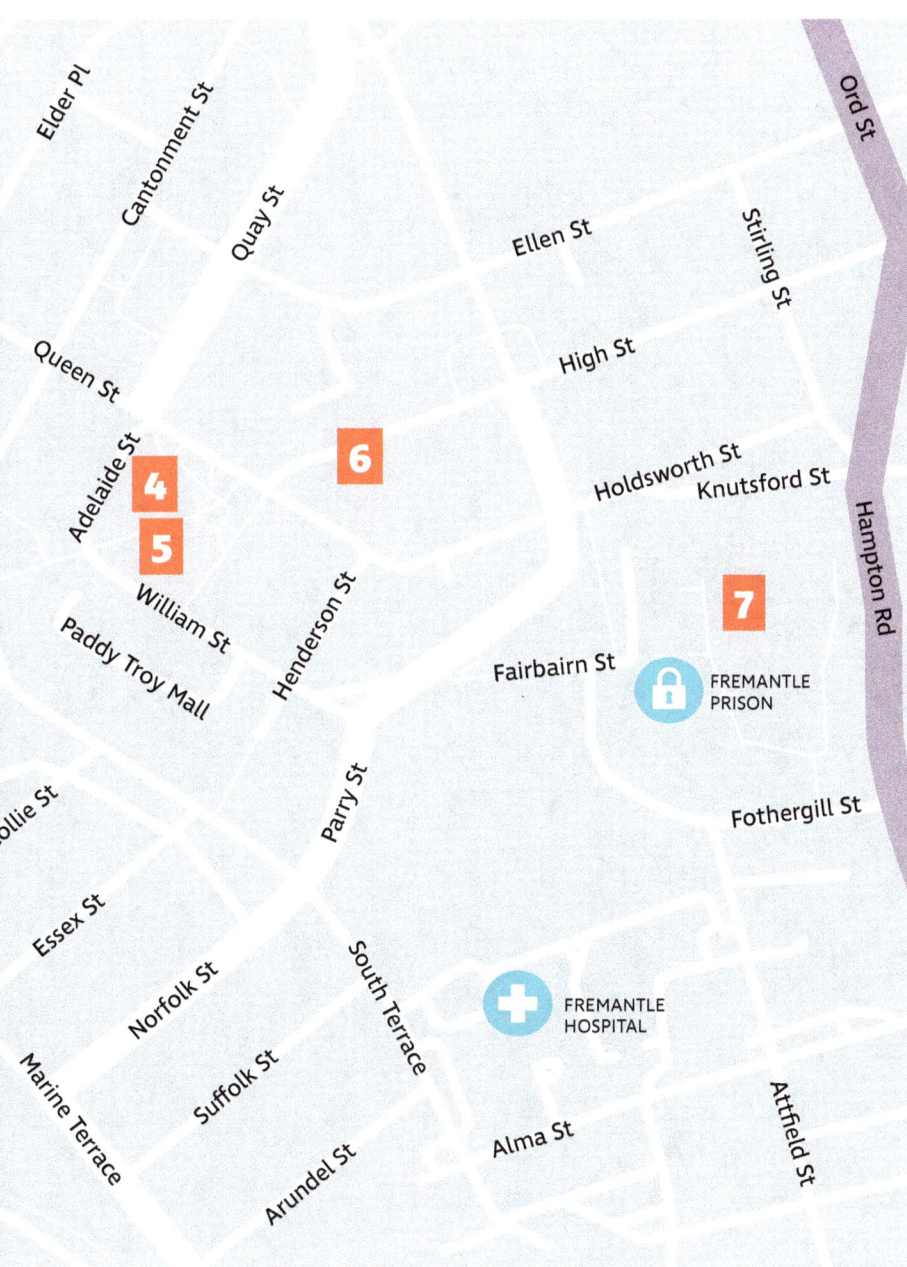

19
Chinese Seamen in Fremantle

Charlie Fox

In the space of two months in early 1942, when their ships had sought refuge in Fremantle harbour after the entry of Japan into World War 2, four striking Chinese seamen were killed, two by Australian security forces in January and two more in mid March by Dutch sailors. It's likely that the dead men were members of the Chinese Seamen's Union (CSU), which in 1921, had been established in Hong Kong, early in the first Chinese republic and during the war was conducting a widely dispersed, international campaign for better wages and conditions. It was a campaign that saw many ships laid up in Australian ports, including Fremantle. But these were certainly not the first Chinese seamen to strike for more pay in Fremantle. That history goes back to the early 1920s.

Thousands of Chinese and other Asian seamen passed through Fremantle in the first fifty years of the twentieth century. From Southern China and several southeast Asian ports, Chinese seamen crewed ships of the many lines that were instrumental in holding together national and imperial economies. These seamen passed socialist, communist and revolutionary ideas between each other and in the ports where their ships berthed. On board they worked as officers, quartermasters, stokers, deck and kitchen hands, and many other jobs, part of a workforce numbering in the hundreds of thousands across the globe. They were employed by labour contractors who sent a portion of their earnings to their families and gave a portion to ship owners for living costs; what little was left the seamen were given to spend as they could. Their pay was always lower than their Australian, American and European counterparts, causing them to look enviously at the higher pay.

In 1922, the union, unhappy with declining wages, staged a big strike in Hong Kong and won a cracking victory. So when Chinese seamen struck for higher pay in Fremantle in 1924, the union was already a force to be reckoned with, as evidenced in China and Hong Kong.

On 24 December 1924, just as the ship *Arabian* was about to leave Fremantle harbour, it was discovered that forty-two Chinese seamen had left the ship. They had been negotiating with the captain for better pay and conditions, but talks having broken down, the local officials of the communist-led Seamen's Union of Australia (SUA) had intervened and may have encouraged the seamen to strike. The captain immediately sought warrants for their arrest for being absent without leave, but they could not be found. The strike was quickly resolved, though, with complete victory to the strikers. Wages were more than doubled, the warrants were withdrawn, and the ship sailed out of Fremantle on 29 December, presumably with a happy crew.

This was an important strike, because Australian unions thought that Chinese seaman were placid and docile and that they worked for low pay, so were used by employers to undercut Australian working conditions. Thus, the SUA fought constantly against the employment of foreign workers on Australian ships. Yet after it became clear that striking foreign seamen weren't a threat to Australian jobs, the SUA supported them. As various historians have pointed out, this is not surprising because seamen have internationalism in their bones.

On 29 and 30 September 1925, surprised onlookers spotted forty Chinese seamen from the British steamer *SS Demodocus* leading a march of British seamen to the Fremantle Magistrates Court to support other British seamen who had been charged for striking. They had arrived in Fremantle in the eye of an industrial storm, the British seamen's strike of 1925.

This monster strike brought together British seamen in ports across Britain, South Africa, Australia and New Zealand. It was a wildcat strike by 15 000 members of the National Sailors' and Firemen's Union, in part against their own union because it had made a deal with the British Shipping Federation to cut its own members' pay. In Australia, seventy ships were held up and thousands of striking British seamen were sent to prison under Britain's *Merchant Shipping Act*, which governed their employment in British and overseas ports. In Fremantle their case was immediately taken up by the SUA.

Facing great odds, the strike in Britain and South Africa was over by 12 October. In Australia the seamen were able to hold out until November because of the involvement of the SUA. But everywhere it ended in defeat.

The *Demodocus* arrived on 26 September. The next day, local SUA leader Thomas Houghton arrived at the ship with 200–300 strikers from other strikebound ships to ask the crew to join the strike. After being refused entry by the captain but following negotiations, the men boarded the ship, talked to the crew and the seamen disembarked with them. Then Houghton invited the forty Chinese seamen. They joined the strike too.

At a meeting at the Fremantle Trades Hall on 29 September,

Ah You and N Pung, Chinese seamen in Fremantle, 1905

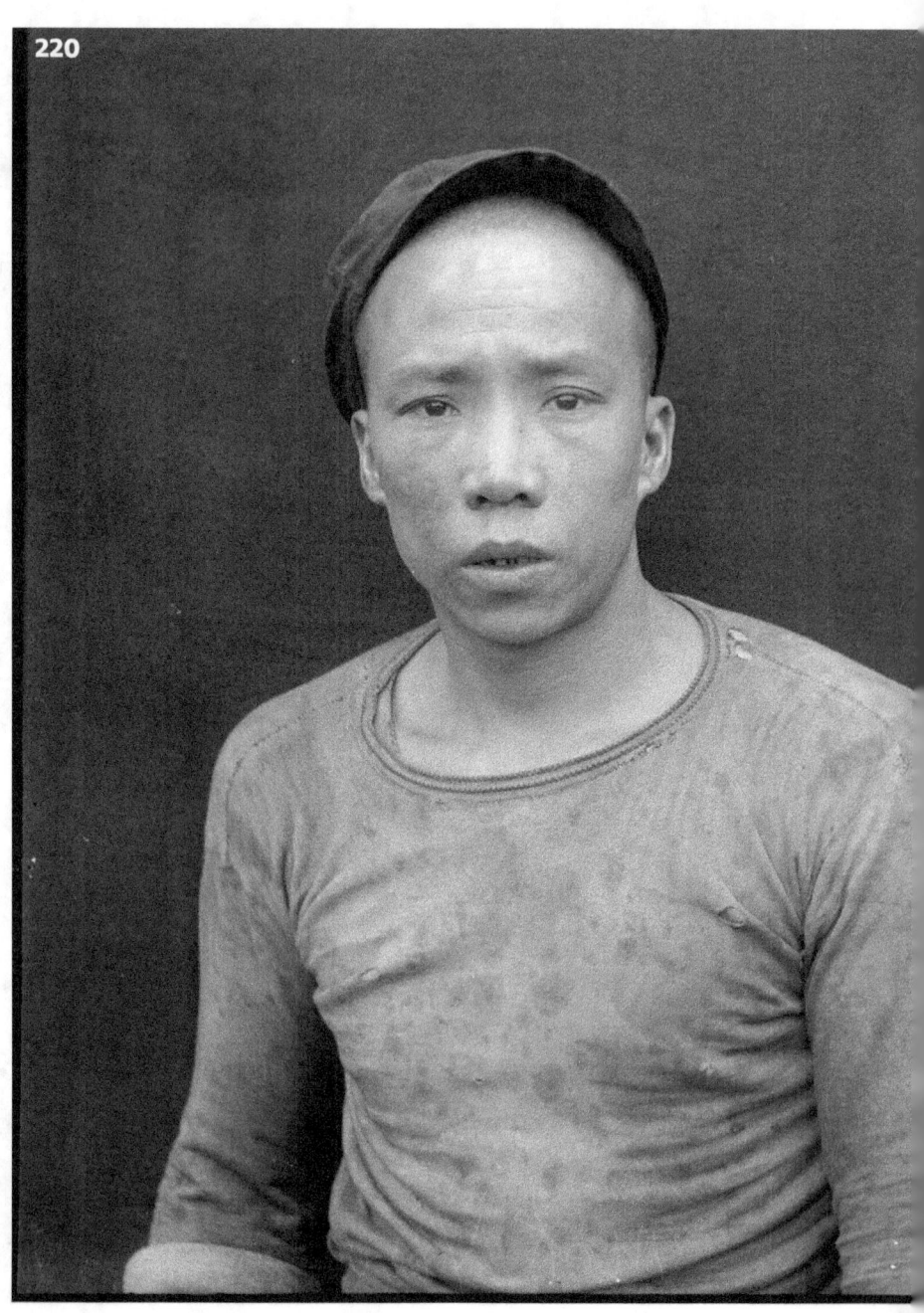

Mock Yow and Lee Sung, Chinese seamen in Fremantle 1905

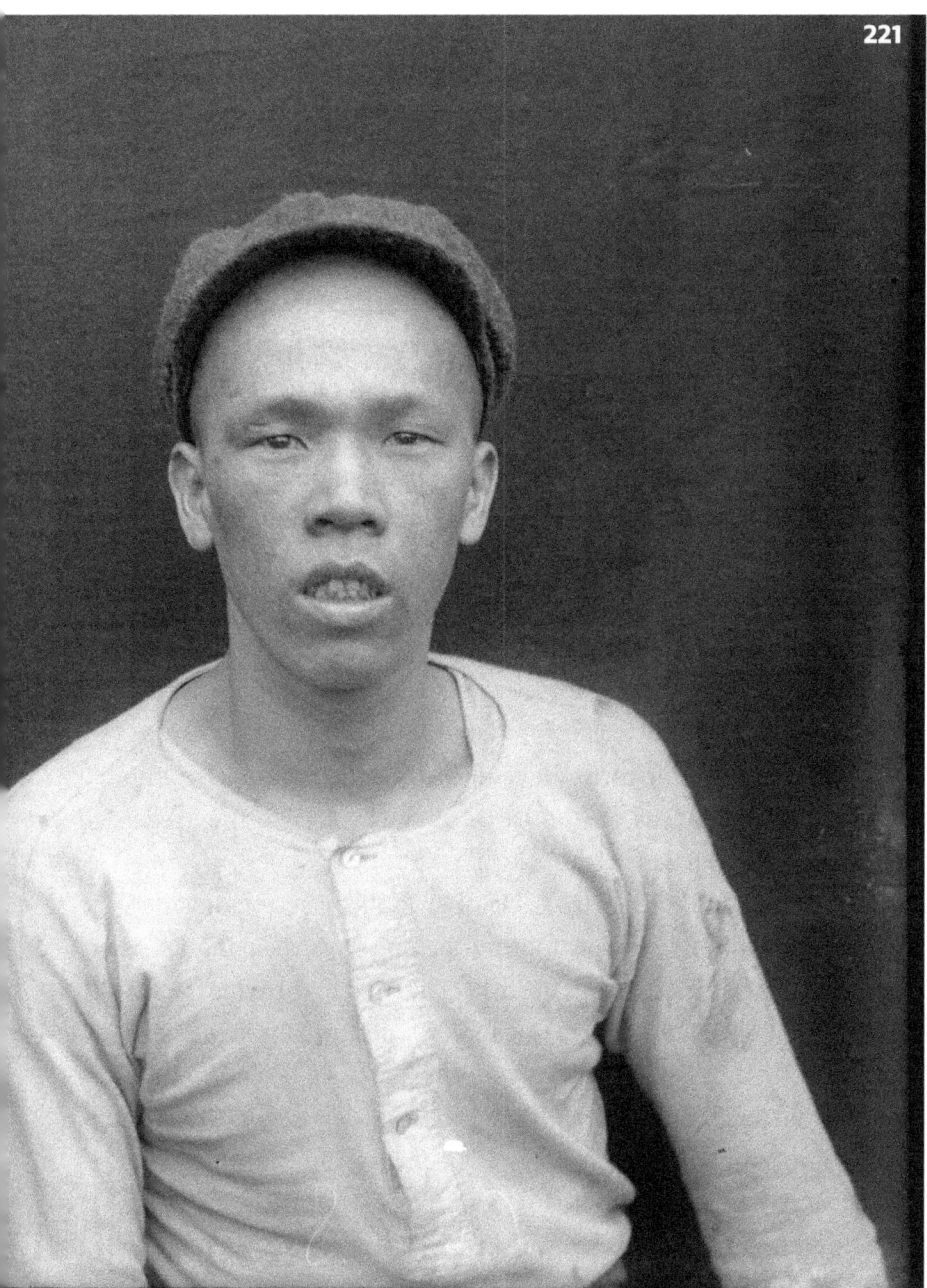

Houghton welcomed the crew to the struggle:

> That this meeting of seamen appreciates the decision of the crew of the *Demodocus* in deciding to fall into line with their comrades in this and other ports in the fight against wage reduction, particularly the Chinese seamen to who[m] we will give every assistance in their demand for equal pay with other seamen doing a similar class of work.

In the meantime, the Chinese crew members were active, giving the lie to claims in the press that British and Australian seamen didn't want their support and wouldn't support them. In addition to twice marching to the court with the British strikers, they also joining in other activities on the waterfront, such as attending a meeting of strikers at the *SS Trelyon*, another laid up ship.

For a week controversy raged around the *Demodocus*. The captain, company agents, British ship owners and federal government all insisted that the crew was intimidated into joining the strikers. As a consequence, the ship owners decided to boycott Fremantle, although it's clear that this was on the cards anyway because they regarded Fremantle as a particularly unruly port.

Then, on the night of the 7 October, police secretly invaded the wharf to thwart strikers preventing the ship from leaving its berth. Alerted by pickets, hundreds of strikers hurried to the wharf but could only watch as the ship moved out and dropped anchor in the harbour. Early the next day it slipped its moorings and sailed for Melbourne. While the local press gleefully called it a defeat for the strikers, Houghton claimed that the crew had been given special consideration to sail and so claimed victory for the strikers.

When Japan entered the war in late 1941, China, which had been fighting the Japanese in the Sino–Japanese war for many years, and Australia became allies. Fremantle became an even busier wartime port and wartime legislation made shipping an essential and protected part of the war effort. Wartime censorship, too, hid from view anything that could be read as undermining the war effort and unsettling the people. One piece of news rarely published was the death rate among seamen in the warring country's merchant marines. As the imperial economies transposed into economies at war, merchant ships carrying war materials, troops, food and commercial cargo were regarded as fair game. They were often sitting ducks for submarines and warships, so the mortality rate among seamen was incredibly high.

Late in 1941, six ships of the British-owned China Navigation Company, all crewed by Chinese seamen, docked in Fremantle. Because the crews demanded higher pay and better conditions, relations between the seamen and their captains had deteriorated. Things were worst on the *Chungking*, where the crew was alleged to have seized its captain and threatened him with violence if pay rises were not forthcoming. A conference between representatives of the men, the captain, the shipping company's agents, the army, the navy and the SUA was held to hammer out an agreement. The union recommended that the men go back to work and a later meeting of the Fremantle District Council of the ALP was full of praise for the 'orderly manner in which they had conducted themselves'. Two representatives of the Chinese seamen attended and expressed their gratitude for the support. Overnight, however, the seamen changed their minds and refused to work.

There are two versions of what happened next, the first by the Australian military authorities. Thirty soldiers with rifles, bayonets and tommy guns arrived on the wharf to remove the Chinese crews from all six ships. When the soldiers boarded the *Chungking*, the crew massed together and attacked them. The first casualty, described as the ringleader, was Tong Yuen Tong, the ship's quartermaster, who ran himself onto a bayonet and was then shot. The other crewmen had tried to flee the scene and run onto another ship moored alongside (the ships being moored three abreast) in an attempt to get to the wharf. The second casualty, Hsu Ping Say, who had run away from the soldiers, was shot in the legs when he refused to stop when called upon, was later found dead.

The second version, compiled by officials from the Chinese diplomatic mission in Canberra after discussions with the seamen, told a very different story. The crew did ask the captain for higher wages but made no threats. After the captain called the authorities, several scores of soldiers arrived with two ambulances, rounded up Chinese seamen on the wharf and, without warning, invaded the *Chunking*. Believing they were about to be forced back to work, the seamen tried to force their way off the ship. At this point the first seaman was killed; the second was shot later as he ran away from another soldier. The representative then alleged that the arrival of the soldiers was unnecessary as there was no sign of violence, that once they had arrived, they should have explained why they were there and that the shooting of the seamen was unwarrantable.

Two inquiries were held into the killings: a police investigation and a coronial inquiry. From the latter several facts are clear. First, the soldier who bayonetted Tong claimed that Tong had run himself into the bayonet, which went into his groin 'or thereabouts'. One witness said he was shot as he continued to rush the soldiers, but another witness, Commander of Naval Intelligence at Fremantle James Rycroft, said that the commander of the troops, Lt McGuckin, shot Tong and that 'Tong was first of all bayoneted in an attempt to stop him, but he had to be shot to stop a riot'. Clearly, the bayonetting was not accidental; Tong was shot in cold blood.

A second fact that emerged was that the soldier who shot Hsu claimed he fired at his legs but the medical report on his death found that he had been shot behind the left shoulder. In other words, he was shot in the back while running away.

It was also alleged that subversives on board were responsible for the violence and that Tong, who had all the 'appearance of a fanatic', was their leader. But in the police investigation a local detective suggested that radicals on shore had engineered the strike.

The coroner found that no blame attached to the soldiers, presumably because he believed that they were in fear for their lives. But in earlier correspondence he wondered why the original dispute was not dealt with in the civil courts. As a result his later, very cryptic, finding takes on extra significance.

> It was very regrettable that these men were killed, but the authorities must have had some excellent reasons for taking the drastic steps, reasons about which it would be better not to know.

Was he suggesting that the military authorities engineered or at least used the confrontation to deliver exemplary punishment to the Chinese?

The upshot of the killings was that the so-called troublemakers were sent to a detention centre in Fremantle and the rest were sent under guard to the quarantine station at Woodman Point south of Fremantle. Of those who were sent to the detention centre, nothing is known of their fate. Of those sent to Woodman Point, eighty-one volunteered to return to sea but only if they were paid British pay rates. Those who stayed were drafted into the labour units of the AMF. There is disagreement about how this happened. One source says they volunteered, another that it was the SUA's idea, another that they were forced to volunteer by the military, and yet another that claims it was the Chinese diplomats' idea. However it occurred, it seems to have been a good result. They were paid Australian military wages and exempted from the Australian *Immigration Act*. While in Fremantle some loaded and unloaded ships at the harbour for the war effort while others picked potatoes near Harvey in the southwest. Eventually, most were sent to Sydney to make barges for the Americans at very high rates of pay. They were repatriated to China after the war.

It was a win for the SUA too. Although some unionists thought introducing cheap labour into Australia was the thin edge of the wedge, the Chinese seamen assured the union that they would never allow that to happen. And three of the six ships sailed off with SUA crews.

Amazingly, the episode was repeated six weeks later. The Dutch tanker *SS Saroena* arrived in Fremantle from Ceylon on the 17 March 1942. The crew had been unsettled since stopping at Calcutta, and although not receiving their asked for pay increase, had sailed on to Fremantle. In Fremantle they made the same demand and when the captain again refused, they demanded to be paid off. He refused and asked the Australian military authorities to arrest the ringleader. When the Australian military replied that this was a civil not a military matter, the captain accused the ringleader of stabbing another crewman and had him arrested.

After the crew demanded he be released, relations on board turned ugly. The captain called a nearby Dutch minesweeper for assistance. Fourteen armed sailors arrived to eject all the seamen from the vessel. The men refused to go. The Dutch, having been instructed by the captain to move them by force, attacked them, bayonetting to death Teong Hok Soong. Other men fled to a ship moored alongside, but the sailors attacked them too, wounding one and bayonetting another.

They were finally rounded up and put on board a nearby Norwegian tanker, but another seaman, Teong Ah Kwai, allegedly tried to escape and was shot dead. Six Chinese men were taken into military custody, although they were released later; the rest returned to the tanker but refused to sail in it. In the meantime, the Dutch authorities, already under pressure from Indonesian and Australian seamen who had black banned Dutch ships in support of the Indonesian independence movement, claimed that the men were fifth columnists and mutineers.

Another coroner's report ensued, with the coroner repeating what the security authorities had told the captain, that the wages case was a civil matter. He then delivered an open finding on the killings.

The matter went to the Crown prosecutor and the state solicitor, who noted that a prima facie case for murder could be laid against the Dutch officer commanding and the two sailors who killed the seamen, but both lawyers decided not to recommend a prosecution on the grounds of justifiable homicide. They wrote:

> The consequences [of taking the case to court] might well be, therefore, that a trial judge would withdraw the case from the jury or direct them to bring in a verdict of not guilty and while ordinarily the existence of a reasonable doubt would not of itself justify a decision not to proceed with an indictment, in this case, the possibility being that the Dutch nationals might feel that they had been unduly persecuted, while an acquittal would not bring any satisfaction to the Chinese, international considerations may justify such a decision.

What happened to the surviving seamen is unknown. Given the level of censorship in Australia, it's also difficult to say with certainty that these were the only killings of Chinese seamen.

This wasn't the end of the violence and repression. Some time in 1943, another Chinese crew threatened to walk off a ship. The details are very sketchy because there were no casualties, no inquest and wartime censorship blanketed any details from the public. Security, headed by a Captain Stahl, blocked the gangplank with armed soldiers as the seamen tried to leave the ship. Meanwhile, hundreds of other seamen had gathered on the wharf. The seamen, the security service report wrote,

> became very threatening and armed themselves with clubs and various implements such as stones, iron bars, meat axes etc. The position looked very ugly when Stahl appeared on deck. He nonchalantly walked down the gangplank among the crowd of howling Chinese, saying in an undertone to the guard as he did so, 'Stay where you are and don't move'. Getting in the middle of the Chinese, he asked who could speak English and without giving them any time to answer, pointed at one and said: 'You, No.1 boy, come here and talk to me.' It was told to me that inside 20 minutes the situation was under control and all the crews had returned to their ships and the particular vessel to which he had been straightening out the trouble sailed on time.

Leaving aside the heroic language, it's clear that industrial action by Chinese seamen was still going on in 1943 and that there was considerable solidarity between the crews.

Over the war years there was a growing militancy among Chinese seamen. Just before the killings a branch of the CSU had been formed in Sydney in January 1942, With the assistance of the SUA and local Chinese residents, the union soon had branches in Melbourne and Brisbane. Angered by the difference between their and Australian seamen's pay, conditions and war risk loadings, they went on strike with increasing frequency. In late 1942 or early 1943, the spectacle of so many striking Chinese crews led the federal government to set up an inquiry into the situation of Chinese seamen in Australia. At its completion, the inquiry recommended they be granted largely Australian standard pay and conditions on board and on shore. Onshore they were also granted exemptions from the *Immigration Act*, which allowed them to live more or less freely, albeit in a restricted range of jobs, until they were to be repatriated to China. All in all, and given the tragedies in Fremantle, it seemed a reasonable result, a tribute to the militancy of the Chinese seamen and the support of the SUA.

20
War on the Waterfront
Bobbie Oliver

Commencing on the night of 7 April 1998, just before Easter, Patrick Stevedores began an assault on the workforce of every major Australian port, including Fremantle. This involved security guards who wore balaclavas to hide their identity, and the use of guard dogs, helicopters and searchlights as intimidating tactics. The ports became war zones as workers formed picket lines and resisted. This chapter concentrates on Fremantle's story, but it is best understood in the context of what was happening nationwide.

In 1996, the Liberal–National Coalition led by John Howard was elected to federal government after thirteen years of Labor administrations. From the second half of 1997, the Howard government turned its attention to the waterfront and in particular the Maritime Union of Australia (MUA), which had formed in 1993 with the amalgamation of the Seamen's Union of Australia and the Waterside Workers' Federation. The government clearly supported waterside employers such as Patrick Stevedores, whose agenda was to de-unionise the workforce.

After an abortive attempt to de-unionise the Cairns waterfront in September 1997, all was quiet for the next few months, as the MUA waited for the next attack. Rumours circulated of non-union workers being trained offshore to replace the unionised waterfront workforce. Patrick Stevedores CEO Chris Corrigan claimed that the workforce was overpaid and unproductive, yet statistics showed that productivity on the waterfront, which is measured in container movements per hour, had increased 75 per cent in the past five years. Wharfies' permanent pay rates at the time of the dispute ranged from $30 000 to $45 000 per annum (Patrick Melbourne Enterprise Agreement 1996, plus 4 per cent increase in 1997, and allowances), which scarcely put them in the high wage bracket. Minister for Industrial Relations Peter Reith claimed that crane drivers on the wharf were earning $90 000 per annum.

The Patrick Group conducted stevedoring business at seventeen wharves around Australia, where it employed 1400 permanent workers and 600 casuals – all MUA members – via four labour hire companies in the Patrick Group. In January 1998, when the National Farmers Federation (NFF) set up a stevedoring company, P & C Stevedoring, Patrick transferred to them the right to use No. 5 Webb Dock in Melbourne, with cranes and equipment. The MUA believed that Patrick and the NFF were colluding to introduce a non-unionised workforce to replace union members.

Then, on the night of 7 April 1998, just before Easter, Corrigan sacked his entire workforce, including 100 workers in Fremantle. Many employees had no indication of what was coming until they heard the morning news on 8 April, informing them that they no longer had a job. In every major port where Patrick's operated, security guards, their faces hidden by balaclavas and accompanied by German Shepherd guard dogs, arrived at the wharf by boat and ordered the employees to leave. Many resisted. In Fremantle MUA branch secretary Terry Buck and sixty other unionists refused to comply until the police arrived. That evening, each of the four Patrick employment companies appointed administrators, who advised the court the following day that they intended to dismiss the employees because the companies were insolvent.

The lockout's impact was immediate. ACTU Assistant Secretary Greg Combet, who coordinated the unions' national response, wrote:

> All of these workers had families, people who depended on them. At a human level, the assault by Patrick and the Howard Government was devastating. Arrayed against them [were] not only their employer but a replacement non-union workforce, including former military men; the federal government from the Prime Minister down; the National Farmers' Federation with a multi-million dollar, anti-union 'fighting fund'; platoons of security guards; squadrons of shock jocks and, ultimately, perhaps, the legal power of the state represented by the courts and police. These workers and their families felt the viciousness and hatred of their employer and the government, and wondered what rights they actually had.

Given its formidable opposition, the MUA's first objective was to survive, then to get members reinstated in their jobs, and then to negotiate waterfront reforms. In order to achieve this, for the first time in its history the union sought a legal solution. Although opposed by some militant unions, the MUA had majority support from its own rank and file, the ACTU and other unions to pursue this strategy, despite the risks involved. On the morning after the lockout, a legal team comprising ACTU and MUA lawyers was in the Federal Court in Melbourne seeking an injunction on the sackings. There followed parallel battles, one in the courts, the other on the wharves.

In defiance of government legislation picket lines were soon set up in Brisbane, Sydney, Melbourne and Fremantle. The dispute sparked an immediate response from port workers' unions around the world, including San Francisco members of the International

Longshoremen's Union, Japanese waterfront unions, the International Confederation of Free Trade Unions in Brussels, and the Netherlands Trade Union Confederation.

The protest at Fremantle wharf received considerable community support, which extended far beyond Fremantle and included UWA academics such as Tom Stannage and Charlie Fox. In a candlelight service on Easter Sunday morning, local clergy blessed the picket line and continued to hold Sunday services throughout the dispute. As had occurred at the Workers' Embassy protests in 1997, unionists and supporters established a community hub nearby, at which they set up a children's crèche, meeting rooms, entertainments and artists, public facilities, power, lights and even a giant television screen. State and federal parliamentarians visited. Former Premier Carmen Lawrence organised a benefit concert that raised $3500 for the families of sacked workers. The TLCWA rallied its affiliated unions to provide a twenty-four hour presence at the picket line and established a telephone tree to contact people quickly when extra support was needed.

At night, helicopters flew in scab workers, and the police played searchlights on the crowd, trying unsuccessfully to intimidate them. On 16 April 700 police, including tactical response group units wearing riot gear, took up positions behind the picket line in order to force trucks through. While violent incidents occurred at other ports around Australia, according to MUA Assistant National Secretary Paddy Crumlin, Fremantle was the only place where the police used the tactical response group against civilians. The MUA's website contained graphic descriptions from participants such as this one:

> When the call came that trucks were on their way, everyone lined up 50 metres from Patrick gate, six rows, of around 120 people, seven deep. They lay prone, linked arms, legs, ankles – whatever grip they could get. The

police moved in. People were put in the back of the paddy wagon, driven 200 metres down the road, let out and made their way back. As soon as they saw no trucks were getting through, they linked arms and stood firm.

Two nights later, in a move instigated by the NFF, a group of farmers attempted to cross the Fremantle picket lines. Again, helicopters and searchlights were used to frighten and confuse the picketers. Again, the tactics were unsuccessful.

Although the MUA asked members not to resort to violence, incidents did occur. After the Fremantle picket abused and spat at non-union labour departing Patrick's terminal on 14 April, Patrick's gained an injunction against the union and several picketers, which would prevent them entering the vicinity of the terminal. Meanwhile, scab labour was unloading ships, although unionists had succeeded in preventing some trucks carrying cargo from leaving the site. Fremantle Port Authority also issued a writ demanding that the wharfies dismantle the site outside Patrick's front gate, which had been called the Workers' Embassy in memory of the 1997 fight (see chapter 16).

In Fremantle, the protest peaked on the night of Monday, 20 April 1998. No containers had left Patrick's Terminal that day, indicating the picket line's success in preventing trucks moving cargo. The NFF threatened to drive trucks through the picket lines in Sydney, Melbourne and Perth by the end of the week. TLCWA Secretary Tony Cooke urged protesters to remain peaceful and professional, to 'stay on the ground and stay with your friends' and not to 'get involved in altercations with police officers. We're expecting them to protect you from any wayward vehicles and from any violent confrontation.' The picket lines were strengthened by 200 Australian Manufacturing Workers' Union (AMWU) members. By 11pm, 1000 protesters were preparing for the arrival of hundreds of police, signalled by an increased police presence during the day and the appearance of a police helicopter that circled overhead in the early evening, apparently trying to assess numbers. There followed 'a long night of tension between over a thousand members of the community and hundreds of police', during which, the ABC reported, 'police could be seen doing riot exercises' and 'a fixed wing aircraft and [a] helicopter kept a constant surveillance of the peaceful assembly'.

Despite the bravado, it was a scary experience for the individuals involved. Charlie Fox, who was there that night, recalled rumours that 'the farmers are coming, now at Midland, now at Claremont'. One of the organisers told picketers that the police

> would try to break another picket line and that our job would be to form a flying V formation and charge (gulp) through them, like the cavalry and come to the rescue of our comrades.

Fortunately, the police held off and such action was unnecessary. Fox also remembered Tom Stannage telling him that on another picket line 'labour lawyers were there to instruct people on their rights and doctors and nurses, too, to assist the injured'. Police discouraged people from walking on Port Beach by telling them to move on. 'It was like an armed camp down there.'

On 21 April in the Federal Court, Justice North handed down his decision that all of Patrick's workers should be reinstated. He ordered the reinstatement of the labour supply agreements between Patrick and the four labour supply companies, despite their insolvency. Furthermore, the labour supply companies must use their former workforce – the sacked MUA members – to perform the work on the wharves. Justice North found that the evidence indicated the workers were sacked because they were members of the MUA. This, arguably, was in breach of the *Workplace Relations Act* and the workers' contracts.

North also ruled that it was 'an arguable case that Patrick owners and Patrick employers have engaged in an unlawful conspiracy'. In Fremantle, unionists celebrated by naming their picket line the Tom Edwards Stand, in memory of another dispute seventy-nine years previously (see 'Fremantle's "Bloody Sunday" ', chapter 21). The full Federal Court dismissed an appeal by Patrick against Justice North's order and his reasoning was substantially approved by a majority of the High Court on 4 May, with one dissenting vote.

But the dispute was not yet over. In May, the MUA succeeded in getting workers back on the wharves, but they were still employees of labour hire firms – the same situation as that existing prior to the lockout. This meant that the wharfies returned to work with no job security and received only a portion of their wages until mid June. Conditions had to be renegotiated: work rosters, penalties and wages. MUA National Secretary John Coombs and ACTU Assistant Secretary Greg Combet scored a major victory in negotiating an end to the notorious double shifts of fifteen hours that wharfies had been forced to work. But there were compromises, too. A settlement between the union and Patrick on 5 August resulted in 738 redundancies nationwide, over one-third of those planned by the stevedoring company. Patrick agreed to drop all charges against the union, to pay over $1.8 million in legal costs and all outstanding wages.

The settlement had its critics. Although Tom Bramble saw the outcome as 'a defeat for union busting', by which the Howard government was 'significantly embarrassed', he argued that the solution brokered by the MUA and ACTU leaderships resulted in a 'miserable deal' for the wharfies. He argued that public support around Australia was sufficient for the ACTU to organise a mass general strike and to hold out for a deal that offered better job security. Instead, the deal 'signed away nearly 50 per cent of the entire permanent Patrick workforce', with maintenance, security and cleaning jobs being allocated to outside contractors. Two-thirds of MUA members would be casuals working 'two hour minimum shifts, on call 24 hours a day 365 days a year'.

Bramble's argument places considerable – possibly misplaced – confidence in union power and solidarity. Once the MUA and the ACTU had decided upon a legal solution, they were obliged to convince the court that the members were 'ready, willing and able to perform the contract of service'. Legal precedent was important here for, according to Rachel Mulheron:

> the employment cases to date indicate, when a plaintiff employee fails to give an undertaking to the employer that there will be no further industrial disruption, the parties are *not* in a position to perform the contract of employment (emphasis in original).

Union militancy aside, in order to have any chance of winning the battle by legal means, the MUA had to eschew industrial action. Bramble's analysis also tends to underestimate the commitment of the federal government to ridding the wharves of union labour. There is a reasonable argument that militant activity would merely have played into the government's hands and achieved its aim of destroying the MUA.

Although the ALP did not win the federal election on 3 October 1998, it was clear that many Australians were unhappy with the Howard government. In Western Australia, sitting Labor MPs Smith, Lawrence and Beazley were joined by four new Labor colleagues: Jan McFarlane, Kim Wilkie, Jane Gerick and Graham Edwards. Nationwide, although the Howard administration held on to government, it was a close call, with Labor gaining eighteen seats and the Coalition losing fourteen on

Mounted police used to intimidate and disperse unionists and their supporters

the 1996 result. More than 50 per cent of the two party preferred vote went to Labor. Among those to lose their seats was former Minister for Transport and Regional Development John Sharp who, with Reith, had masterminded the plan to reform the waterfront. Given that the government was revealed to be supporting the employer in illegal actions against some of its own citizens, it is disappointing that the verdict of the Australian public was not harsher.

Tom Edwards' funeral cortege pauses outside Fremantle Trades Hall 9 May 1919

21
Fremantle's Bloody Sunday

Bobbie Oliver

A century ago this year, Fremantle was still reeling from events that had happened during the previous fortnight. On 4 May 1919, over a thousand wharf labourers, or lumpers as they were called, their wives and children had mobbed the wharf, thrown bricks at the premier, faced armed police, and seen one of their own killed and others injured in the event that has since been termed a riot or Bloody Sunday, and referred to as Fremantle's Eureka. At the time, the Fremantle branch of the ALP hailed the lumpers' stand as 'the finest exhibition of solidarity in Western Australian history'.

For several days after the event, police officers feared for their safety on the streets of Fremantle. The funeral of Tom Edwards, the lumper who died of injuries incurred on the day, brought not only Fremantle but also the whole state to a standstill. When the Labor movement later proposed a memorial for Edwards, the authorities deemed it too inflammatory to be set in the street. The drinking fountain that today stands in Kings Square was originally constructed in the Fremantle Trades Hall. Since then, Bloody Sunday and the name of Tom Edwards have been invoked in industrial disputes from striking female tea room workers in 1921 to objections to live sheep exports in the 1980s. His sacrifice has been commemorated in May Day marches. How was it that such events occurred in Fremantle and that feelings about it should continue to run to strongly for many years afterwards?

The union at the centre of the dispute, the Fremantle Lumpers' Union (FLU), was formed in 1889, in the days when unions were still illegal in Western Australia. The Lumpers, who later become a branch of the Waterside Workers' Federation and are now part of the Maritime Union of Australia (MUA), had to be militant because their work was dangerous and their conditions were very poor. In 1919, mechanisation was limited to the crane that lifted heavy cargo onto the deck and then down into the holds. Accidents were common.

In those days, a man could never be sure whether he had a day's work until he was hired at the bull pen, the area where workers congregated each day on the wharf to try to get work. Even then, if he was given a shift, he would not know how long the shift would be. Working twelve and fifteen hour shifts was not uncommon. The bull system benefited the young and strong and disadvantaged older and less proficient workers. No money was paid for simply turning up. If a man was unemployed, he had to wait for the next pick-up time and hope that something came up then.

The cause of the industrial dispute that sparked Bloody Sunday lay in the winter of 1917. Although Western Australian unions were not involved in the general strike that gripped the eastern states, in August the FLU had refused to load a ship with flour for the Dutch colony in the East Indies (modern day Indonesia). They believed that Australian flour was finding its way to Germany via the Dutch East Indies. Rumours abounded that Australian soldiers discovered wheat bags, clearly marked as being from Australia, in German trenches.

Meanwhile, former ALP member turned conservative Prime Minister Billy Hughes' solution to the general strike in the eastern states was to form rival national workers' unions in critical industries such as railways, mines and ports. The National Waterside Workers' Union (NWWU), its members drawn from the ranks of the unemployed, scab workers, non-unionists and volunteers ranging from university students to farmers, began operating in ports around Australia. At Fremantle, the FLU stayed on strike for fourteen weeks before finally capitulating and accepting the appalling conditions forced upon them by the Australian Steamship Owners' Federation. These conditions included granting preference to NWWU members, payment in some cases of weekly wages instead of an hourly rate, and employing foremen who were not waterside workers.

From September 1917 until May 1919, Fremantle wharf was a battleground where violence occurred daily. The police force was stretched to its limits trying to protect NWWU members from attack, either in the form of 'accidents' on shipboard (easy enough to bring about in the dangerous working conditions of the wharf in the premechanised era) or brawls on the way to and from the railway station or at pick-up times. Under the new conditions, entry to the wharf was by means of a metal disc (which the lumpers referred to as a dog tag) and a registration card that even those employed on the North Wharf had to present at the pick-up office in Cliff Street before and after each day's work. This provided plenty of opportunities to be waylaid and set upon by out of work, angry lumpers with hungry families to feed.

When the Employers' Federation complained of insufficient police protection for NWWU members, they admitted that sufficient protection would mean stationing a police officer at every hatch of every ship being loaded or unloaded. The police commissioner reminded Colonial Secretary Hal Colebatch that this level of protection would require more than sixty constables to be employed throughout each twenty-four hour period. Nevertheless, police were obliged to provide protection during the pick-up times, a situation that continued throughout 1918. The armistice on 11 November was celebrated by a midnight battle between the rival unions in High Street.

Sailing into Fremantle Harbour in April 1919, with influenza victims among its passengers, the coastal steamer *Dimboola* provided the lumpers with a long-awaited opportunity to redress the grievances of the past hungry months. The ship was already the centre of a dispute between Hal Colebatch, now premier, and Acting Prime Minister William Watt, who objected to the seven day quarantine period imposed by the WA government. Watt believed that this would mean ships carrying cargo would be needlessly lying idle. Although the chamber of commerce supported Colebatch's seven day quarantine, when the FLU moved to enforce it by refusing to unload the *Dimboola* and making sure that no one else did, the union's action was branded as subversive.

During the last week of April, the centre of Fremantle was the scene of two major demonstrations at which the FLU canvassed for donations to support the strikers. *The Fremantle Wharf Crisis of 1919*, published by the ALP in 1920, was an eye witness account of these demonstrations:

> The sight of hundreds of women, many of whom carried little babies, or to whose skirts clung tiny, ill-clothed children, marching at the head of a column of men numbering thousands, was distressingly impressive. For many long months they had watched their little ones suffer, going short of necessary food and clothing; they had seen what little nest-egg might have been accumulated in better days ... gradually diminish and vanish; and with the spectre of hunger hanging continually over them

and their children, both men and women were determined, once and for all, to settle the issue and demand the right to work on the wharf. In no industrial trouble before did the women folk stick to their men as did the wives, daughters and sweethearts of the Fremantle lumpers, and in the achievement of final victory they are entitled to claim an honoured place.

Watt put further pressure on Premier Colebatch, insisting that the state government must honour its 'pledge to the loyalist workers'. On 30 April, the state government took control of the wharves, despite the FLU making a compromise offer permitting soldiers to unload perishable goods from *Dimboola*. The state ALP supported the lumpers' stand, insisting to the premier that there could be no industrial peace on the wharf while the two rival unions existed. The NWWU had not been granted preference in the Arbitration Court, and because it was not registered under the Commonwealth law, it had no legal status and could not be recognised by any of the court's decisions.

In these discussions, the premier gave no indication of what action he planned to take on Sunday, 4 May. Saturday passed quietly. Preparations were made to transport a party of blacklegs down the river to the wharf early on Sunday morning to erect barricades around the *Dimboola* so the ship could be unloaded without interruption. As soon as Colebatch's intention became known, at around 10 o'clock on Sunday morning unionists were alerted to come to the wharf. Meanwhile, police who had been brought secretly to the wharf and quartered in B Shed, came out and took up pre-arranged positions. They were joined by a force of fifty mounted police – some of whom had been brought from country stations – who made a cordon across the wharf entrance.

Although the first few lumpers who gathered moved when the police requested them to, the crowd on the railway bridge was not so compliant. As the launches carrying the premier and scab volunteers passed underneath, the crowd began hurling bars of iron, lumps of road surface and rocks, despite attempts by police with drawn bayonets to stop them. After the launch passed, the crowd rushed from the bridge to the wharf where its numbers reportedly swelled to over 1000. The police were unable to prevent the lumpers surging back onto the wharf and throwing missiles. They headed for the pick-up bureau between B and C sheds, intent upon throwing the barricades into the harbour.

The police on the wharf were ordered to fix bayonets; at that point their rifles were not loaded with ammunition. As one of the lumpers, a man named Brown, ran towards the spot where a group of employers and National unionists were erecting the barricades, police grabbed him and, according to William Renton, the Lumpers' president, 'seemed to bayonet him' despite Brown being unarmed. Renton claimed that prior to the incident, 'there had been absolutely no trouble between the lumpers and the police', which conflicted with accounts of lumpers hurling rocks and other missiles. Renton later insisted that no missiles were thrown until after the bayoneting. He asked the police to let him go to aid the injured man, but they refused. Renton stated that three or four police surrounded him 'with rifles and stones in their hands'. One said, 'Get him' and Renton was hit on the head with a missile while he was facing the police. He was knocked down, and when he tried to get up he was again knocked down with a baton, which inflicted a wound that required bandaging. Another lumper, Tom Edwards, who went to assist Renton, was also hit on the head with either a police baton or a rifle butt and fell to the ground with a fractured skull. Tom's wife Jane, who was also present, waited with him until an ambulance arrived and took him to the Fremantle Hospital.

Police Commissioner Robert Connell, his senior officers Inspectors

Mann of Perth Police and Sellinger of Fremantle, and two labour officials, ALP State Secretary Alex McCallum and the Member for Fremantle Ben Jones, held an emergency meeting in C Shed. McCallum obtained a guarantee from the premier that the parties leaving the wharf would not be attacked. He then addressed the crowd from the footbridge, urging people to leave the wharf quietly. Unfortunately, at this point, a car arrived with ammunition for the police and a sergeant began issuing cartridges to the foot constables.

At some point, the *West Australian* reported, the *Riot Act* was read, although Inspector Mann did not mention this in his report. That the small force of 150 mounted and foot police was not immediately overwhelmed by several hundred angry lumpers probably says more about the unionists' respect for police and authority than any lack of provocation. The chief inspector quickly stopped ammunition being issued. McCallum secured the premier's guarantee that he would leave the wharf, and promised that his launch would not be attacked as he went back up the river. The lumpers then withdrew to the O'Connor Monument. Twenty-six police officers and seven lumpers had been injured. Tom Edwards, the one fatality, died at Fremantle Hospital on the evening of 7 May. He was forty-one years of age and left behind a widow and three children.

From Sunday to Wednesday, following the confrontation on the wharf, Fremantle was rocked by riots. On Sunday afternoon, the lumpers regrouped and threw the hated barricades into the harbour. On Monday night, two police constables were beaten up in High Street. A several thousand strong crowd gathered outside the Federal Hotel and attacked the armed officers who went to their colleagues' aid. Alex McCallum was called to an emergency meeting with Renton and Fremantle Trades Hall Secretary Fred Baglin at King's Theatre.

The labour officials managed to defuse the situation and quiet the angry crowd.

At midnight on 7 May, Colebatch and Deputy Premier James Mitchell finally agreed to withdraw the NWWU from the wharf, shut the National Workers Bureau and return to the pre-August 1917 status quo. There was to be no victimisation on either side. Until an agreement was reached in the Arbitration Court, the FLU and the Tally Clerks Union would continue to work under their existing awards. Any difference of opinion would be settled by arbitration. Lumpers' families in urgent need of assistance were to receive government aid, and Mrs Edwards and her family would be compensated. Eventually, she received £686. Shortly afterwards, Colebatch resigned after only one month as premier; he was succeeded by his deputy, James Mitchell. The FLU had won.

Thousands attended Edwards' funeral on 9 May. The procession was headed by Renton riding a black horse, and a band, which played the *Dead March*. Every Labor politician in the state attended and unions sent representatives from as far away as Albany and Geraldton. In Fremantle, flags flew at half mast, the vessels in the harbour dipped their ensigns. Elsewhere in the state, public transport and work ceased for three minutes. Kalgoorlie shops and hotels closed as a mark of respect. Photographs of the funeral show the size of the procession and Edwards' grave in the Anglican section of Fremantle Cemetery smothered in wreaths. Later the FLU erected a fine monument, far more impressive than the resting places of his fellow lumpers.

But the government and employers, having grudgingly compensated Edwards' widow, were very reluctant to accept any blame for his death or to acknowledge his sacrifice. The ALP state executive's minutes show that, a month after Bloody Sunday, the

Fremantle Harbour Trust advised the ALP's Fremantle District Council that it refused permission to erect a memorial to Edwards in the Fremantle Port area on the grounds that it 'would not be conducive to public harmony'. Also the inquest recorded Edwards' death as accidental. The ALP erected a memorial drinking fountain in the Fremantle Trades Hall; it was later reclaimed from the ruins and placed in its present location in Kings Square. The inscription reads:

> This memorial fountain was erected to the memory of Comrade Tom Edwards, working class martyr, who sacrificed his life on the Fremantle wharf on Sunday, May 4, 1919. 'Greater love hath no man …'

Proceeds from sales of *The Fremantle Wharf Crisis of 1919* were directed to a fund for Mrs Edwards. Five hundred copies sold in six months to buyers all around Australia. With the money raised, the labour movement built Jane Edwards a cottage. She later remarried, and died in 1964 at the age of eighty.

The immediate impact of Bloody Sunday was that the FLU was successful in getting the rival NWWU driven from the wharf. Its victory inspired a similar action on the Melbourne wharves on 21 May, but because the wharves there were enclosed and as a result more easily guarded, this action failed. This was not the end of the Nationalist unions, but over the next two years, other industrial battles were fought in the mines and on the wharves until they finally disappeared.

Tom Edwards' martyrdom remained a powerful symbol for the working class movement. It was invoked by striking Esplanade Hotel workers in 1921, and also during the Seamen's Union strike in 1925. Bloody Sunday has also become associated with May Day, because of the date on which it occurred. In 1937, the wharfies' journal, the *Waterside Worker*, retold the story. In 1950, the Maritime Unity Committee, an association of the major waterfront unions, organised a march to the Tom Edwards Memorial and laid a wreath. In 1954, the first May Day procession held in Fremantle gave pride of place to Jane Edwards and commemorated the events of 1919. In the refurbishment of Fremantle in the 1980s, Edwards' memorial fountain was restored and rebuilt in Kings Square. Also in the 1980s, when the wharfies went on strike over the live sheep export dispute and farmers threatened to load the sheep, a small, handmade plaque appeared on the wharf bearing the message, 'Remember Tom Edwards'.

Today, if you climb the stairs of the MUA's offices in North Fremantle, you will still see the large photograph of Tom Edwards, holding pride of place on the wall. Whether or not many of the MUA's members know his story, its significance – the need to maintain a strong union presence on the waterfront and to fight for rights and conditions – was emphatically brought home to them in 1998. This story is now a century old but its message is as relevant in the twenty-first century as it was in 1919.

22
John Curtin at the *Worker*
Bobbie Oliver

Early in 1917, the *Westralian Worker,* the weekly newspaper of the Western Australian Labor Federation (ALF, later ALP), employed a new editor after the previous editor John Hilton had been sacked for his 'pallid prose' and his pro-conscription views. The ALF wanted a firebrand who would argue eloquently against any attempt by the federal government of Labor rat W. M. 'Billy' Hughes to reintroduce military conscription for overseas service in World War 1 after a 1916 plebiscite on the issue failed by a narrow margin. They hired the right man.

John Curtin was born on 8 January 1885 in Creswick, Victoria, to Irish immigrants John and Catherine Curtin. His father's health was poor, and he experienced a childhood of poverty, which he later described as an existence of 'tea without milk and bread without butter'. From an early age, Curtin dedicated himself to changing the social conditions of the poor. By 1907, he was president of the Brunswick branch of the ALP and was writing articles for the *Socialist*, the journal of the Victorian Socialist Party. In 1911, aged twenty-six, he was appointed Victorian secretary of the Timber Worker's Union (TWU). Curtin founded a monthly union journal *The Timber Worker* in 1913, aimed at informing 'the rank and file of essential questions of life and death'. Topics included Marx's theory of wage slavery, a call for a people's constitution and support for a proposed referendum by the Fisher Labor government seeking to grant the Commonwealth the same powers as the states over labour laws and create a nationally recognised workers' compensation scheme. Curtin, who was a centralist with a national vision was to maintain his faith in the federal system of government, despite demonstrating his awareness that it did not always benefit states with smaller populations, such as WA and Tasmania.

After leaving the TWU, Curtin worked for the 1916 campaign against conscription for overseas military service in World War 1, speaking at Melbourne's Yarra Bank and in other public places throughout Victoria, often in front of hostile crowds. He was gaoled for three days after failing to comply with the governor-general's proclamation ordering all single males, aged from twenty-one to thirty-five, to enlist in the armed forces. The trauma of his imprisonment and the strain of living under the threat of physical violence, coupled with bouts of heavy drinking, broke Curtin's health, causing him to spend some time in a convalescent home. Meanwhile, his friends worked to secure his appointment as editor of the *Westralian Worker*, and when early in 1917 this was achieved, Curtin moved to Perth. The prospect of a steady income enabled him to marry his long-time fiancée Elsie Needham. Their relationship provided much needed stability in his life. The couple married in 1917, settled in the beachside suburb of Cottesloe and had two children.

The *Westralian Worker* had been founded by the ALF as an outcome of the 1899 trades union congress in Coolgardie. The first edition appeared on 7 September 1900. Early editors included Wallace Nelson, a Scot from Aberdeen who had previously worked on

The *Westralian Worker* office in Stirling Street, where
John Curtin was editor 1917 to 1928

the *People's Newspaper* in Rockhampton, and Julian Stuart. Initially housed in offices in Kalgoorlie, the *Worker* (as it became known) moved to Perth in 1912 where it gained status as the statewide voice of the labour movement rather than simply a goldfields newspaper. The move coincided with Labor's improved electoral fortunes in WA, with the first majority Labor government, led by John Scaddan, having been voted into parliament the previous year. In 1915, the People's Printing & Publishing Company bought the *Worker*. Figures estimated on the income from yearly subscriptions (set at 5/- in 1916) indicate that circulation rose from around 4200 in 1917 to almost 14 000 in 1928. This was undoubtedly boosted by the AWU taking over the paper in 1919 and issuing copies to all of its members. It was housed in a building in Stirling Street, later home to the *Sunday Times*.

When John Curtin arrived in WA in 1917, he continued his public speaking, in Perth mostly on the Esplanade and in Fremantle mostly outside and occasionally inside the town hall. He spoke on issues such as conscription and Fremantle's Bloody Sunday. Meanwhile, at the *Worker*, the change of editorial style was instant. Some of Curtin's most powerful and eloquent criticisms about the conduct of the war, the peace settlement and the inequality of sacrifice suffered by working people were written in the first few months of his editorship. He attacked profiteering, which he saw as an outcome of warfare, and reiterated his belief that only capitalists benefited from war. He wrote that the working class gained nothing from the conflict and yet paid the biggest sacrifice.

This inequality between classes was most pronounced in the matter of conscription for overseas military service. Hughes' nationalist government – a coalition of some ALP members of parliament and the Liberal Party that had been re-elected in May 1917 – took the course of action that anti-conscriptionists had feared they would since the failure of the first referendum: it once again appealed to Australians to vote in favour of introducing conscription for overseas military service. Prior to the second conscription referendum, set for 20 December 1917, Curtin was at his eloquent best, demonstrating his ability to argue convincingly. He claimed that voluntarism had not failed, but that Prime Minister Hughes had 'got his sums completely wrong'. In 1916 Hughes had claimed that 16 500 voluntary recruits per month was the minimum number necessary to provide enough reinforcements for the front without introducing conscription. In 1917, he revised the figure down to 7000 per month, but Curtin asserted that even the revised figure was excessive.

Curtin's arguments focused on three main points. First, the British government had requested five Australian divisions (100 000 men). There were already enough men recruited and in camp to provide the necessary reinforcements for these divisions, hence the threat to break up the Australian Imperial Force (AIF) if insufficient Australian men enlisted was an empty one. Second, there were only about 30 000 single men aged between twenty and forty-four left in the country, including those who were medically unfit. In order to maintain his monthly quota of 7000, Hughes would soon have to recruit married men with dependents, despite promising that he would not do so. Third, Curtin argued, Australia should attend to its own defence needs before those of the empire, a theme he returned to several times over the next few years. WA had gained not only an effective advocate for the anti-conscription campaign but also a fearless critic of imperialism and war.

Curtin wrote much on the futility of war before and after the November 1918 Armistice. His editorials expressed outrage at the war mongering of world powers supposedly dedicated to pursuing peace. Reflecting on speeches made at Anzac Day ceremonies in 1923, for example, Curtin stated that, 'The war did not add one single good thing to civilisation, but drained it of the stuff of progress and security'. He pointed out that 'More men are under arms now that the world has allegedly been made safe than in 1914, when it lived on the verge of a volcano'. Furthermore, war and preparation for war created an economic climate in which some suffered because nations gripped by 'industrial paralysis' failed to provide adequate employment for their citizens, and yet others were able to make 'vast gains'. The economic provisions of the peace treaty had created an unforeseen situation in which 'German workers have jobs that yield them a miserable standard of subsistence while the British workers have not got jobs, and are told to migrate to Australia'. In the 20 March 1925 *Worker*, he asked rhetorically: 'Are we to repeat eternally the follies that went into the incubation of the so-called "great war"?'

On the subject of Australia's postwar relations with the British empire, Curtin argued that, as a British colony, Australia could never take its place in world affairs. It would continue to be a recruiting ground for empire wars, and to be bound up in Britain's international plans. When the Prince of Wales visited Australia in July 1920, Curtin objected to the heir to the British throne being used as a missioner (or emissary) for 'psychological propaganda', paving the way for an imperial reconstruction of the postwar world. In line with ALP policy, Curtin criticised the imperial federation proposed by British Secretary of State for the Colonies Lord Milner because he believed that it would result in 'a contraction in Dominion autonomy'. Ceasing to be a colony had been one of the major incentives for the Australian colonies to become a federated nation but a quarter of a century later, Australia was still a British colony. Curtin used the examples of India, Egypt and Ireland to prove his argument that imperial interference pushed countries towards independence rather than cementing them in the empire. 'Loyalty does not demand that we consent to any expansion of imperial authority,' he wrote. Using the Prince of Wales as a 'missioner for doubtful causes' put Australians in a very awkward situation. To speak out against the cause would embarrass the future king, to remain silent suggested acquiescence. The heir to the throne, he argued, should never be placed in such a position.

In November 1923, returning to the need for Australian autonomy from Britain, Curtin wrote that, in the eyes of Prime Minister S. M. Bruce (1923–29) and his class, workers were merely material to be used for 'productive, exporting and exploiting purposes in peace and wholesale gun fodder in war'. Reiterating that 'Australian sentiment must begin, end and stay at home', he urged Australia to become self-contained. 'America has done it – why not Australia?' The USA had kept itself free from aggression by 'minding its own business'. Curtin believed that for Australia to continue close defence ties with Britain was dangerous rather than advantageous.

While such arguments suggest that he advocated isolationism, Curtin's view of the international situation was well informed, realistic and even (sadly) prophetic. In several editorials in 1924, 1925 and 1927, he insisted that a peace based on the conditions of the Versailles Treaty would not be an enduring one: history proved him to be correct. He criticised the Western powers for refusing to consider total disarmament, and regretted the failure of the several disarmament conferences held by the League of Nations.

In the so-called booming 1920s, Curtin continued to draw the attention of his readers to the vast inequalities that he saw existing in Australian society. In a particularly angry editorial on social inequality dated 8 October 1920, he wrote:

> Yea! While rose-smothered drawing-rooms and thousand-guinea parties manifest the frightful inconsequence of the parasitical class, there reek in narrow streets and stifling alleys the sad-eyed labourers whose exertions have made possible the squandering of the rich.

By 1923, Curtin was a homeowner with a mortgage. While some may have regarded this as adopting a capitalist way of life, Curtin firmly believed that workers should strive 'not merely to be better paid slaves' but for full emancipation from servitude. The worker, therefore, had the same right to live in comfort and own his home as the employer did.

The John Curtin statue in Kings Square, Fremantle

The theme of working class poverty continued in editorials throughout the 1920s. Curtin attacked the 'paradise for the workers' myth, stating that it was irrelevant whether the Australian working class was better off than their counterparts elsewhere in the world. The point was whether 'our standard of living is as good as it ought to be'. While Australia's virtues were praised by those 'whose bellies are filled with meat', there were thousands 'compelled by poverty to buy cheap – and therefore nasty – stuff to eat, to drink, and to wear'. He believed that Australia was like any other country in that it contained extremes of wealth and poverty, 'beautiful houses and miserable slums, class hatreds, strikes and lock outs, employers versus unions'. In 1922 he wrote with the empathy of personal experience, of breadwinners and their families being 'tormented by the possibility of a hungry tomorrow'.

Writing on child welfare, Curtin commented on a report in the *West Australian* of Premier James Mitchell opening a kindergarten demonstration in July 1922, at which 'barefoot kiddies' made their way among the dignitaries. He stated that, despite scientific advances, the child mortality rate was on the increase and the birth rate was falling. The obvious reason for this was poor health practice. Curtin wrote indignantly: 'Barefoot kiddies! In the depth of winter! In the richest country in the world!' The problems of child welfare, he wrote, were not primarily about the provision of kindergartens but about adequate means of subsistence for the fathers on whom the children were dependent.

> There is a complaisant superstition that in Australia things are so wonderfully regulated in the matter of wages, that the activity of public bodies in the matter of child welfare takes the form of lessons on how to nurse the baby. This idea is woefully astray. The evidence – it is located

in public documents laid on the tables of Legislatures – leaves it beyond all doubt that families of five on the basic wage, even when the father has continuous employment, have always been straitened, and in the past four years, severely straitened.

Curtin saw evidence all around him that extreme poverty limited the prospects of working people and their capacity to participate fully in society.

Worker editorials also took aim at the Christian church. A particularly bitter editorial published on Boxing Day 1919 (which may have been written by Curtin's father-in-law, Abraham Needham) attacked the churches' attitude to charity. The editorial reminded readers that Christ was 'on the side of the poor and the oppressed' and suggested that he would not be found in churches. If Christ's life meant anything, it meant 'peace on earth and goodwill to men rather than the establishment of cults which clutch a text book in one hand and gold and the sword in the other'.

Returning to this theme for his Christmas 1923 editorial, Curtin wrote:

> No failure of the Churches has been more tragic than their failure in brotherliness.
>
> Our Xmas greeting therefore is a call to definite social achievement. We cannot love our fellows if we permit any to go hungry, or homeless, or ill-clad; and as Bread is the foundation of existence, the means whereby bread is produced and distributed are essential phases in the 'Kingdom of God upon earth'; no churchmen, no professing followers of Christ can sincerely celebrate the Xmas festival without resolving to engage in effecting that transformation in society which will enable the human family to live as brothers, sharing in the fruits of the earth, and commonly holding a proprietary title to all of it.

In the 18 December 1925 issue, he wrote that for 'peace and goodwill among people' to be attained there had to be 'a new Social Order with a new Social Spirit'. It is interesting to note here the similarity to that of his phrasing in 1919. He reflected that the 1914-18 war – 'the war to end all wars' – had 'pushed peace farther away than ever' because modern imperialism was 'as imperially anti-Christ as was Rome under the brutal Nero'. The editorial concluded on a more socialist note, urging that the people 'must effect Christmas for themselves' and 'men must become their own saviours'. However,

> any day, and every day, is Christmas Day that sees Christ at the heart of things, prompting governments to altruistic legislation and causing exploiters and monopolies to relax their grip of the people's rights. And December 25 is never Christmas Day where these things do not obtain.

In 1927, Curtin chaired a committee that recommended the establishment of a federal government funded child endowment scheme, and the payment of 13/5d a week (rather than the government's proposed 5/-) on the third and subsequent children in a family. This recommendation was based on the belief that two children were provided for by the basic wage that had been implemented as a result of the 1907 *Harvester Judgement*. The committee's report strongly opposed any move by the Bruce government to means test endowment or to pay for it by reducing the wages of single or childless workers. Curtin was emphatic that child endowment was a federal responsibility:

> The Federal government, which is the voice of the whole nation, demands the people's sons as soldiers, while at the same time it welcomes the daughters as potential mothers of more soldiers, therefore, the same executive which strips the subject of his children in the time of national feud, should shoulder the responsibility of assisting over-burdened mothers in the proper rearing of their children in times of peace.

The *Royal Commission on Child Endowment*, which was conducted during 1928, decided against instituting any scheme of child endowment.

In that year, Curtin resigned from the editorship of the *Worker* when he was elected as the federal Labor member for the seat of Fremantle. Curtin became prime minister in 1941, and within two months of entering office was confronted with the prospect of Australia's invasion by numerically superior Japanese forces at the commencement of the Pacific war. Even in the midst of war, his government enacted welfare measures such as unemployment, sickness and pharmaceutical benefits. Thus Curtin's concern to ensure, as far as possible, equality of sacrifice in wartime did not desert him during the crisis. Despite some views to the contrary, John Curtin stayed true to the convictions he had formed as a young man, living a life of poverty with unsugared tea and unbuttered bread. As for the *Worker*, its high point was past, and although it continued in publication until 1951, no editorial successor matched Curtin's eloquence and capacity for advocacy.

23
Hard Hats, Heritage and Hope

Riley Buchanan

'GREEN BANS TRAVEL WEST TO PERTH' declared Sydney's *Tribune*. It was the beginning of 1974 and union leader Jack Mundey, representing the National Council of the Builders Labourers' Federation (BLF), had just announced to the 800 strong crowd gathered at The University of Western Australia that a green ban would be placed on the Palace Hotel, the then 140 year old Romanesque structure at the intersection of St Georges Terrace and William Street. Widely touted since its opening in 1897 as the finest hotel in the southern hemisphere, the Palace Hotel had been purchased by the Commonwealth Bank in 1972 and now faced demolition. A high-rise office building was to be built in its place, a fate shared, throughout the 1960s and 1970s by the other three corners of the intersection, as well as a number of other buildings along St Georges Terrace. Mundey's message was met with great enthusiasm despite, as the *Tribune* reported, the 'obvious discomfort of the conservative section at the meeting which wished to avoid the involvement of workers in the struggle'.

Yet, as the Sydney newspaper's readership undoubtedly knew, workers' actions, specifically those of the NSW BLF since 1970, were fundamental to the fight to preserve sites of ecological and heritage value. The Australian green bans movement, which had its origins in

Saved but dwarfed by steel and glass: The Palace Hotel, Perth city

NSW, was carried out by construction workers who refused to work on projects that they deemed ecologically or socially irresponsible. By the time the union announced the green ban on the Palace, the NSW BLF had already imposed some twenty-five green bans on Sydney locations of environmental, historical or social significance. By mobilising the collective industrial power of workers, the green bans movement was, within just a few years, successfully contesting development as usual mentality and preventing unnecessary and harmful destruction of urban and natural environments.

The first green ban was instigated by a group of concerned citizens (who were dismissed by their council as 'thirteen bloody housewives') and imposed by the BLF in June 1971 on Kellys Bush, a forested public reserve on the southern foreshore of the Woolwich Peninsula, a place of significance ecologically and for its surrounding community and traditional owners. The 4.8 hectare site was to be destroyed to make way for twenty-five luxury houses. The success of this ban was greatly encouraging for the movement, evidence of the power that could be harnessed by construction workers and their unions insisting that their labour not be used in socially and environmentally irresponsible ways. Mundey, state secretary of the NSW BLF, articulated the green ban movement's ethos in a letter to the *Sydney Morning Herald* in 1972:

> Yes, we want to build. However, we prefer to build urgently-required hospitals, schools, other public utilities, high quality flats, units and houses, provided they are designed with adequate concern for the environment, than to build ugly unimaginative architecturally bankrupt blocks of concrete and glass offices ...Though we want all our members employed, we will not just become robots directed by developers – builders who value the dollar at the expense of the environment ... Progressive unions, like ours, therefore have a very useful social role to play in the citizens' interest, and we intend to play it.

And they did. More than forty green bans were imposed by the union in NSW, about half of which successfully prevented the destruction of significant buildings or green areas. Now, with a green ban imposed on the Palace Hotel, the movement had arrived in the west.

Concerns about the environmental and social impact of urban development were evident in Western Australia well before 1974. We need only think of the campaign against plans to build an Olympic swimming pool on bushland in Kings Park in the late 1950s, of Bessie Rischbieth facing off against bulldozers threatening Mounts Bay in 1964 and the battle to save the Old Barracks and Barracks Arch from demolition in the later 1960s. Taken together they demonstrate the beginnings of conservationist thinking in Western Australia. Such campaigns gained even more traction during the construction boom of the late 1960s and 1970s. Initiated and sustained by several interrelated factors including the mineral boom in the 60s and an increase in population that Perth was largely unprepared for, the rapidity of demolition and development unsettled – and emboldened – many.

When the Commonwealth Bank's plans to demolish the Palace Hotel became clear in 1972, a number of residents, workers and state officials immediately began to push back against its plans. The National Trust of WA recommended to the National Estate Task Force (established by the Whitlam government to ensure the preservation of 'the best buildings of our past and the best features of our natural environment') that the Palace be financed to ensure that it avoided demolition, yet the efficacy of this request was uncertain. 'Preserving good things costs money; new developments make it', as Perth journalist Athol Thomas put it. In October 1973, an ambitious solution was put forward by two concerned workers: Robert Roberts, a chartered quantity surveyor and Len Ravenscroft, a professional house mover. Their plan was to save the hotel by relocating it. By raising the building about 8 feet (2.5 metres) on specially constructed rubber wheeled dollies, the Palace was to be carried alongside the one way traffic on William Street downhill to its new location on the Esplanade, the site once occupied by the Hotel Esplanade, itself only recently demolished.

Needless to say, Roberts' and Ravenscroft's idea did not bear fruit. But their passion and pragmatism are indicative of the mood growing among residents, workers, heritage bodies and, eventually, a number of city councillors. A public lobby group known as the Palace Guards soon formed to save the Palace and encourage the people

Victoria Hall, High St, Fremantle

of Western Australia to lobby decision makers. By the end of 1974 they claimed to represent some 23 000 people. The Guards were well represented at the meeting at which Mundey announced a green ban had been placed on the hotel, but his message was also directed quite specifically toward builders labourers:

> What is the use of winning a 35 hour week, higher wages and better conditions if we are going to choke to death in cities that are devoid of parks and where streets never see the sun?

Yet his address was also brimming with questions that must have resonated with other members of society, because their moral implications undoubtedly affected (and continue to affect) every member of society:

I believe that you have to ask: Is it enough to have full employment rights but to ruin cities? Is it right that workers should build the iron monster that is slowly strangling cities and other resources on this earth? ... I agree that we must stand for egalitarianism while we are in a capitalist existence, but the important thing surely must be quality of life.

A number of key stakeholders rejected the arguments put forward by Mundey and the Palace Guards, including town planner and architect Gordon Stephenson, who was appointed in 1952 together with Town Planning Commissioner Alistair Hepburn to develop a plan for the Perth metropolitan area. Stephenson's view was that 'because of the site's value ... the Palace cannot remain as it is – a charming but relatively small hotel'. The fate of the Palace Hotel was still at risk, so lobbyists continued their campaign at a national level. They successfully pressured the Commonwealth Bank to postpone its decision to demolish the Palace until after the National Estate Committee, headed by Justice Robert Marsden Hope, released the *Hope Report*. This was, as Jenny Gregory has pointed out, a groundbreaking report that led to the implementation of the *Australian Heritage Commission Act 1975*. The *Hope Report* was, in essence, a 'call for government agencies and statutory corporations to set a better example in preserving sites of ecological and heritage importance'.

In the end, the Commonwealth Bank's proposal did not go ahead. As Gregory pointed out, the Commonwealth Bank, having been forced by mounting public pressure to await the results of the *Hope Report*, could 'scarcely demolish the building in the face of the [report's] strong stance'. The threat of the Palace Hotel's destruction sharpened the growing realisation that, to quote Athol Thomas once more:

> progress does not necessarily mean more skyscrapers. It might also countenance the preservation of the good things of the past – and

understanding that progress is not necessarily wrapped up in living concrete poured at the rate of 1000 tons a day.

This push for a more humane civic vision that respected the value of heritage and future community needs was also present in Fremantle, to an even larger degree than in Perth due to the presence of the Fremantle Society, a community action group formed in 1972 to 'provide a responsible voice on matters affecting the overall character and development of Fremantle and to encourage the interest of residents in civic affairs'. The Fremantle Society, inspired by a similar conservation movement in the country town of York, drew some 400 people to its first meeting. Among them were many well-known Fremantle personalities, including communist trade unionist Paddy Troy.

Despite the strong community support for the Fremantle Society's objectives, many Fremantle city councillors remained unconvinced about Fremantle's worth as a historic port city. This meant that a number of iconic Fremantle buildings risked demolition, including Victoria Hall on High Street. The neoclassical church hall, constructed in 1895, was designed by prominent architect J. J. Talbot Hobbs. Originally the St John's Parish Hall, it was renamed for the diamond jubilee of Queen Victoria. As Ron and Dianne Davidson relate in their book *Fighting for Fremantle: The Fremantle Society Story*, the hall was owned by brothers Bob and Norm Wrightson during the 1960s and 1970s when it was principally used as a music and dance hall. The hall's vaulted ceiling of polished wood meant that it could be played like a musical instrument by those with the right singing technique. From 1973, there were strong moves for its destruction.

Not only was Victoria Hall a significant place in terms of the social history of Fremantle, but it was also one of the few goldrush era buildings still left standing east of the town hall. It was likely

Old Peninsula Hotel, Railway Pde, Maylands. Now a community centre

that the destruction of the hall would provide the impetus for the widening of High Street by more than 5.2 metres on either side, a proposal outlined back in 1955 in Stephenson and Hepburn's plan for the development of the port city. The Fremantle Society wasted no time in organising protests against the proposal. Once again the implementation of a green ban proved a highly effective strategy in ensuring the preservation of the building. Committee members wrote to the secretary of the NSW BLF to request that a green ban be placed on Victoria Hall to prevent demolition. The Fremantle Society had strong connections with the federal BLF and with Jack Mundey, but by the time the letter arrived Kevin Reynolds had taken on the role of secretary of the WA branch and he wanted evidence of strong community support before a green ban was imposed. Ron and Dianne Davidson describe what followed.

> BLF organiser and Fremantle Society member Bob Olsen set out to gather such evidence:
>
> He disguised himself with soot and oil, threw aboard some picks and shovels and parked his Simca and trailer outside Victoria Hall. Then he proceeded to make the noises of a demolition gang; he knew these noises well.

Then he waited. Eventually, a crowd gathered to stop what they thought was preparation for the demolition of the hall, and Olsen disappeared. The next morning he reported back to the BLF the public interest that he had provoked, albeit with a bit of strategic deception. A green ban was imposed.

A council meeting held some weeks later voted to allow the demolition of Victoria Hall; the owners scheduled an auction. Ron and Dianne Davidson write that during the auction 'two figures emerged from the crowd and announced that there was a green ban on the building'. The crowd began to leave, heeding the implication of the green ban, the auction was abandoned and Victoria Hall was saved.

It is clear that by 1974 the green ban movement held significance and, more importantly, efficacy, in the minds of people concerned about the rate of development; people believed that such bans could ensure the preservation of places they did not want to lose. The green bans had changed people's ideas about what was possible: workers' interventions in projects they deemed socially or environmentally harmful emboldened other community members to become active in decisions about what kind of place they wanted to live in. The Fremantle Society's efforts to prevent socially and environmentally objectionable projects being carried out in their city won many other successes throughout Fremantle. Their work continues to this day.

The Fremantle Society and the Palace Guards were not the only community action groups that mushroomed concurrent to and in solidarity with the green ban movement. There was also the Peninsula Association, a local action group that formed to lobby against the Swan Brewery's proposal in 1974 to demolish half of the Peninsula Hotel in Maylands to make way for a carpark. By the time demolition was set to begin in 1976, the activity of the green bans movement in Victoria and NSW had virtually ceased: a year earlier, Victorian branch and Federal BLF secretary Norm Gallagher intervened in the NSW branch and subsequently nullified all green bans. The Peninsula Hotel was therefore never specifically subject to a green ban. Yet the fight to save it can certainly be placed in the context of the green ban movement, because it was bolstered significantly by the role of the Trades and Labor Council (TLC), which intervened in plans to destroy the hotel on a number of occasions. Demolition was suspended in May 1976 when TLC Secretary Peter Cook held an urgent meeting with Swan Brewery executives and convinced them to stop further work on the hotel for four weeks, giving the Peninsula Association time to organise a submission on alternative uses for the hotel and to raise funds to cover the cost of restoration. The fight was hard won, but in 1980 the company finally bowed to public pressure and the ownership of the Peninsula Hotel was transferred to the Association, which restored parts of the hotel with community-raised finances and converted it into a community centre for not for profit organisations.

The green bans movement had long term ameliorative effects in Perth and Fremantle. Although the bans were not implemented to the same extent as they were in NSW, the ethic of social and moral responsibility that they came to represent emboldened many people to intervene in the plans of powerful decision makers to ensure that sites of historical, environmental and social significance were preserved for future generations. Workers asserting their authority in deciding whether a development project should take place – and at what cost – also helped to foster a strong sense of solidarity for community members eager to take a stand against development. As academics Verity Burgmann and Andrew Milner put it, 'Because builders labourers had questioned the products of their own labour, the resident activism at this time queried the nature of production under capitalism'. Mundey was acutely aware of just how crucial this could be for the green bans movement and beyond: he wrote about how unions linking up with community action groups such as the Palace Guards, Fremantle Society and Peninsula Association could become 'a powerful countervailing force against institutionalised bureaucracy and the power of the developers' dollar'.

The green bans movement represents a powerful moment in Australian labour history and in environmental politics. As well as saving many valuable environmental and heritage places for future generations, the green bans movement also had a profound impact on community cultures, public attitudes and changes in environmental legislation and planning regulations nationwide. In Western Australia, the ethic of social and environmental responsibility harnessed by workers and communities continues to embolden people to intervene against socially and environmentally harmful development projects, an action that is still important in today's social and political landscapes.

24
The Anti-Vietnam War Demonstrations
Bobbie Oliver

It was November 1971 and students were sitting their end of year exams in UWA's majestic Winthrop Hall. Among them were Bill Thomas and Wayne Henderson. Both men were on the run from the police – they were draft resisters who had gone underground to avoid imprisonment – but they had managed to enter the examination venue undetected. Another student tipped them off that two plain clothed police officers were waiting at the exit to arrest them as they left. A small door next to the impressive pipe organ provided an alternative exit. Bill and Wayne climbed out on the roof, made it to the ground and escaped. The student who tipped them off was David Parker, later a Minister and then Deputy Premier in state Labor administrations in the 1980s and 1990s. All three were student activists who opposed Australia's involvement in the Vietnam war and the conscripting of young men for military service.

The *National Service Act*, which the Menzies government passed in 1964, required 20 year old Australian males to register for military training that involved two years continuous service, followed by three years in the Army Reserve. Unlike earlier compulsory military training schemes, the period of national service would interrupt employment or education. Even more significantly, it could involve active service in an overseas conflict.

In 1962, the federal government had committed military trainers to assist the forces of the South Vietnamese government defend their country against communist infiltration from the north. The Perth branch of the Union of Australian Women (UAW) was one of the few voices raised in protest against this decision. A student protest group, Youth Campaign Against Conscription (YCAC) formed in Sydney in November 1964, two weeks after Menzies announced the re-introduction of the National Service scheme. Their specific aim was to abolish the scheme. They dedicated their early efforts to helping the ALP win the 1966 federal election. A branch formed in WA in 1966.

In 1965 Australia's commitment in Vietnam was expanded to include active service troops who would fight alongside US forces. The government decided that conscripted national servicemen with a year's training would be included in Australia's troops. This decision, more than the reintroduction of national service (a scheme that had operated throughout most of the 1950s), stirred up opposition to conscription and Australia's involvement in the Vietnam war. Between 1965 and 1972, over 804 000 men registered for the National Service Scheme, 63 735 of them conscripted in the birthday ballot system, of whom 19 000 served in Vietnam. The conscripts comprised 44 per cent of the 42 700 Australian soldiers who served in the conflict and 200 of them represented 45 per cent of those killed in action.

Initially, most Australians supported the government's decision, but by 1969 this had changed to majority support for troops to be withdrawn. Although dissent was evident even before Menzies' announcement that troops would go to Vietnam, 1966 was the year when antiwar demonstrations took off in WA as elsewhere in Australia. On 1 April, Rupert Gerritsen, a UWA arts student and

Save Our Sons group at demonstration. Joan Davies (right) threw her shoe at Prime Minister Harold Holt

member of the University Labor Club, together with several others staged a midnight protest in which they placed a 15 foot (4.5 metre) wooden cross near the State War Memorial in Kings Park and set it alight. This demonstration was repeated on 8 June, when the cross was accompanied by a placard declaring, 'Ours not to reason why, ours but to do and die in Vietnam'. Gerritsen was arrested, charged with wanton damage to cables belonging to the Kings Park Board and fined $10 and $20 restitution. He refused to reveal the names of his fellow protesters.

Save Our Sons (SOS), formed on 29 March 1966, was another of the earliest antiwar groups in Perth. According to member M. Henderson in a 1966 report of its activities, SOS aimed to 'give West Australians an opportunity to protest against Australian intervention in Vietnam, conscripts and the sending of conscripts to war'. Unlike most other SOS branches, the Perth branch included men in its membership and had a male secretary, Raymond Collie. SOS organised its first protest only four days after forming. Carrying antiwar placards, about fifty protesters marched from Forrest Place to the Perth Esplanade. Their protest was reportedly well received by the public and was featured in the media.

This was also the year in which Joan Davies achieved notoriety by throwing her shoe at Prime Minister Harold Holt at Perth Airport on 21 April. Joan was staging a protest with other SOS members on a balcony about 5 metres above the tarmac where Holt's plane landed. As Holt walked from the plane into the airport, he looked up and smiled at the protestors. This provoked Joan and she hurled her shoe at him. The shoe missed the prime minister but struck another member of his party on the head. Joan was arrested and charged with creating a disturbance. She was fined $20. The *West Australian* of 22 April featured the incident on its front page, complete with a photograph, under a banner headline, 'PM's smile angered Perth shoe thrower'. Joan Davies, interviewed after her court appearance, was quoted as saying, 'I don't think war is a laughing matter'. Neither did the SOS, but the group distanced itself from her actions. Collie immediately rang the press, dissociating SOS from any violent action and said the shoe incident had not been planned.

A large protest in Forrest Place on 11 June, jointly organised by YCAC, SOS and the Vietnam Action Committee, attracted about 500 people. The rally turned violent when police moved in to take the name and address of a young man addressing the rally. Some of the crowd abused the police, calling them fascist pigs. An opposition group comprising Young Democratic Labor Party (YDLP) and Democratic Labour Party (DLP) University Society members urged the police to shoot the demonstrators. Police arrested four university students for burning their draft cards and charged them with disorderly conduct. Despite the *Sunday Times* the next day labelling these events the Battle of Forrest Place, eventually all of the offenders were acquitted.

As the war continued and allied casualties mounted, the numbers of protests and protesters increased. An ABC TV screening of *Mills of the Gods*, which presented graphic images of the battlefields, including child victims of napalm attacks, provoked a strong public response. After this event there were large attendances at antiwar rallies. Some people who objected to the arrest of those who had burned their draft cards, expressed their displeasure and concern in the *West Australian*, although there were those who supported police action and criticised the objectors, one suggesting that their stance was based on cowardice rather than rational belief.

The police took a fairly lenient attitude to a street march held in Perth on 6 August 1966 that deviated from the approved route, as well as towards a 'Picket for Peace' that CPA members set up outside the US consulate at 171 St Georges Terrace some weeks after the Battle of Forrest Place. Protesting specifically against recent US bombings and the escalation of the war, the picketers handed out thousands of pamphlets and leaflets to passers-by. Reportage in the *West Australian* focused on counterprotestors rather than the Picket for Peace, but *Daily News* coverage was more even handed, including images of antiwar protestors and their placards. Although police disbanded the demonstration after three days, CPA Secretary Sam Aarons told the *West Australian* they had received a fair go.

Opponents comprised many different groups with varying attitudes to war. Some, such as the Women's International League for Peace and Freedom (WILPF) and the Society of Friends (Quakers) were pacifists who objected to all wars. SOS, also non-violent, had been formed in the eastern states in 1965 specifically to oppose conscripts being sent to the Vietnam war. The Draft Resisters Movement (DRM), founded in Melbourne in early 1968, set a new tone for civil disobedience and direct action. The DRM formed not to oppose conscription but to wreck it. Its members refused to register as conscientious objectors or to seek deferment because to do so meant they recognised the validity of the National Service Scheme. Instead, they were non-compliers, refusing to take any part in the scheme's requirements, which meant they were disobeying the law. Gary Cook was the first WA man imprisoned as a non-complier.

Other groups had a specifically pro-Labor ethos. In a 2008 interview, Bill Thomas recalled that the membership of the WA branch of YCAC was 'a group of guys ... who were trying to form a Young Labor Association'. Members included Les Heinrich, Rupert Gerritsen, Keith Taylor, Tony Lloyd, Kevin Edwards and Bill Thomas. Like SOS, YCAC refused to sanction violent or illegal activities, such as burning draft cards. Heinrich stated prior to the 11 June demonstration in Forrest Place that any draft card burning would be the action of individuals and not official YCAC policy. SOS and the university branch of the ALP supported the demonstration. Many antiwar and anti-conscription movement members saw UWA as a focal point of student activism and draft resistance. Bill Thomas believed that 'UWA *was* the DRM in WA. There really wasn't anything else outside the University.'

While much publicity was given to the three moratorium mass marches that were held across Australia in May and September 1970 and June 1971, the Anti-Vietnam War Moratorium Campaign (AVWMC) was ongoing, only suspending its activities late in 1971 after the federal government committed itself to withdrawing the bulk of Australian troops from Vietnam. On 7 August 1970 about twenty-four students conducted a sit in against conscription in the National Service Registration Office on St Georges Terrace. The demonstrators chained themselves across a passageway so that no one could enter or leave the building. Some carried placards showing a child impaled on a bayonet, with the caption: 'Be conscripted. Learn a trade.' Perhaps this message was too sickening for some people to take responsibility for it. Although organiser Peter Griffiths claimed that protest was organised by DRM, including young people from UWA and the WA Institute of Technology (WAIT) and members of the public, *Pelican's* writer said: 'No particular group or faction organised it.' Another project, Peace Now, was organised by WAIT lecturer Tony Watts with Judy Forsyth and the Reverend Keith Wilson.

Usually, marchers managed to remain peaceful while suffering extreme provocation. In the September 1970 moratorium march, demonstrators were pelted with eggs, lemons and water, and were sprayed with fly spray. While demonstrations in Adelaide and Sydney were marred by violent incidents, the Perth march remained peaceful. Campaign organisers reminded participants that violence merely played into the hands of the government and helped to maintain stereotypes that protestors were, in Minister for Labour and National Service Billy Snedden's colourful phrase, as reported in the *Sydney Morning Herald* of 6 May 1970, 'Political bikies pack raping Democracy'.

1971 moratorium march

The CPA and the ALP opposed the war and gave support to the resisters. In Western Australia, Harold Peden, an official in the Boilermakers Union, TLCWA office bearer and member of the CPA, was an organiser of Perth's first moratorium march on 8 May 1970. While small compared with numbers in other capital cities – some estimates placed the Melbourne march at 100 000 – it drew 10 000 marchers. In later years, many former party members recalled that they and their family members had taken part in marches and demonstrations.

ALP Senator John Wheeldon addressed an antiwar rally in Perth in May 1965. At a 1966 May Day rally at Fremantle Town Hall to celebrate the ALP's seventy-fifth anniversary, a panel of speakers addressed issues relating to the Vietnam war and conscription. The university branch of the ALP asked the state ALP to lead an anti-Vietnam protest, which it did. Wheeldon and Peter Dowding (later state premier) defended draft resisters in a legal capacity. Premier John Tonkin marched at the head of the moratorium procession on 30 June 1971 in Perth, flanked by TLCWA President Jim Coleman and ALP State Secretary Joe Chamberlain. An estimated 6000 people turned out, compared with 10 000 in Sydney, 20 000 in Melbourne and 5000 in Brisbane. The WA Branch of the ALP supported Calwell's staunch opposition to the war, but they were out of sync with Whitlam's softer position.

Tonkin served as patron of the WA Vietnam Moratorium Campaign until that body passed a motion urging young men to disobey the law by refusing to register for national service. Tonkin did not disagree with the campaign's right to pass the motion, but stated that it made his position as its patron untenable. As WA premier he was sworn to uphold the law. Tonkin incurred the wrath of the antiwar movement when his government became the first Labor administration in

Australia to gaol a non-complier, Gary Cook. Bill Thomas regarded Tonkin's position on conscription as 'political myopia'.

Like the antiwar organisations who supported them, the protestors were a diverse lot. Many, such as Bill Thomas and Wayne Henderson, were university students. Among the student activists writing for *Pelican* was Carmen Lawrence (Labor premier 1990–93), who supported the position of non-compliers. Some UWA activists were very persuasive. In an interview in 2000, Tony Pointon recalled that having a brother at university influenced his opinions and brought him into association with anti-conscriptionists. His father, who had served with the British Commonwealth Occupation Force in postwar Japan, also taught him that war was wrong. When Tony went to register, he wore a badge inscribed, 'Don't register for National Service'. He applied to register as a conscientious objector and stated that he wouldn't go to Vietnam. When his case was heard in 1971, his parents and cousins supported him in court and his father spoke as a witness. Tony thought 'Gough Whitlam was God'. He was very glad when Labor won government and Whitlam freed all the draft resister prisoners.

As in other parts of Australia, the experiences of one objector differed widely from another. Some, such as Douglas Thorpe of East Fremantle, were granted total exemption from military service. Thorpe, whose case was heard on 18 July 1967, said he believed that war was futile and that peace could be achieved and maintained through education and teaching tolerance. Earlier, in June 1967, a different magistrate in a different court dismissed the application of Douglas Panther of Nedlands, who objected to the army taking away his right to make moral decisions for himself. In the same month, in other courts around the Perth metropolitan area, Robert McMullen's application for total exemption was upheld, as were the applications of two Jehovah's Witnesses, Peter King and Robert Warren, while David Rupe was granted exemption only from combatant duties.

Perhaps nowhere was the serendipitous nature of court decisions more evident than in those concerning men who applied for exemption after enlisting in the army. Two Western Australians, John Poole-Johnson and Desmond Phillipson, experienced strong revulsion during training at Puckapunyal, where dummies were filled with red fluid to simulate blood. Poole-Johnson deserted, was arrested and taken to Karrakatta Barracks where he was given another medical and ruled unfit for the army. Phillipson, who did not desert but who lodged an application for military service and then refused to obey any further orders, had his application, and then his appeal, dismissed.

While no WA draft resister or conscientious objector gained the public profile of Michael Matteson, Bill White or John Zarb, WA had its well-known resisters. Gary Cook, a UWA student from Toodyay, was one of the first to defy conscription call-up in WA. Initially, Cook complied with the law. He registered for national service and applied for deferment. In 1969, when his call-up came through, he attended the medical examination, was found fit and told to report to Irwin Barracks in January 1970. He chose not to comply, instead informing the Labour and National Service Department that he was not going to attend military training. He published his decision in the *Perth Independent*'s 4 March 1970 issue in an article titled 'Hell no, won't go to Vietnam'. Cook appealed to a wider public because in appearance he was short haired and clean shaven, not the bearded, long haired hippy stereotype.

Amendments to the *National Service Regulations*, gazetted 27 August 1970, introduced a new Conscientious Objector Referral scheme, which enabled the government to force draft resisters into compliance with the Act. Under section 32A the minister for labour and national service could direct a registrar of national service to 'refer the question of a person's objection on the grounds of conscience to taking part in military service to a competent court'. Non-compliers would be summoned to appear in court to be examined as a conscientious objector.

In October 1970, Gary Cook became the first WA non-complier to be referred. He did not attend the hearing but had prepared a statement, which Derek Schapper read to the court on his behalf. Senior Magistrate T. Ansell found that Cook 'did not hold beliefs which prevented him from engaging in military service'. Cook found refuge with draft resistance groups in Melbourne. After police issued a warrant for his arrest, he joined the Melbourne-based underground movement, the Draft Resisters Union (DRU) established in June 1970 to provide protection for draft resisters hiding from police. No comparable underground movement existed in WA. Cook appeared at the Melbourne moratorium on 30 June 1971, where about 5000 demonstrators protected him and other underground resisters from arrest.

Cook returned to WA in August 1971. He was arrested when he appeared at a huge student protest rally in Perth. Demonstrators gathered outside St Mary's Cathedral, initially intending to march to the Commonwealth Police offices. When Cook and Bill Thomas, who had also been in hiding, appeared with a statement of resisters' reasons for continuing to oppose the draft despite the Gorton government's announced withdrawal of combat troops, they marched instead to the Department of Labour and National Service. Cook, Staples, Schapper and Thomas were arrested. While the others were released after their fines were paid, Cook was sentenced to two years in prison for his defiance of conscription laws. During his court appearance, an unruly demonstration erupted outside. Prior to his trial, Cook urged his supporters not to wage a free Cook campaign because it would detract from the anti-conscription campaign. Thus, he encouraged a departure from established tactics of anti-conscription groups when their members were gaoled.

Cook provided inspiration for the DRM even though he was not a member. Peter Vintella refused to register, although, as a married man he would automatically have been exempted. Kevin Booker wrote to the pacifist newspaper *The Peacemaker* and added his name to paper's list of non-compliers. Vince Bresland recalled that those early non-compliers made it easier for others to follow in their footsteps.

The DRM made political use of its underground members. Henderson featured in a dramatic appearance when he was whisked onto campus at a UWA anti-conscription rally. He arrived riding pillion on a motorbike, jumped off and was shown briefly to the masses before jumping back on the bike and roaring off again. Thomas was similarly exhibited. Filmed by ABC TV, Thomas, disguised in sunglasses, also arrived in front of a huge crowd outside the Reid Library on the back of a motorbike. Bodyguards carrying walkie-talkies surrounded him. One bystander carried bolt cutters, reminiscent of Michael Matteson's dramatic escape from Sydney University when a quick thinking student with a pair of bolt cutters cut through his handcuffs and freed him from his police escort.

Despite the glamour of such events, being underground could be 'pretty scary', as Wayne Henderson recalled. He was always aware of the impact on others of his decisions, and tried to avoid causing trouble for family and friends who gave him shelter. The police parked outside his parents' house for weeks at a time, forcing him to climb over the back fence when he wanted to visit them. On the lighter side, sometimes they parked outside the wrong house so he was able to walk straight past without them recognising him.

Protests evolved from individuals trying to avoid being conscripted to a concerted attempt to smash the draft system. According to historian Beatrice Laufer, some former resisters believed that those who registered and sought deferment of their national service were not making a stand and that they didn't register on the radar screen of political resistance. Indeed, seeking deferment was seen as an easy way out, despite those who gained deferment early in the conflict having to face the prospect of eventually being called up, as happened to Gary Cook. Thomas even asserted that, 'to participate [by registering] in it is to be an accomplice to the Vietnam war'. Laufer writes that even the high profile eastern states objector Bill White stated that, in retrospect, he wouldn't have taken the path of registering as an objector if his case had come up two years later. But this statement says as much about the impact of protest as it does about White. The early days of the war were a lonely time to be a resister; it is hardly surprising that many took the route of registering their objection, which had worked for some even in World War 2.

What did the antiwar movement achieve? Did the protests change public opinion or were they merely an expression of changing opinion? Early protests often took the form of the SOS' peaceful and silent vigils, a few demonstrators risking the ridicule of a public who overwhelmingly supported Australian military commitment in Vietnam. These few swelled to the masses who took to the streets in 1970 and 1971.

Perhaps the most profound change happened in the lives of those who dared to protest for the first time. Taking to the streets educated them in methods of dissent and removed the fear of being arrested and imprisoned. Some later worked for prison reform. Others sought to save the environment or prevent nuclear war. Yet others – draft resisters, objectors and their supporters – entered politics. The demographic of the protests against Australia's involvement in the wars in Iraq and Afghanistan at the beginning of the twenty-first century – comprising a large proportion of baby boomers and younger people – gives a fair indication that the anti-Vietnam protests did, indeed, radicalise a generation.

25

May Day: The Workers' Day

Charlie Fox

Perth's first May Day meeting was held in 1897, seven years after 1 May was established by the Paris International Socialist Congress as the international workers day, a declaration that was inspired by the great eight hour day struggles in the USA. It soon became a day to demonstrate for the advance of the worldwide working class movement. As it spread across Europe and the world, it characteristically demanded three things: the strengthening of fraternal relations of the world's working classes, the overthrow of capitalism in favour of some form of socialism and an end to its wars. But divisions quickly surfaced. In an attempt to get consensus at the International Congress, the character and structure of the day was left up to national working class movements. As it turned out, revolutionaries marched on 1 May, reformists marched on the first Sunday following. In Australia, with some exceptions, both marched on the Sunday.

But May Day had a much longer history. In the northern hemisphere 1 May is the first day of spring so May Day had long been a festival of fertility, rebirth, regrowth and regeneration, celebrated with fetes, gatherings, holidays, May queens and maypole dances. But, as Europe industrialised, May Day in this spring festival form became somewhat anachronistic and, in the southern hemisphere where spring begins on 1 September, incongruous. Yet its themes of renewal and regrowth infiltrated May Day in Perth and the May Queen and maypole kept a foothold in May Day celebrations for probably seventy years.

For many years May Day in Perth and Fremantle ran in opposition to Eight Hour Day and Labour Day celebrations. Eight Hour Day, which was first celebrated in late October 1891, was labour's grand day, a day to celebrate winning the eight hour working day, an affirmation of workers' pride and respectability. Watched by thousands and led out by political leaders and rousing bands, long rows of decorated floats created by unions to celebrate their trades rolled through Perth's (and sometimes Fremantle's) streets followed by dozens of union members, sometimes as many as hundreds – just as many people as organisers could get to come. Sometimes commercial floats displaying the wares of local manufacturers took part too; when they did, the whole procession was a mile long. A meeting on the Esplanade followed, and a sporting carnival, usually at the Claremont Showgrounds, was held in the afternoon or the next day.

Then, in 1919, Eight Hour Day became Labour Day, and in 1921 the Labor Party's Labour Day Committee, shifted it to the first Monday in May to bring it into line with the worker's day in the rest of the world. But this wasn't May Day. The new day and name didn't mean a radical change in the nature of the celebration, it was in many ways still the old Eight Hour Day procession, held on the new Monday Labour Day holiday, followed by the usual meeting and the same sporting carnival. But sometimes the Labor Party also staged meetings on the Sunday preceding and these were May Day celebrations. The Labour Day processions ran intermittently for another fifty years, until, in the face of dwindling numbers, union apathy and diminished public interest, they were finally abandoned in 1972.

The first May Day meeting was on Perth's Esplanade on Sunday, 2 May 1897, under the auspices of the Democratic Reform League and the nascent Labour Church. William Mellor and Fred Davis, two stalwarts of the early radical movement in Perth, moved and seconded the major motion.

> That this meeting of citizens of Perth and district hereby send their fraternal greetings to all fraternal organisations which are striving to improve the social and industrial conditions of toiling humanity in all parts of the world, recognising that the cause of labour is universal, and we hereby pledge ourselves to endeavour to bring about a better and more equitable state of society, based upon mutual cooperation and human brotherhood in place of the commercial anarchy at present prevailing.

These were Labour Church ideals. As we have seen, the brotherhood of man was the rock on which its philosophy for change was built. There was no mention of socialism, except in the general statement of 'mutual cooperation', or peace. Nor was there mention of anarchism, riot, violence and revolution, which was how May Day in Europe was ordinarily reported in the local press.

Gradually, May Day moved towards the common themes of May Days everywhere. In 1899, after fraternal greetings were sent to the workers of the world, Monty Miller moved a motion attacking 'uncontrolled private capitalism' and monopoly and the misery that they caused. In 1902 he moved that 'This meeting declares that the interests of labour is everywhere peace and denounces all wars (by whosoever waged) as capitalistic in their origins and serving only capitalistic ends'. Then contemporary and pressing issues were dealt with: the election of pledged Labor candidates to public office and a grab bag of current demands, including, early on, the introduction of the single tax.

Perth's radicals organised these first meetings. In 1902, it was the Social Democratic Federation, in 1912 the Western Australian Socialist Party and during the war, the Wobblies. On several occasions, though, for example in 1905 and 1907, the Labor Party organised them. In keeping with tradition, in 1905 the major motion called for the socialisation of the 'means and instruments of production, distribution and exchange'.

On the afternoon of Sunday, 30 April 1922, the day before the big Labour Day parade, there were two May Day meetings. At the first Wobbly Charlie Reeves, by then in the One Big Union, preached red revolution to his crowd in what the *West Australian* called a long, impassioned address. Later, in the Labour Day Committee's meeting, John Curtin spoke about 'the oneness of working people of all countries' and called for the overthrow of the capitalist system so as to end poverty and unemployment. In 1925, the *Great Southern Herald* reported that at a 'monster May Day meeting' on the Sunday – organised by the Labor Party to replace the Monday procession – speakers again introduced motions advocating the abolition of capitalism and war and for the continuation of the wage struggle against the exploiting class.

This radical rhetoric was common in the Labor Party before and after the war, because socialism was a common aim in early Labor Party discourse. During the war, the Party had expelled the conscriptionists; after it adopted the socialisation plank. The ALP was probably more radical then than it has ever been since. But while the May Day motions were radical, the speeches were not. Union secretary and ALP parliamentarian May Holman thought that socialism would come by constitutional means; another ALP luminary, E. H. Barker, thought a revolution was 'evolution with a bit of a move on'. But this was reform rather than revolution. In parliament Labor was moderate, constitutional and accustomed to the exigencies of governing.

By the time the Great Depression arrived there was a new revolutionary party in Perth. The Communist Party of Australia (CPA), which had first formed in Sydney in 1920, and then in other Australian capitals, from then until the 1960s dominated radical celebrations of May Day. For most of this period the Party was in thrall to the Soviet Union, trying hard to follow the sometimes contradictory directions required of it. Its presence in WA was still very small, but in 1926 a Workers' Educational Union, probably a forerunner of the Party, held a May Day meeting in a city hall and was addressed by Bill Mountjoy and Mrs Throssell (Katharine Susannah Prichard), two noted members.

In 1928, the *Sunday Times* reported that communists met under a red May Day flag and a sign that read: 'Capitalism means Murder, Machine guns and Misery. Communism means peace and prosperity.' They were dispersed by police. The Party seems to have planned a May Day meeting in the city on 1 May 1931, chalking messages on walls calling for people to turn up. Whatever was planned, though, was forestalled by hundreds of police who descended on the city.

After that the Party accepted the inevitable and in venues such as the Protestant, Rechabite and Manchester Unity Halls, all just north of the railway line, celebrated May Day on 1 May with an evening dance, meeting and concert. With their singing, dancing, revelry and speeches the Party called these nights free and easy socials, and boasted that every chest was emblazoned with a red rosette. Mountjoy and Mrs Throssell were regular speakers at the socials. In 1936, Mountjoy spoke on the history of May Day and Mrs Throssell on the celebration of May Day in the Soviet Union.

Through the later 1930s and World War 2, as often as it could, the Party celebrated May Day on the Esplanade as well, decorating the platform with banners bearing May Day slogans, advertising and reporting on them in the *Workers' Star*. By this time too, the Party had moved on from its early sectarianism; now, with communism in Europe facing the threat of fascism, it began to call for working class unity. In 1938, the *Workers Star* wrote a May Day call to women:

> Let our voices mingle with the voices of our sisters in every capitalist country, with the joyous shouts of the millions of Soviet women demonstrating their freedom.
>
> For a better life.
>
> For peace, freedom and democracy.
>
> For unity of the working women against war and fascism.

It's fair to say the call for unity in Australia never worked and the relocation of May Day from Perth to Fremantle had much to do with postwar rivalries between Labor and the communists. After abandoning them during World War 2, the ALP revived the Labour Day processions in Perth in 1947 and 1948 but banned communists from marching under their own banners and criticised those who carried placards calling out the Labor Party for its anticommunism. Then, in 1950, it decided to shift Labour Day to March, pleading that the weather would be better and that unionists had lost interest anyway, but probably more because it wished to dissociate itself from the military parades in Moscow, which they believed characterised May Day in the public mind. In any event the Labor Party did not hold a procession for another nine years.

Thus the door was opened for Fremantle's Maritime Union Council to organise its first May Day celebration, so in 1950 it did with a rally on the Esplanade after the police refused permission to march around the town. But the arguments continued. Labor refused to be involved in the early years and formidable Labor Party Secretary Joe Chamberlain tried to sabotage the meetings, threatening ALP affiliated bodies who joined in with suspension or disaffiliation and warning off interstate guests with threats of suspension or expulsion. The Fremantle District Council of the ALP organised the event in 1956, 1957 and 1959 and tried to stop Fremantle's communist identity Paddy Troy from speaking. Chamberlain even came down to make sure nobody stood on the platform with him.

But even with Fremantle's enthusiasm, May Day was intermittent. It continued through the later 1950s and early 1960s until, in 1966, the celebrations were cancelled in favour of union participation in the Labour Day procession, organised for the first time by the new WA Trades and Labor Council. It seems to have returned in 1972 (the evidence is a little confusing) only to disappear again until 1978, although in 1977 a committee for a May Day march held a march in Perth. The march disappeared again in 1979 but returned in 1984 and has been held every May since, organised by either the maritime unions or the TLCWA in Perth.

Fremantle's May Days were a new beginning. For the first time, May Day meetings were preceded by a procession. Hundreds of marchers marched or strolled in a set order, either from the Esplanade to Princess May Park or later, winding through Fremantle's streets from and to the Esplanade. Then came the meeting and, in the evening, May Day dinners in Fremantle hotels.

In these early years the processions were led out by marching bands or marching girls followed by floats on the backs of trucks representing Left wing unions, their members, many carrying their own signs, followed on foot. Women marched in union women's auxiliaries, others carried placards and marched behind the Australian Union of Women banner. A little later, the Communist Party brought its own display along and was joined by the Eureka Youth League, the Australian Peace Council and New Theatre. Not surprisingly, the language was largely about the tried and true May Day themes: international brotherhood, peace, and socialism (the celebration of socialism in the USSR was always prominent). But there were other themes: demands for Aboriginal rights, money to support 'retarded' children, opposition to US bases, and 'Friendship between Women of all Races'.

Some have described these May Days as sombre affairs, but serious is a better word because these were serious times: the Cold War, Bob Menzies' attempt to ban the Communist Party, fights by Left political factions for control of trade unions, all made life tough for radicals. Even so, there were many moments of humour. In 1950, papier maché models of dictators Hitler, Mussolini and Tojo appeared alongside one of Menzies under the slogan, 'Tip the Can on Menzies' ban'. In 1963, when nuclear disarmament was the main theme, one banner on an ancient car read, 'The Only Bomb My Family Wants'. In 1964, on the eve of the Beatles' Australian tour, one banner read, 'Better Beatle cuts than wage cuts', and another 'The Beetless. We Love Equal Pay for Equal work. Yeah, Yeah, Yeah'. (The Beatles were obviously still new to the latter banner makers.)

Also in 1964 the CPA's float celebrated forty-one years publication of its newspaper, *Tribune*, the AEU proudly displayed Harald Vike's famous modernist union banner, and in 1966 banners opposing the Vietnam war began to appear. Yet the organisers still retained some of the older May Day traditions. The march was led by a truck bearing candidates for May queen. By now though, the crowds were small. Photos of the processions show stalwarts marching through often empty streets. Of course, most shops were closed on Sundays so, beyond the procession, there was little incentive for people to go to Fremantle.

In 1978, Fremantle's May Day got a new face when the celebrations were held on a Saturday. New times, a new generation and a changing Fremantle all demanded a thorough makeover. Now, an afternoon fair followed the traditional march and meeting to encourage people to make a day of it. There was folk dancing, music, theatre, craft exhibitions, food stalls, children's activities and even the return of the maypole, but the May queen contest had disappeared. The absence of May Day in the late 1960s and 1970s meant that WA escaped the conflicts over the May queen as had occurred in the east, where the women's liberation movement, members of which marched behind feminist banners, objected to her.

The procession and meeting became more diverse. New social movements such as environmentalism and women's liberation appeared in the march, alongside banners advocating socialism and the Campaign for Nuclear Disarmament (CND) advocating peace. Even the pensioners movement turned up. Peace was even more important in the 1980s, a time when the local peace movement gained momentum. In 1985 the march was followed by a meeting in the Freo Town Hall, where peace activist Senator Jo Valentine spoke.

By 1990 the day had become bigger, louder, more light hearted, more artistic and colourful. An explosion of colour replaced the traditional red of the CPA. The Fremantle Foo Foo band wearing its pink, yellow and red costumes led the way. The dull blues and greys of men's and the subdued colours of women's clothing were replaced by the rainbow coloured hues of post 1960s fashion. More activist

Over the decades, May Day marches changed from 1929's sober but triumphant parade of unionists headed by a marshal on a white horse to a wide variety of groups with floats, such as peace demonstrators in the march from Fremantle's Princess May Theatre in 1988

groups joined in. Fremantle had become a centre of Perth's peace and environmental movements which saw new participants marching and a wider range of unions attending. As anti-union Liberal governments attacked workers' rights, the union movement responded. A teachers' strike in the early 1990s saw hundreds of teachers join in. In the late 1990s and early 2000s waves of industrial reforms by the state and federal Liberal governments that attacked workers energised unionists.

In 1987 a new generation of union banners was unfurled, showcasing contemporary realities of work. If the older banners were heavily masculine, created when unions and workers were mostly male, now men and women appeared together – in the Municipal Officers Association's banner, for example. In other banners the faces became multi-ethnic as immigration changed the face of the workforce. In 1990, Bob Hawke, Margaret Thatcher and Alan Bond were lampooned by big papier maché models and the Foo Foos enlivened proceedings with their maracas, kazoos and drums. The fair (renamed a community festival) was now an integral part of the day to which parents brought their children along and fed them icecream. Marchers quenched their thirsts in beer tents while they listened to contemporary rock bands, and a multitude of groups set up their tables to sell books, pamphlets, food or other items.

As Fremantle changed, the watching crowds grew. The city had gentrified. It had discovered its architectural heritage, which, with the changes wrought by the 1987 America's Cup, drew tourists to the town. As Sunday became a shopping day the procession now wound through busy streets where shoppers and Cappuccino Strip habitués in South Terrace watched it go past with either applause, amusement, hostility or a lack of interest.

As the day changed some of the old faithfuls disappeared. The

CPA, which was wound up in 1991, had gone. Socialism and peace, once the key demands of the march, faded too as immediate concerns such as wages and conditions, attacks on the union movement, and the environment came to dominate the meetings. The organisers, UnionsWA (formerly the TLCWA), began to present the day as the modern manifestation of Labour Day: 'The traditional purpose of May Day is to seek a balance of work, rest and play,' wrote one official.

Yet the variety of radical and progressive organisations and causes taking part continued to widen: unions that had never participated or marched before, human rights organisations, educational groups such as the Labour History Society, women's and Aboriginal groups, the Greens, national liberation movements, socialist organisations and the new Communist Party. May Day had become a dizzying inclusive display of causes. The marchers continued to give it its traditional radical flavour.

26
Fremantle's Counterculture: India and the Orange People
Charlie Fox

Fremantle, the workers' town, began to change in the 1970s. The first container ship arrived on the wharves in 1969 where they were worked by the massive gantries built to unload and load containers. As a consequence, the waterfront workforce had by the 1990s fallen by 80 per cent from its 1969 level. Many Fremantle families, old and young, Anglo and continental European, moved to newer suburbs to new jobs or became Fremantle commuters. Fremantle's population began to fall, but new kinds of people moved in: young, white, Anglo, middle class, who bought up cheap older houses to renovate and live in. Then, as prices rose, more old families moved on. Gentrification had begun.

The establishment of Murdoch University in 1975 was important, too. Murdoch was different. It cultivated an egalitarian image, radical lecturers staffed the schools of social inquiry, human communications and education and like-minded students were attracted to their courses. Many Murdoch staff and students settled in Fremantle, bringing with them new tastes in culture, the arts and middle class politics: the environmental, peace, antinuclear and anti-uranium movements and community politics. Staff from education, for example, helped start Perth's first two community schools, the

Lance Holt and the Fremantle Community Schools, and John Raser, the radical foundation professor of peace and conflict studies became well known in Freo through the 1980 regular columns he wrote for the *Fremantle Gazette*.

Fremantle's art world grew anew, too. Artists set up studios and exhibition spaces, musicians ran music venues, and actors established theatre groups, to the extent that by 1980 Fremantle had six theatre companies. In 1970, after a campaign to save it from demolition, the old Fremantle Lunatic Asylum was restored and in 1972 became the Fremantle Arts Centre, hosting, among other things, a growing art and craft culture. Many old Fremantle councillors were displaced by new ones committed to the city's architectural heritage, who began legislating for the preservation of old buildings, a movement begun in large part by the new Fremantle Society, established in 1972. In 1976 Fremantle Arts Centre Press was established, so literature obtained a foothold in the new Fremantle as well.

Then came the counterculture. It set itself up against the old age of industrialism and unlimited material growth, of technocracy, alienation, competition, exploitation and competitive individualism. The new? Think the harmonised self-supporting communities at Nimbin rather than the revolutionary politics of Marxism, Maoism and anarchism. One stream of Fremantle's counterculture was an eclectic mix of spiritual doctrines dedicated to transforming the self, releasing, unlocking or awakening ones 'true' being. Some of these ideas were reworkings of older European thought but more came from India, the Hindu and Buddhist India of the youthful Western imagination: authenticity, meditation, yoga, oneness with the universe, music, gurus, clothing, chants, food, the end point of the hippie trail, everything the West wasn't. It was from this Indian

The old Fremantle Trades Hall, renamed Ikkyu House by the Rajneeshees. Now a private residence

spirituality that the Rajneeshees derived.

The Rajneeshees were not the first devotees of Hinduism in Australia but they were a part of the 1960s and 1970s flowering of mostly Hindu orders and ideas in Australia. The best known were transcendental meditation, which was introduced in the 1960s, having been popularised by the Beatles, the Hare Krishnas, who arrived in 1969, the Ananda Marga, whose members were framed for the Hilton Hotel bombing in Sydney in 1978, and Sri Chinmoy, which set up shop in Australia in 1979 and mixed meditation with jogging.

Nor were the Rajneeshees the first Indian order to arrive in Fremantle. Perth's first yoga centre was set up in North Fremantle in

1971, then, in 1976, moved across town to South Fremantle where it became an ashram. In 1979 its patron, the Swami Venkatesananda visited. In 1977, Indian Buddhists arrived to talk about Buddhism; transcendental meditation workshops were being held in the city as well. The search for enlightenment had established a foothold in Fremantle. Indian spirituality had arrived.

The North Indian neo-Sannyasin guru and scholar, Bhagwan Shree Rajneesh, set up the first big Rajneeshee ashram in the Indian city of Pune in 1975, which is where many Westerners first came into contact with him. Pune was big, but the main growth in the sect was after June 1981 when Rajneesh secretly fled India for the USA because of growing hostility among locals scandalised by rumours of sexual extravagance, and threats from government, in part about unpaid taxes. Rajneesh set up his new community in Oregon and began building Rajneeshpuram. It grew rapidly, ultimately housing a permanent population of 6000, with visiting Rajneeshees from the whole Rajneeshee diaspora making for a fluid population. It became a self-sustaining city, a giant commune, built on voluntary Rajneeshee labour for the material and spiritual needs of Rajneeshees. It was also a beacon that drew the world's Rajneeshees into its embrace.

As it grew, the commune's inhabitants went to war with local residents and state and federal governments, to the point where guards with submachine guns began to accompany a somewhat paranoid Rajneesh wherever he went. Rajneesh mystified Americans, who wondered at his extravagant displays of wealth (ninety-two Rolls Royces, expensive watches and gorgeous outfits). By late 1985, Rajneeshpuram had become increasingly bizarre, manifested in a fortress mentality, growing authoritarianism, mass poisonings, even attempted murders.

Then in September 1985, Rajneesh and his second in command, the abrasive and confrontational Ma Sheela, fell out. Rajneesh denounced Ma Sheela as the cause of all the movement's problems. The next day, she, with several followers, fled to Europe. Then Rajneesh left too, deserting the smoking ruins of his community and, after being excluded from twenty-one countries, returned to Pune, changed his name to Osho, and began again. Disillusioned followers and the still faithful went home if they could; many left the movement altogether. Others stayed, blaming Ma Sheela for everything and remaining loyal to Rajneesh. The recent Netflix documentary *Wild Wild Country* provides an excellent insight into this organisation and to Ma Anand Sheela in particular.

Who were these Rajneeshees? Surveys of Western Rajneeshee ashrams have shown that initiates were white, mostly female (one Sydney Rajneeshee estimated three women to every man) middle class, young (in their late twenties and early thirties), mostly single or divorced and often highly educated. They were rarely involved in wider radical politics but were likely to have been in similar orders or to have explored meditation and yoga. Some described themselves as seekers, unhappy or world weary. To become an initiate or neo-Sannyasin seemed pretty simple. Once you had become adept in meditation, listened to Rajneesh's discourses and felt ready for it, you could take Sanyas, a kind of induction into the order, which those in Poona or Rajneeshpuram did from Rajneesh himself, but most did by writing to him to ask for it. They promised to dress in orange (the colour of sunrise and hence the name, the Orange People), wear a mala (a small portrait of Rajneesh on a necklace of 108 beads), perform meditations and other programs and go by new names, with the prefix Ma for women and Swami for men.

Rajneeshism arrived in Western Australia in 1976 when psychologist Jim Coventry, now named Swami Indivar, returned from Pune and set up a meditation centre in the outer suburb of Forrestfield. Two years later it had become a residential community and was joined by another centre in Victoria Park. Then, in late 1981, Kerry Marwick, a wealthy young York farmer renamed Swami Kerry, moved to Fremantle, became a Rajneeshee and bought the Oceanic Hotel in Fremantle's Collie Street to accommodate a new ashram. He also leased the old Fremantle Trades Hall building next door, which the order renamed Ikkyu House. Setting up a holding company, the ashram turned to business to raise funds to support itself, which it did extremely successfully. It ran restaurants, a building company, a contract cleaning company and many more enterprises.

After serving as a residential commune for some time, the hotel was turned into luxury residential apartments and leased or sold, leaving Ikkyu House to become the centre of the order's activity. It housed a Zorba the Buddha restaurant on the ground floor and a function centre on the upper where the community resided. Savita House, a property on Wray Avenue in Fremantle, became a therapy and massage centre until, in 1982, it was voluntarily closed and its functions moved upstairs in the old TLC. About 100 of the perhaps 500 Rajneeshees in WA, including twenty children, were accommodated there, living – it must be said – a pretty Spartan life. Many more lived outside, mixing everyday life with Rajneeshism. At some point, the administration decided that the ashram would no longer accommodate people, so residents moved into share houses around Fremantle, journeying to the ashram for meals, work, meditation and encounter sessions, the latter of often bruising confessions of one's hangups. It is possible that the move may have been made because of an order from Colorado that a portion of the money from every ashram in the world be remitted to finance Rajneeshpuram.

Typically, women held the senior administrative positions in the ashram in Fremantle. Devotees worked for nothing, doing all the work necessary to run them successfully, staffed all of the institutions of the Rajneeshees. Workers in the ashram cooked, washed and cleaned; others worked in the restaurants or other businesses, or in the homes of Rajneeshees who lived elsewhere. If they resided in the ashram, they received a small allowance, their accommodation and food. Many worked outside, some to raise money to go to Rajneeshpuram for the annual festival, but they also sent money in to help provide everyday necessities.

What did the Fremantle Rajneeshees do? Information on daily life in the ashram and elsewhere is sparse. Local Rajneeshees never talked about it much, preferring to present an image of love, life and laughter whenever they met outsiders. They talked about comradeship and friendship, sharing the work, meditations and encounter sessions, as well as the gossiping, conversation and badinage carried on by any group with a fixed focus on life. They certainly worked hard and when, in 1983, Rajneesh redefined Rajneeshism as a religion (necessary for US immigration and tax regulations) and declared that work was now a form of worship, they dutifully worked even harder.

What made Rajneeshees different from other Hindu sects and indeed other *Sanyassins*, was their particular quest for self-discovery and enlightenment. They were not ascetics who disavowed desire and material good for poverty, celibacy and abstinence. Rajneesh had no time for poverty. He was a fan of US capitalism and an opponent of socialism, he loved luxury. He was eclectic and revolutionary, lifting Sannyasinism from its Hindu roots, mixing it with countercultural

Western psychology and philosophy, providing a way for materialists but requiring devotees to find their inner, real selves. It was a doctrine for enjoyment of everything, a freeing from the constraints of society, culture, family, religion and contemporary morality.

These doctrines usually required a guru, an instructor and a guide. Rajneesh certainly was one, although he insisted that followers should not follow rules or programs but seek and find their own individual true selves. Aveling remembers him saying, 'You are totally free, you must fly alone', but, as we will see, Rajneeshees viewed Rajneesh with adoration (look on YouTube at the eyes of the crowds waiting for him on his famous drive-bys in Rajneeshpuram and you see them shining with joy) and unequivocal obedience.

The typical Rajneeshee program included a range of meditations. Rajneesh invented a particular form of dynamic meditation. It entailed twenty minutes of vigorous breathing, twenty minutes of catharsis (shouting, screaming, throwing oneself about), twenty minutes of jumping up and down shouting 'Hoo', and then ten minutes of standing completely still. (You can see an example at Rajneeshpuram on YouTube.) Devotees often described a feeling of pure bliss that followed the performance of these meditations.

The program also included listening to Rajneesh's discourses on tape. These were usually ninety minute elaborations of religious, philosophical or other themes and were followed by a range of encounter and other therapies designed to free devotees from social, cultural and psychological conditioning. They would include encounter and tantra sessions, some designed to free the sexual drive from repression and on into self-realisation. Certainly, many Rajneeshees rode a freed up sexuality with great energy.

The Rajneeshees settled into Fremantle quite well, appreciating the atmosphere of community, diversity and tolerance. Conservative Christian groups and some sections of the Perth media were hostile, but most Fremantle people seemed to tolerate, even accept, them: their businesses were well regarded, they were admired for their hard work and their vegetarian restaurants were successful. However, things began to deteriorate in late 1984 during an ill-fated attempt to set up a school and a business in Pemberton, a timber town in the southwest forests. Faced with the prospect of another Rajneeshpuram (convincingly slandered by Perth interests hostile to the order) locals opposed it, and when Ma Sheela arrived in Perth in early 1985 as part of an Australian visit to extend control over the local ashrams and abused all those who opposed her, the venture collapsed. Fremantle people began to turn against the Rajneeshees.

When Rajneeshpuram crashed and burned so too did the Rajneeshee institutions in Fremantle. Disillusioned, people left; the restaurants, Ikkyu House and other centres around the city all closed. Perhaps because of growing public hostility, custom for their businesses fell away and with the fall in membership, the free labour of devotees dried up. Also, given that on his departure from Rajneeshpuram Rajneesh had decreed that his followers no longer needed to wear orange or the mala, they disappeared into everyday clothing and probably thought it prudent to lower their profile.

But they didn't go away. With the help of another wealthy devotee, Jay Harman, in December 1985 they moved into Dalkeith House, a heritage listed mansion in Fremantle that acted as a meditation centre, therapy rooms, library, coffee shop, business offices and communal dining hall. They named it the Rajneesh Meditation and Healing Centre, then the Rajneesh Academy of Body Artistry and the Rajneesh Institute for the Miraculous. Here they ran the usual meditations and counselling sessions, sold books and tapes, including Rajneesh's (now Osho's) discourses, held seminars and workshops and short residential courses. They survived Osho's death in 1990, but later in the decade, now a shadow of their former selves, they moved on from Dalkeith House to teaching meditation courses from other premises.

What can we make of Fremantle's Rajneeshees? Although they certainly stood out as an exotic feature of Fremantle cultural life, for those living in the ashram their way of life was quite revolutionary. Much of what they did was not really new. Many Indian orders arrived in Australia in the 1970s and 1980s, promising members the path to enlightenment. Some communes, such as Nimbin, the Universal Brotherhood at Balingup, one or two others in Fremantle and even Billy Lane's socialist commune, New Australia in Paraguay, to name but a few, preceded them. Their heightened sexuality certainly separated them from other Hindu orders and was probably a bit much for many conservative Western Australians, but it was just one manifestation of the sexual revolution of the 1960s. Their approach to capitalism was new – no other Indian orders adopted it so readily – and Rajneesh himself was a great advocate for it. Yet, the Fremantle ashram was an urban commune, as were many Rajneeshee institutions, so it had to buy what it needed with money from its businesses and by trading its skills. It was in a strange way, individualist and collectivist.

After Rajneeshpuram collapsed, one ever-hopeful Fremantle devotee spoke of how he believed Rajneesh planned the collapse of his US empire to illustrate that 'nothing is permanent'. In the end, in Fremantle, it was Rajneeshism that proved to be impermanent. By the turn of the century it seemed to have become nothing more than one New Age body competing for influence among many.

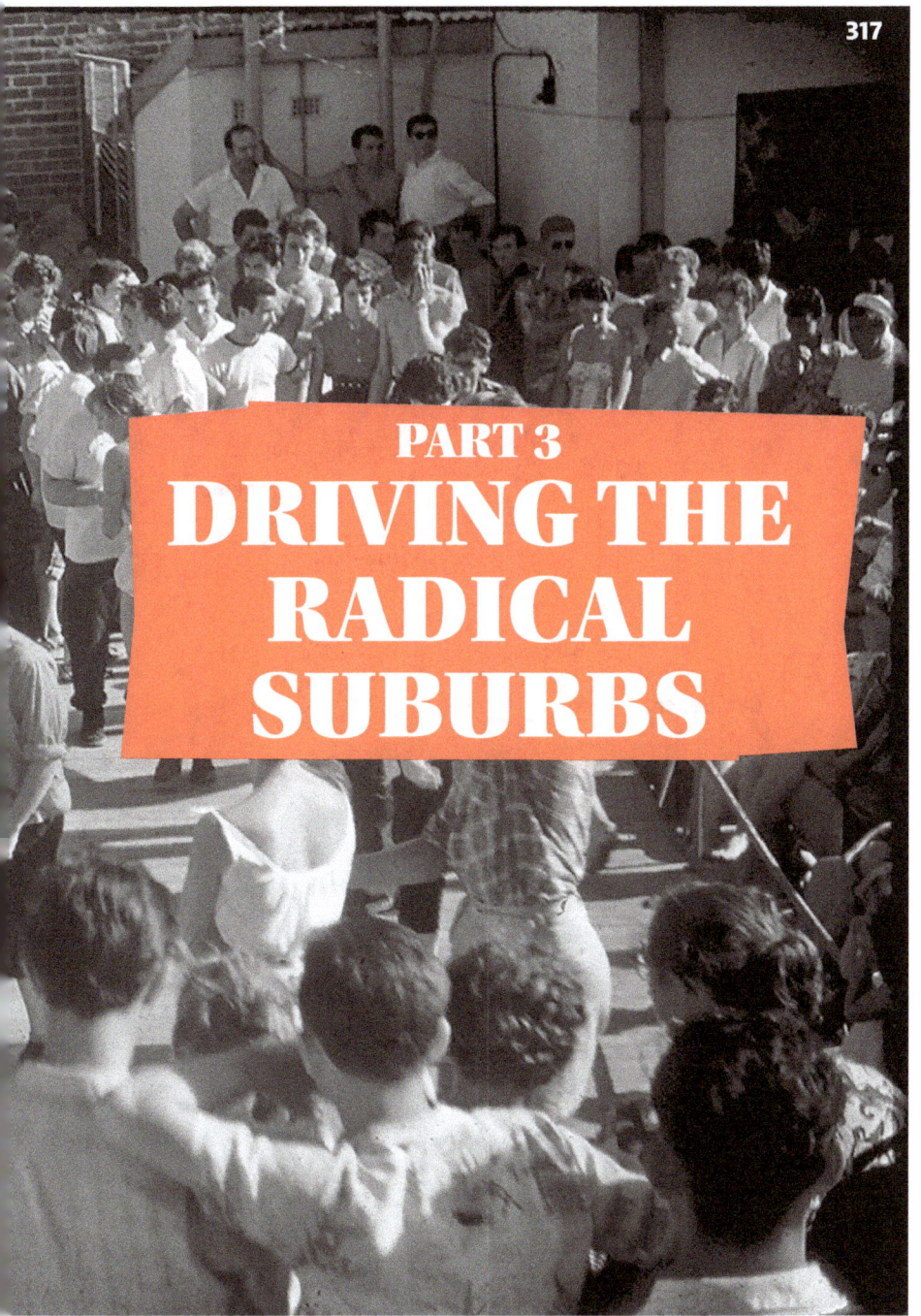

PART 3
DRIVING THE RADICAL SUBURBS

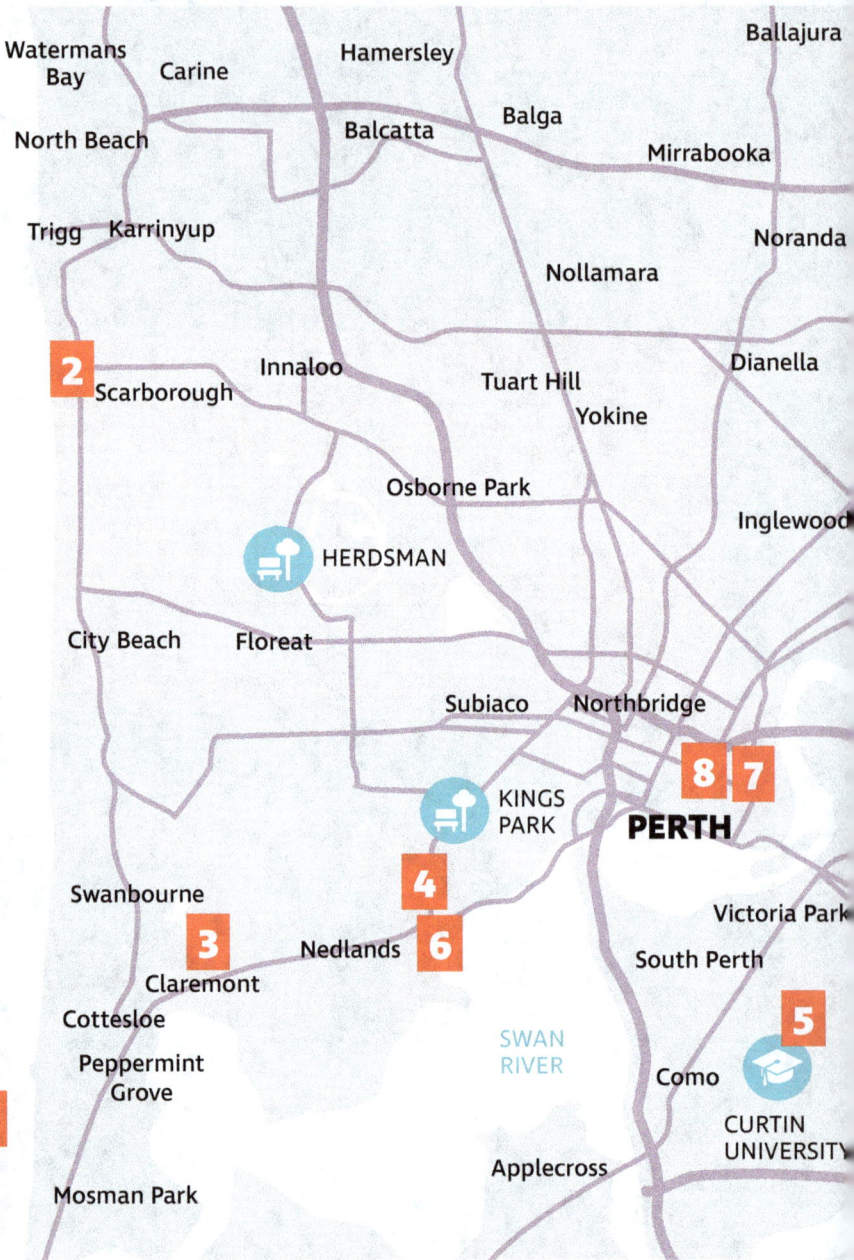

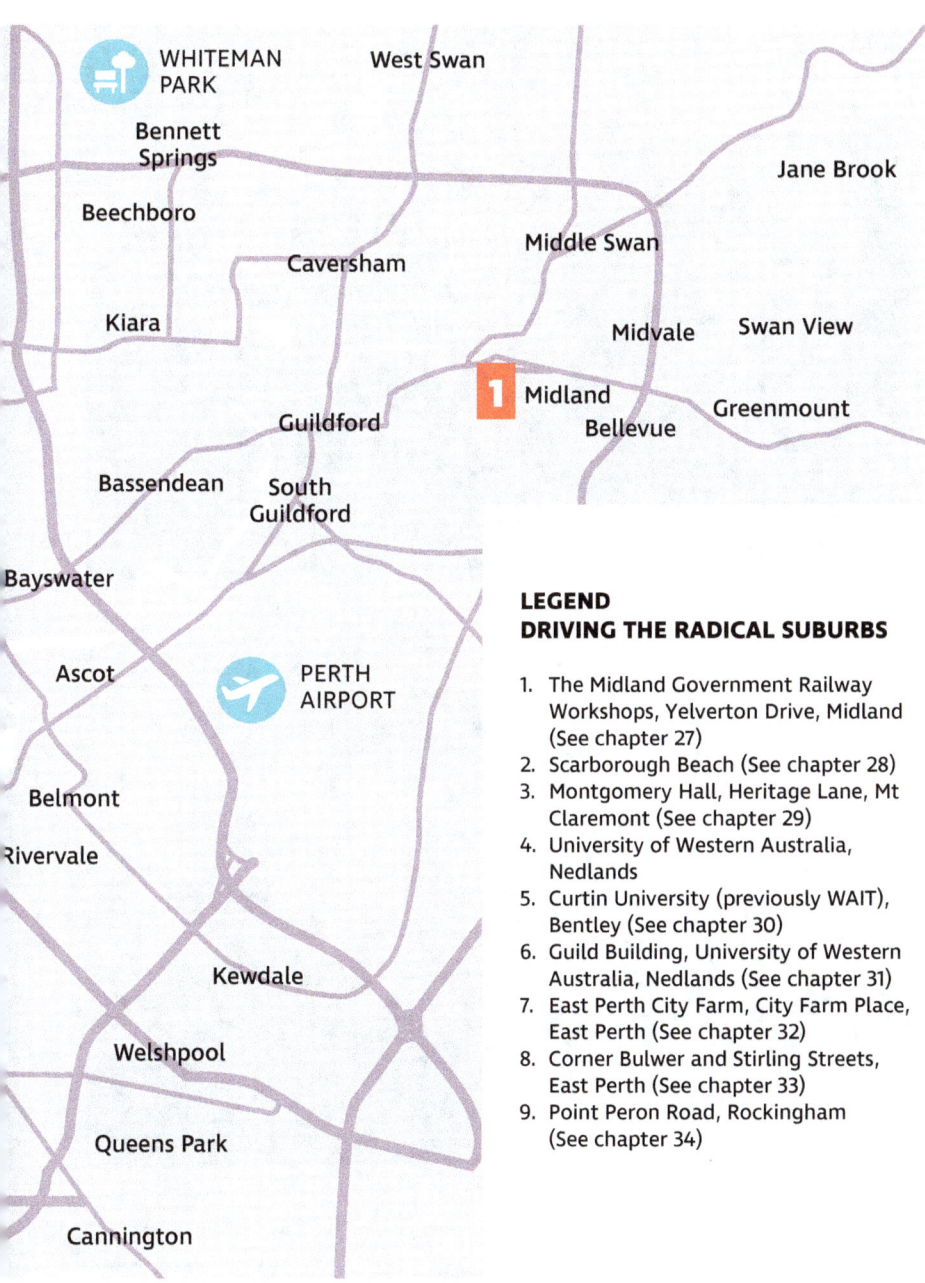

LEGEND
DRIVING THE RADICAL SUBURBS

1. The Midland Government Railway Workshops, Yelverton Drive, Midland (See chapter 27)
2. Scarborough Beach (See chapter 28)
3. Montgomery Hall, Heritage Lane, Mt Claremont (See chapter 29)
4. University of Western Australia, Nedlands
5. Curtin University (previously WAIT), Bentley (See chapter 30)
6. Guild Building, University of Western Australia, Nedlands (See chapter 31)
7. East Perth City Farm, City Farm Place, East Perth (See chapter 32)
8. Corner Bulwer and Stirling Streets, East Perth (See chapter 33)
9. Point Peron Road, Rockingham (See chapter 34)

Protests against the closure of the Workshops in 1993 included street marches and an attempt to drag a diesel locomotive back to the Workshops

27
Red Square and the Flagpole
Bobbie Oliver

During its ninety year history, among its workforce of thousands the Midland Government Railway Workshops had many characters. One of the best known was Jack Marks, a fitter and turner at the Workshops in the 1950s, and a shop steward for the Amalgamated Engineering Union (AEU). A raucous but gifted orator, Marks' stage was either at the flagpole or in a section of the machine shop that became known to workers as Red Square. To the modern worker, the Workshops would seem a far from ideal work site: hot, incredibly noisy, dangerous and crowded. Before the 1980s, the workers lacked even basic safety equipment and endured primitive facilities on a site where they were locked in from morning to evening. While these conditions did not generate much industrial militancy, these two places still excite the memory of past employees and catch the imagination of visitors decades after the Workshops' closure: the flagpole and Red Square.

Built in 1916 as a memorial to Workshops employees who died on active service in World War 1, the flagpole was relocated to its present day site in front of Block 1 (the carriage shop and wood mill) in 1924. The shift took place in preparation for the erection of the peace memorial, which permanently commemorated the war dead who had worked at the Workshops. The flagpole soon became a focus for workers' gatherings when there were grievances to be aired, as well as a forum for political candidates and other public figures wishing to address the assembled workforce. In the Workshops' 1950s heyday a gathering of up to 3500 workers around the flagpole made an impressive sight.

Anyone wanting to organise a flagpole meeting had to get permission from the works manager. Management provided a loud speaker and an electrical tradesman employed at the Workshops was allowed to set up the platform and amplification system in work time. By sanctioning properly organised flagpole meetings, management gave the workers a means of letting off steam and airing legitimate industrial grievances; they also provided a platform for the communists, including candidates for state and federal elections and agitators.

During the 1950s, management decided that workers were abusing the privilege so they banned flagpole meetings. Undaunted, the workers invited speakers to lunchtime gate meetings, held at the main gate where, from the back of a truck parked outside, the speaker would address workers assembled inside the fence. One of the visitors who spoke at a gate meeting in June 1958 was well-known communist Federal Secretary of the Waterside Workers' Federation Jim Healy. Although flagpole meetings were reinstated after state Labor government Minister for Railways Bert Styants revoked the ban, Works Manager Bill Britter still refused to permit US singer and political activist Paul Robeson to give a concert on the premises during his visit to WA in December 1960. To the delight of hundreds of workers, Robeson defied the ban by performing on the back of a truck parked outside the perimeter fence. He then proceeded to a civic reception hosted by the mayor of Midland, thus making the Workshops management look rather petty.

Jack Marks spoke at many flagpole meetings in his capacity as shop steward and as a CPA candidate in state and federal elections. He was especially popular as a flagpole orator; workers often asked if he would be speaking when a meeting was called. The blokes appreciated his coarse humour. According to his biographer, Jolly Read, it was Marks who coined the name Bullshit Castle for the chief mechanical engineer's office. As a shop steward for the AEU, he was often a member of a deputation to the management to discuss some industrial issue. Afterwards, he would tell the workers assembled at the flagpole: 'Well apart from an aching anus, I got nothing!' Or he would ask, 'Have you seen the daily sausage wrapper today?' referring to the *West Australian* newspaper, noted for its conservative viewpoint. Even some of the Workshop managers appreciated Marks' qualities. Ron Wadham recalled in a 2002 interview that Marks was

> a great guy and always good-natured *outside the battle zone* ... a remarkable character ... a fine controller of men and a persuasive speaker. He would stand at Flagpole meetings and point towards the Management buildings and decry the exploitation of the workers and pronounce the ineptitude of the Manager.

Wadham was well aware that Marks was a master at manipulating the power relationships in the Workshops, a place that Wadham himself described as being 'a natural battleground' between employers and unions.

> Jack Marks' other stage was an area in the Machine Shop section of Block 3, where his work was to operate one of the heavy Dean and Grace lathes. The space between the double row of 14 lathes became known to the workers as Red Square or Red Alley because of the unofficial

activities that took place during lunchtime. In the lunch break, Marks would impart communist propaganda to any of his fellow workers who were prepared to stop and listen. Young apprentices like Rod Quinn regarded the Workshops as a university where they developed the self-confidence to have an opinion. Quinn and others came to listen and absorb political ideas.

Marks carried out his lunchtime activities under the gaze of the foreman whose elevated office overlooked the entire workspace. Meeting in Red Square to discuss their grievances in full view of the foreman was a calculated act of bravado and defiance. To workers on the shop floor, the subforemen and foremen were a race apart – men who had been tradesmen like themselves but had crossed the divide to side with the bosses. Most did not become foremen until they were in their mid fifties, and they were generally selected for their management and trade skills, although workers who experienced bad foremen had their own ideas about who was promoted and why. The elevated office accentuated the foreman's status above his former fellow workers; his job was to see that everyone else did his job. Much of his time was spent at the office window, looking up and down the factory floor. Consequently, he was regarded as a policeman or even, in Dave Hicks' words, 'a little tin god'.

The foreman had a clerk to do his paperwork. If a worker needed to leave the premises for any reason during working hours, such as to attend a doctor's appointment, he had to climb the stairs to the elevated office in full view of everyone and get a leave pass from the clerk. The foreman had absolute control over workers' freedom to move around the shop. Apprentices had some freedom because their training required them to gain experience in different shops and to attend classes, but tradesmen were not supposed to leave their shop without good reason. Even if an employee went to another area on the site as part of his duties, the foreman had the authority to demand to know why he was there. Employees were always under scrutiny and dependent upon the foreman's good grace. The authoritarian regime with its strict control, even to the extent of confining employees to the grounds at lunchtime and timing toilet breaks, made many feel as if they were in prison with the foreman as their gaoler.

In this atmosphere of constant supervision and suspicion that existed even during their free time, the activities of Red Square constituted a thumbing the nose at management's representatives. The foreman, of course, could never be one of the mob because it was his job to make his workshop function as efficiently as possible and to report regularly to the management on such matters as the output and performance of men and machines, accidents, industrial disturbances and any other factors that influenced work productivity. Above the foremen was the management hierarchy, often hated by workers, who adhered to a strict them and us culture, which included never talking to anyone in a white shirt. On the factory floor, the foreman was merely the ever-present reminder of this autocratic system.

The communists were a small but active group at the Workshops in the 1950s. They produced their own newspaper *Unity* on roughly a monthly basis. Although most took little notice of their rhetoric, they impressed the men because they were committed unionists who, as shop stewards, worked hard to obtain better pay and conditions for their fellow workers. No doubt some workers hung around Red Square at lunchtime to learn something about what the communists believed, and possibly because the communists' political zeal made them curious; others did so because they were entertained by Marks' oratory and enjoyed his coarse humour. Marks and other shop stewards such as Denis Day, Jack Coleman and Rod Quinn, all went on to careers as paid union organisers outside of the Workshops.

Communism never flourished in Australia, but perhaps Western Australia, noted for its political conservatism, was particularly hostile territory in the middle of the twentieth century because the ALP controlled the Trades and Labor Council. This arrangement denied non-ALP unionists a voice in the state's industrial councils and discriminated against unions whose officials belonged to another political party, be it Communist, Democratic Labour or Liberal. Most union activists came from the state's few heavy manufacturing, mining or transport industries, located on the goldfields, the wharves, the Collie coalfields, or at Midland's private or government railway workshops. Changes to goldmining technology in the 1930s drove a number of skilled tradesmen to seek work in Midland. Ted Zeffert, who was employed at the Workshops for about three years, Jack Coleman and Bill Stronach, a shop steward in the fitting shop before the World War 2, were all from goldfields families with similarly militant backgrounds in the sustenance work camps of the 1930s.

Although workers were generally confined to their particular area in the Workshops, some had better opportunities to mingle. Zeffert met many fellow communists while distributing *Tribune* around the Workshops. Also, his work took him into each of the three main blocks where he met many goldfields men, most of whom were tough, cool headed, industrially militant individuals, used to working in dangerous conditions. The communists were very active in the Joint Unions Committee, a body that coordinated responses to issues affecting more than one union at the Workshops. Consequently, men would gather in a convenient spot in their workshop during the lunch break to discuss any grievances with their shop steward. Red Square has endured lasting fame, possibly because of Marks' larger than life persona, but there were many such gathering places.

In union politics, Marks was elected repeatedly to the AEU executive and was branch president in the early 1960s. He was shop stewards' convenor at the Workshops, represented staff on the Punishments Appeal Board, and was the metal trades federal delegate. But people were reluctant to have him represent them in parliament. Marks and other prominent communists such as Joan Williams and John 'Rivo' Gandini stood for the House of Representatives and the Senate during various campaigns in the 1950s and 1960s but none came close to victory. The little Workshops local rag, *Unity*, boasted that the communist vote in the federal electorate of Swan had almost doubled from 493 in 1959 to 801 in 1961 – but it was still not nearly enough to secure a seat in parliament. Even the communists' program for the Midland Workshops, which promised more jobs by expanding and modernising the railway system, including electrification of the metropolitan rail service, gaining more overseas contracts, improving amenities for workers and increasing margins did not guarantee votes. Some workers felt that if Marks had joined the ALP instead of the CPA he would have soon become a member of parliament because he could talk people into anything.

Many who frequently gathered at Red Square were veterans of the unsuccessful six month metal workers' strike that occurred in 1952, a strike that was bitterly remembered in the 1960s when tradesman would still point out to new apprentices which workers had been blacklegs. The Australasian Society of Engineers and the Moulders' Union both refused to take part in the strike, which their officials claimed was communist inspired. Marks' lathe was superseded as a gathering place once he departed from the Workshops, and Red Square ceased to exist except in legend. Later, the marking off table at the opposite end of the lathes from the foreman's office – but still well within his view – became the spot. The flagpole continued to be a gathering place throughout the life of the Workshops. It was there at 2 pm on 27 April 1993 that workers were summoned to be told the devastating news that the Workshops would be closed in a year's time. The Workshops closure, on 4 March 1994, brought many careers to an end, and set others in a different though not always satisfactory direction.

Today, although the main buildings and structures on the site (including the flagpole) remain, protected by heritage legislation, the only trace of Red Square is the section of floor in Block 3 where the lathes once stood. The Rail Heritage Centre, so long fought for by labour historians and heritage practitioners, has not materialised and does not look like ever eventuating. Consequently, the level of interpretation necessary to explain the significance of sites such as the flagpole and especially Red Square, from where the fabric has been removed, does not exist, and this is tragic. To the rare visitors who gets access to the buildings today, the empty floor has little meaning, but to the men who worked there, especially in the environment of increasing powerlessness and a decreasing workforce that prevailed during the last years, it is not surprising that Red Square and the flagpole became the stuff of legend, representing the Workshops' glory days when unions had power and unionists stood up to Bullshit Castle.

28
The Scarborough Snake Pit
Charlie Fox

The Snake Pit was just a few square metres of open air dance floor out the front of a little cafe on the Scarborough beachfront in Perth's north where, for a few years in the later 1950s, young people would go to rock'n'roll. For a few weeks in February 1958 it became the centre of a storm when Perth's afternoon paper, the *Daily News*, ran a campaign against it. Its defenders argued that it was just harmless fun. But local shopkeepers didn't like the crowds and older people thought it was a den of adolescent iniquity, populated by bodgies and widgies – a working class subculture conservatives viewed as simply gangs. In these postwar years Perth was a conservative town that didn't take rebellion lightly. The pressure on the Snake Pit's owner was enormous, so much so that after the short campaign he shut down the Snake Pit.

The Snake Pit began probably around 1955 (the dates are a bit iffy) when Don Errichetti and his wife Rosanna Rifici bought a kiosk on the corner of the Esplanade and Manning Street and set up a cafe they called La Spiaggia. Wanting al fresco dining they put tables outside and began playing Italian melodies on their record player. But just a few days after it opened, some bodgies turned up and asked – demanded – that they play rock'n'roll. Errichetti, as he said later, 'just went along with it'. And so the Snake Pit was born. It proved to be a great place for

The Snake Pit open-air dance floor on the Scarborough Beach Front

young people. The dancing was fun and free, the music was new and exciting, you could cool off in the sea, your parents weren't there and the police didn't bother you.

The Snake Pit – so named because the dancers looked like writhing snakes – began small and grew. It's said that at its peak a thousand people were dancing or watching at any one time. After a while Errichetti built a wall round the dance floor, in effect sinking it, so spectators and dancers could have a seat and a break. This created a livelier atmosphere and, incidentally, trapped the heat and made it as hot as hell. But it soon got a reputation. The mix of rock'n'roll, uninhibited jiving and the presence of bodgies and widgies alarmed their parents, who began warning their children, especially their daughters, not to go there, so of course, they did.

The arrival of the Snake Pit accompanied the arrival of rock'n'roll in WA so like rock'n'roll itself it always had an air of rebellion about it. Indeed, the arrival of the cafe and the music was probably the first time Perth was confronted with the new postwar teen culture. It was bigger and more public than milkbars, where bodgies and widgies hung out, but where adults did not go. Of course, crowds at the Snake Pit were much bigger too.

In the early days Errichetti played the music of the great US rockers: Bill Haley, Elvis Presley, Little Richard, Jerry Lee Lewis, Buddy Holly, Chuck Berry, Eddie Cochran and Fats Domino, and sometimes the great US female singers Brenda Lee, Lavern Baker and Lillia Briggs. Because it closed in early 1958, it was too early for great Australian rockers such as Johnny O'Keefe, known as J.O.K., and Col Joye and the Joy Boys, but sometimes Perth's rock'n'roll bands played there, bands such The Saints, The Roulettes, and Bill Blaine and the Dynamics.

Some say young people came from all over Perth to dance at the Snake Pit but it's more likely they were northern suburbs working class youth already lured there by the beach, Luna Park, milkbars, cafes, rollerskating, juke boxes, minigolf and the Scarborough Hotel for the over twenty-ones. It was already an entertainment centre, and a raffish one at that. Indeed, it was quite unlike Perth's other beaches, which were more sedate, respectable and still largely undeveloped. So Scarborough was different.

Photos of the Snake Pit show the dancers: male–female couples, sometimes two males or two girls dancing together, sometimes girls dancing by themselves. The Jive was the favoured dance but the Creep, a slow motion body on body stroll around the dance floor, and rock'n'roll, were also popular. Perth scandal rag the *Mirror* thought the Creep was a bodgie dance and described it as 'the type of thing done by sensation seeking drug addicts in the low dens of London'. There were also jive competitions and exhibitions. To dance on weekends you had to be something of an exhibitionist, not scared of the crowds looking on. The audience was doubtless there to watch the spectacle, spend some time between swims and learn some moves. But perhaps some came hoping for trouble.

Interviewed years later on the ABC, most dancers recalled dancing, having fun, drinking Coke and eating Italian icecreams. A few men remember sex in the Scarborough sandhills but no one recalls drugs or drinking alcohol. A few remember trouble. The so-called king of the bodgies, Andy Andros, claims he and his fellow bodgies kept the place in order, seeing off troublesome rivals such as a roving gang of Leatheries. It's unlikely though that there was much trouble, otherwise it wouldn't have lasted as long as it did and it would have been more heavily policed. In any case, Don Errichetti policed it himself – he had been a US marine in an earlier life and was well able to keep things orderly; Constable Tony Martin from the Scarborough Police Boys' Association watched over it as well.

Several people have claimed that it was mainly bodgies and widgies, identifiable by their clothes and their hairstyles, who danced at the Snake Pit. Bodgies wore black stovepipe trousers, black shirts and black desert boots and had Elvis Presley haircuts. For widgies it was tight slacks, tight skirts and blouses or flowing skirts or dresses over rope petticoats that spun out in wide circles when they danced. Yet contemporary photos don't show a preponderance of bodgie and widgie gear. They showed people in bathers and bare feet, shorts and shirts, dresses, yes, baggy and ordinary trousers with light coloured shirts and, yes, a smattering of bodgie gear.

Did parents know that their kids were at the Snake Pit? Gwen

Donaldson's mother didn't, otherwise 'she'd have had a fit'. Patricia Grey (the girl in the leopard skin bikini as she is famously known) would go there any time she could because 'I just wanted to dance'. Her father didn't know she went. Patricia once said that he thought she was just at the beach. Perhaps this is what led many to say that the Snake Pit was their place, where they could enjoy themselves in their own way, differentiating themselves from adult culture, dancing to music that began as youthful defiance and which, for some years to come, carried overtones of rebellion.

In March 1957, the *Daily News* printed two letters about the Snake Pit. Dancing there was fun, wrote one, 'Just youthful high spirits, getting plenty of exercise and having a whale of a time'. Another put the fun atmosphere down to the presence of Constable Martin and the Police Boys' Association turning 'what could have been a trouble spot into a source of exercise and innocuous fun'.

What a difference a year made. Then, in early 1958, with the Snake Pit firmly in its sights, the *Daily News* began its campaign to 'clean up the Scarborough beachfront'. Front page headlines such as 'We've Had Enough Of Beach Louts' and ' "Out With The Louts", Says Scarborough' set the tone as the paper lined up angry letter writers, police, local dignitaries, residents and members of parliament to slam 'the great unwashed', 'stupid cowardly louts', 'ill mannered, dirty and badly dressed youths' who were wrecking Scarborough Beach for families. One correspondent blamed the Police and Citizens Boys' Club for sponsoring rock'n'roll competitions at the Snake Pit. Others blamed outsiders, youths from working class suburbs such as Maylands, Inglewood and Bayswater. Under pressure, Don Errichetti chimed in, telling the *Daily News*:

> The past three weeks have been the worst and I've been running the show at a loss. The bodgie hooligans aren't good for business – they drive away genuine customers. They have smashed tables and chairs and done more damage than they're worth.

He promised to ban the bodgies and shut down the Snake Pit. And he did. On the following Monday, the *Daily News* gloated:

> The general quietness on the Promenade and the absence of bodgies and widgies coincided with the cessation of rock-n-roll and banning of bodgies from the beachfront centre known as the Snake Pit.

What were the bodgie crowds supposed to have been doing? Well not much, if the *Daily News'* front page exposé was right. A young couple with a pram was forced off the footpath as bodgies remarked, 'Out of the way Shorty'. As one woman made her way through a crowd she was embarrassed by obscene language. A young man 'had the shirt torn off his back' as he walked along a footpath.

Groups of young men can be pretty scary if they decide to be obnoxious, but this catalogue of misbehaviour doesn't really seem sinister enough to shut down the Snake Pit. Indeed, a *Weekend Mail* reporter, writing in July 1960, had seen the police file but found only a few incidents and nothing of any note. But perhaps the presence of bodgies and widgies wasn't the only reason the Snake Pit was closed down. The very next week, the Scarborough Surf Club was to host a national surf carnival and a festival of entertainments was planned as part of the weekend, including a ball in a nearby park on the Saturday night. The last thing the powers that be would have wanted was bodgies and widgies, rock'n'rollers, jivers and troublemakers spoiling the party.

Many people were angry after the Snake Pit closed. Much later Gwen Donaldson, wrote:

Our summer Sundays were spent jiving at the Snake Pit, another of this fair city's dens of iniquity. What could be healthier than dancing to the latest rock'n'roll beat in the open air, drinking the ubiquitous Coke and having fun? No, once again our behaviour was considered outrageous.

Constable Martin recalled in 1960 that maybe the kids did make some noise, but 'That was because they were alive – not half dead like some of their critics – but there wasn't any harm in them. Time has proved that.' Errichetti regretted closing it down. 'It still makes me sore,' he said later. 'In fact I'm sorry I closed the joint. I shouldn't have been so easily swayed by the unfair adverse publicity.'

Bodgies and widgies had jived in Perth since 1950. Early on they were portrayed as mere neophytes, 'progressive dressers' and not much more, although more than one dance club closed its doors when they showed up. It was in the eastern states where the bad ones were, as local papers such as the *Mirror* loved to point out, publishing scary stories about 'bodgie and widgie cults staging sex and drinking orgies, marihuana and Benzedrine parties, violent brawls and vicious crimes'.

By the mid 1950s a new bodgie cult had arrived in Perth. Stories began to appear about brawls in Fremantle, Cottesloe, Midland and elsewhere, describing bodgies protecting their turf, staging sex parties to initiate widgies into gangs, escaping from juvenile detention centres, assaulting police, running marijuana parties, playing chicken on the roads in their cars and congregating aggressively around their favourite hangouts – milkbars. Such were the waves they were making that in 1955, the head of the Perth CIB declared war on them and set up a special anti-bodgie police unit. A year later the WA parliament passed legislation aimed at the gangs (and Southern Europeans) outlawing the carrying of offensive weapons such as knives and knuckle dusters.

Naturally, experts began looking for causes. Some called the bodgies psychologically unbalanced, others blamed working mothers for neglecting their children. Yet others blamed the decline of the great socialising institutions – church, school, family and home – while others blamed movies, comics and books. The more expansive regarded juvenile delinquency as a symptom of vast social disorder. Said one, 'We all are to blame'. The more specific blamed rock'n'roll.

Music historians say that rock'n'roll arrived in Australia in 1955, when the US movie *Blackboard Jungle* hit the screens. Part of the score was Bill Haley and the Comets' classic, 'Rock Around the Clock'. In April 1956, the *Mirror* warned its readers about the growing popularity of rock'n'roll in Perth and breathlessly described the rioting, violence and mayhem that seemed to follow it round the USA. One US critic wrote in the *Mirror* of Elvis Presley:

> This fellow is supposed to be a singer. But if his howling and yowling, wailing, screeching and caterwauling be a form of song then a tomcat on a back fence deserves the title of the world's greatest vocalist ... And all this while his face is distorted in suggestive smirks and leers. The picture – wittingly or unwittingly – appeals to the lowest instincts of the viewer – animalism at its rawest ... No wonder there have been so many reports of teenage riots and other outbursts in towns and cities where Elvis has made personal appearances.

It was called jungle music. In the USA it was identified with African Americans in a kind of racist musicology. It was animalistic, instinctive, sensual, sexual and obscene; it caused young, impressionable listeners to throw off their inhibitions and let nature in the raw take over. The release of Bill Haley's own movie, *Rock Around the Clock*, which arrived in Sydney, Melbourne and Brisbane in 1956, seemed to prove the point: wild dancing and rioting was conducted by bodgie and widgie gangs, who joyfully tore up seats at cinemas and fought each other in the streets. *Rock Around the Clock* was received much more peacefully in Perth but respectable citizens were worried.

Yet rock'n'roll was slow to move in Perth, partly because none of the big stars who toured Australia in the 1950s – Little Richard, Big Joe Turner, Bill Haley, Buddy Holly, Eddie Cochrane and others – crossed the Nullarbor from the east. Movies took their place. *Rock Around the Clock*, *The Girl Can't Help It*, *Don't Knock the Rock*, *Rock Pretty Baby* and *Rock, Rock, Rock* all arrived in 1956–57. Movie chains began to feel the power of the teenage dollar.

Radio was where most people heard rock'n'roll. Even though television arrived in 1956 it took a few years for TV bosses to discover the teenage audience so TV rock'n'roll didn't begin in Perth until 1960, well after Perth produced its own rock bands. These bands played at dances in suburban halls (the Maylands hall dances were bodgie haunts), the better known played gigs at the big dance venues such as the Canterbury Ballroom and the Embassy; the best later got gigs on television.

Rock'n'roll was readymade for dancing and jive was readymade for rock'n'roll. As we have seen, bodgies and widgies were jiving in Perth in 1951. By 1953 jive was still exotic but slowly moving to the mainstream. In 1953 a Perth bandleader organised a jive contest for the New Year but the Embassy ballroom allowed just one jive each Friday night. In December 1956, the Lido staged a weekly jive night but some months earlier the *Mirror* had reported that local dance schools wouldn't teach rock'n'roll dancing, one dance teacher describing it as 'sexy hooliganism in jive time'.

In January 1957, the *Daily News* portrayed the jive as a bodgie dance, assisted by a willing young bodgie who remarked in an interview that

Everyone can jive in the mob. Jiving starts you off. You start to feel good and feel as though you can beat up anyone. The rhythm gets you. You get up, get a sheila and start jiving.

Someone must have been in touch, because shortly afterwards the *News* ran another story declaring that the Education Department was teaching the jive to all comers at its twenty-five centres. In the same year, Perth staged a rock'n'roll dance marathon (the winner danced non-stop for seventy-six and a half hours). Then, in October 1959, radio station 6IX staged a hop at the Embassy for 1400 'casually dressed teenagers'. Through all the arguments, suburban bodgies and widgies jived to bands in local halls and around juke boxes in their local milk bars. It seems that the jive had won over Perth.

The Snake Pit proved to be collateral damage in the war on bodgies and widgies. It closed leaving a hole in the summertime recreation of northern suburbs youth. People moved on; certainly bodgies and widgies did, turning up at other dance venues that took one look at them and promptly shut the doors. More places began staging rock'n'roll, which increased its presence on commercial radio, appeared on television and big acts began to come from the east. Bodgies and widgies continued to go to Scarborough. In 1961 and 1963, the *Weekend News* complained about 'the worst type of juvenile delinquent' causing trouble on its Sunset Strip, that raffish street on the Esplanade where the Snake Pit once stood.

For many years memories of the Snake Pit remained sharply divided. It wasn't until the twenty-first century that the venue was fully rehabilitated. Scarborough Beach now hosts Snake Pit revival nights where ageing rockers jive the night away, that is, if they're not too tired.

I wish to acknowledge Erin Gothard-Fox for her valuable research assistance on this essay.

29
Closing the Asylums
Charlie Fox

Since 1904 until its closure, Claremont Hospital had been the state's major hospital for the insane. It housed generations of people with mental illness and intellectual disabilities. Officially opened in 1908, Claremont was closed by the state in 1972. But in a way it wasn't a real closure; its disappearance was simply a change of nomenclature, done to rid its replacements of the stigma, which over the years had been attached to the name Claremont. In its place, it simply renamed its two divisions, Swanbourne and Graylands.

Fourteen years later the government demolished Swanbourne. After the demolition only a couple of buildings remained, one of which was Montgomery Hall, the centrepiece, named after its first superintendent, Sydney Montgomery. Graylands remained. What had happened to make these changes possible? It was deinstitutionalisation, the process that has left, with some exceptions, the hollowed out shells of hospitals for the insane empty and desolate across the Western world. Much later many would be turned to other purposes, such as expensive apartments, convention centres and, more appropriately, community centres.

This is the story of the deinstitutionalisation of Claremont and its successors and their replacement by ideas of community care and

Montgomery Hall once the centrepiece of Claremont Hospital for the Insane. Now a convention centre

inclusion. These huge changes weren't simply about hospitals for the insane; they were also part of an international movement that attacked all confinement institutions, from hospitals for the insane to prisons and juvenile detention centres. For some, such places were pillars upholding the system. For others, the logic was:

> That such institutions did not work, that they caused more problems than they solved; and that the community, where those problems had their origins might be the best place, after all, to look for solutions.

Built in optimistic Victorian times when the European Enlightenment made reason a defining premise of sanity and when a cure for mental illness was thought to be possible, many countries built new, grand hospitals where the insane might be cured. As these countries industrialised and populations grew, the number of patients rose, which meant the hospitals quickly became overcrowded and unworkable, becoming instead warehouses where troubled and troublesome people lived and died. In Britain in 1827, for example, there were just nine hospitals for the insane, each with an average population of 116. By 1909, there were ninety-five, each with an average population of 1008.

Fremantle Lunatic Asylum, built in 1865, was the first purpose built hospital to which the insane and intellectually disabled were sent before Claremont was built. Then, in 1929, Claremont was supplemented by Heathcote Hospital in Applecross, a reception hospital for 'curable' patients on the road to recovery. South of the city, at Whitby Falls, was a farm colony where fifty patients produced food for the hospital system; Lemnos at Shenton Park was a home for shell shocked ex-soldiers.

Until deinstitutionalisation, there were two ways of getting out of Claremont: discharge and death. As historian Philippa Martyr has shown, death was easier and more frequent. The 1955 *Stoller Report* of 1955, a national report on mental health across Australia, damned Claremont as overcrowded, understaffed, inefficient, rundown and out of date. Over the years various changes were made, trial leave was instituted and rehabilitation facilities were built. In 1966, two wards were set up as therapeutic communities where staff and patients worked together and where patients took a role in the management of the ward. In 1967, the wards were given the names of Perth suburbs, which replaced simple letters or numbers, and nurses were given modern uniforms in an attempt to soften the hospital's image.

The first obvious sign of deinstitutionalisation was in 1959, when

Claremont set up its first day clinic, Graylands, the brainchild of the new Inspector General of the Insane Dr Digby Moynagh, who imported the idea from the UK where similar clinics were being created. Hitherto, all patients at Claremont were inpatients, but voluntary patients who were not sick enough to be admitted as inpatients but were too sick to be left untreated could now come to Graylands for day time medical treatment and therapy. It was the first such place in the country. Seemingly, it worked.

By the 1960s the reign of the mental hospital was on the brink. Critiques came from everywhere: psychiatry, sociology, the media, even popular culture. Exposés by crusading journalists in the USA and Australia painted dismal pictures of drab wards, forgotten and abused patients, who in some cases were casualties of the medical procedures designed to cure them. Ken Kesey's 1962 novel and the 1975 film, *One Flew Over the Cuckoo's Nest*, showed how powerless patients were in even apparently open hospital wards.

Anti-psychiatry arrived in Australia early. Writing in the 1960s, psychiatrists including Briton R. D. Laing, Hungarian American Thomas Szasz and French philosopher–historian Michel Foucault, in their different ways denied the existence of mental illness. They attacked psychiatry, its institutions and the idea that insanity was an objective, observable, somatic fact. Rather, madness was at some level socially constructed, a label imposed on troublesome people to constrain and confine them.

Sociologists joined in. In 1961, US sociologist Irving Goffman charged that hospitals for the insane were 'total institutions' where surveillance, control and the 'destruction of the self' were used to recreate patients in the image the hospital wanted. In 1973 again in the USA, David Rosenham famously sent students into mental hospitals to fake symptoms of mental illness and concluded from their reports that hospitals couldn't distinguish between the sane and the insane. In 1974, Perth psychiatrist Robin Winkler did the same in his own pseudo patient experiments. Hospital psychiatry was increasingly regarded, even by its practitioners, as a dismal science.

Although the psychiatric profession in Australia tried hard to close ranks against these ideas, in the 1970s there were many who were persuaded. One result was the growing emphasis on the patient's rights to refuse treatment, involuntary admission and hospitalisation. Then, of course, as living in the community implied, the right to community treatment, and then full citizen's rights became a cornerstone of the critics demands.

New psychotropic drugs that mitigated mental conditions also drove deinstitutionalisation. Becoming increasingly available and effective meant these drugs could be administered to people at home or at least somewhere other than Claremont. By 1967–68 the number of beds at Claremont fell from 1500 to 1100. For Harry Blackmore, the new psychiatric superintendent who had been appointed in 1967, the benefits were obvious.

> It is better for ex-patients to walk down a suburban street, do their own shopping and attend work if practicable rather than live permanently in the secluded and protected environment of a large institution.

In 1970, Claremont was divided into dementia and deficiency divisions with 300 beds each and a psychotic division with 450 beds. It was now possible to abandon Claremont Hospital altogether. The psychotic division became Graylands Hospital, the Dementia and Deficiency divisions became Swanbourne. In the latter, patients were mainly older with organic brain problems and older intellectually disabled patients. From the start it was disastrous: old, dilapidated, backward, understaffed and custodial. Photographs taken of the same ward in 1912 and 1977 show very little had changed; after sixty-five years there were still long rows of wire beds in drab surroundings. Mental Health Services knew it was bad, so bad that even Director Fred Bell could call it 'outmoded, inconvenient and depressing'.

Where did the deinstitutionalised patients go? In those early years most went to twenty hostels or lodging houses, which, in 1973, housed about 500 people. Patients who could be were sent home, others moved to private hospitals, respite and nursing homes, and to mental health units in mainstream hospitals. Treatments were provided by these hospitals and new outpatient clinics where specialist staff provided medical and other assistance. By 1976 there were nine full time and seven part time outpatient clinics; a year later there were more patients outside approved hospitals than in them.

Yet problems soon arose. Governments promised that the money available from either selling or closing hospitals for the insane would be spent on community care but it wasn't. Indeed, in Australia, state governments spent more on mental hospitals even though most mentally ill people were living in the community. As a result the process of building clinics was too slow and there were many unmet needs.

At first the hostels couldn't accommodate all those who wanted to stay in them. Then, later, there were so many complaints that in the late 1970s the government was forced to license, regulate and supervise them. Many patients who had been moved into the community returned to Graylands because they couldn't afford to live outside, they preferred the companionship there or refused to take their medications. There were greater demands for admissions to Graylands too, as more people with drug and alcohol problems turned up, but there was not enough staff to provide for them.

There was also continuing opposition to deinstitutionalisation from within the system. Some doctors and nurses, who were used to their old ways, stood in the way of the new, some actively sabotaging the process. In 1984, just two years before Swanbourne was demolished, the Commonwealth government and the states formulated a new national mental health plan. With the promise of extra money, things seemed to be looking up.

There's a similar story about those with an intellectual disability. If, in WA in the 1960s, you had tried to find where children with an intellectual disability lived you would have been sent first to Claremont Hospital for the Insane. Let Guy Hamilton, the key figure in the deinstitutionalisation of people with intellectual disabilities in WA and a world leader in the field, describe the infamous J Block:

> The care was appalling. In the male children's ward, J Block, there were people who lay in bed with bed sores until they died; there were cot cases for whom little but basic nursing was provided; there was no policy of training and the care of 40 people in a ward by two or three nursing staff was inadequate. At meal times they were seated at arm's length from each other, so that they couldn't grab each other's food, which I suspect they did simply because they were hungry. Many who were incontinent were often hosed down outside, even in winter in the so-called airing court. There was no individual care, no love, there was no care at all and bad behaviour was coped with in the medical fashion, using what some used to call 'chemical warfare' against them … It was the only place in the world where I have found children as young as two years being referred to by their surnames … They were receiving worse treatment than animals and most certainly were not being treated as children.

Or you might have been sent to Nathanial Harper Homes where fifty or so profoundly disabled children lived. Or perhaps the Slow

Learning Children's Group (SLCG), which embattled parents who kept their disabled children at home worked hard to fund, find and provide services in the hope that they might live a relatively decent life.

Then in the later 1960s things began to change, led largely by Hamilton, himself a father of an intellectually disabled child and from 1964 the head of the new independent Mental Deficiency Division (MDD) of Mental Health Services. Hamilton was charged with providing for people with intellectual disability in Claremont and in the community. Hamilton had learnt from the work of Jack Tizard in the UK that treating children as children and adults as adults and both as human beings meant treating them in the community, not in institutions. So began this second process of deinstitutionalisation in Western Australia.

The process was premised on three principles: that families should look after their disabled children, that institutions that housed people with intellectual disability not take any more, and that such institutions close and their patients be transferred to the community. Two doctrines became important: normalisation, a Scandinavian doctrine that proposed that people with intellectual disabilities should live in as close to normal living conditions as possible to enable them to reach their full human potential, and social role valorisation, introduced by US sociologist Wolf Wolfensberger, which involved training people with intellectual disabilities in valued social roles (worker, student, homeowner). Ideally, integration into the community would follow as people accepted them in their new roles.

Further changes followed. The social model of disability displaced the medical model. The idea that disability was to be found in the body gave way to the idea that disability was caused by the disabling practices of society. Two things followed: that doctors would no longer be the key profession for people with intellectual disabilities – educators, psychologists and therapists would be. If the problems they faced originated in the wider society the social model said, then the solutions were also to be found there.

In Perth, the motors of change moved quickly. From 1964 Claremont stopped taking any more children; babies were now expected to live at home with their parents. Resident children were gradually moved out of Claremont into hostels and other institutions in the community that had specialist services. Also in 1964 the MDD took over Irrabeena, an assessment and diagnostic centre set up earlier by the SLCG. In 1966 the newly established Pyrton Training Centre in Guildford was opened and a new occupation, social trainer, was introduced. This person was to work with children (usually those sent from Swanbourne) on new programs. Children worked through progressive stages of development, which would ultimately lead, it was hoped, to a house in the community and a normal life.

Next it was the adults' turn. In the very early 1980s responsibility for residents with intellectual disabilities was transferred to the Division for the Intellectually Handicapped (DIH), which replaced the MDD, until, by the end of 1983, there was no one left in Swanbourne at all. About the mass transfer of now former residents, the director of MHS wrote in his report for 1981–82: 'This will be an achievement of which MHS and DIH can be extremely proud.' Many were moved to Pyrton to undergo training that would enable them to live independently.

Earlier, some people thought to be capable of living in the community went to hostels such as Croyden in Subiaco. By 1973 there were seven such hostels from where they graduated through other hostels until it was thought that they, too, were ready for some kind of independent living. The group home was the end stage of the process in which groups of people with intellectual disabilities might become able to live in neighbourhoods as everyday citizens. In 1974 the MDD had just two such properties that housed six women, but fifteen years later the Authority for Intellectually Handicapped Persons (AIHP), which had replaced the DIH, had 138 and there were many more run by other bodies such as churches and the SLCG, facilities where people with intellectual disabilities lived with the support of social trainers who helped with therapies, new skills and outlooks. State and federal governments began to increase the number and range of services to help people and families provide for, educate and train their children.

The United Nations introduced the Declaration of Rights of the Mentally Retarded in 1971, which required nations to introduce their own parallel legislation. Ten years later the UN declared 1981 to be the Year of the Disabled. In the 1980s, Australia began to introduce legislation that outlawed discrimination against people with intellectual disabilities. New parents groups sprang up to advocate for their children, disabled people began to advocate for themselves and a disability rights movement was born. A key moment in this history was in 1986, when the AIHP replaced the DIH as a separate and independent body. Some began to argue that disabled people had become just one part of a new world of diversity and inclusion.

The speed at which the process of deinstitutionalisation took hold in Australia was astonishing. But how successful has it been? The answer: 'depends'. Report after report has found that the situation of people with mental illnesses remains dire and that the promises of governments to fully fund a complete system of community care hasn't happened. The *Burdekin Report* of 1993 found that the human rights of mentally ill people were constantly breached: homelessness, imprisonment, unmet needs, funding shortfalls, serious neglect and lack of services continued to prevail. The hoped for support and inclusion by the general public hadn't happened either. Incredibly, reports today say the same thing. Yet lest we think that deinstitutionalisation was a mistake, when patients in those hospitals were asked by Burdekin where they would rather be, they invariably said 'In the community'.

The deinstitutionalisation of people with intellectual disabilities worked better but perhaps this is because their situation was so dire. Parents of Claremont's adults weren't thrilled when their children were moved out, as they hadn't been told it was going to happen and feared their children wouldn't cope in the community. Divisions surfaced between those who favoured different models of development. Programs in places such as Pyrton used controversial techniques and many hostels still resembled institutions. Some other crucial institutions such as schools were very slow in coming to the party. Divided responsibilities between state and federal governments caused problems and there was never enough money to provide all the services that people wanted and needed. Even though it would be hard to argue that the community had wholeheartedly included people with intellectual disabilities (unemployment is high, as is violence against them) there is no doubt that their lives today in practically every respect, would be unrecognisably better to people fifty years ago.

Cover of UWA student newspaper *Pelican* June 1971

30
Student Radicalism in the 1970s
Alexis Vassiley and Chris MacFarlane

The University of Western Australia (UWA) and the Western Australian Institute of Technology (WAIT, now Curtin) could not have been more different. The former, opened in 1911, a bastion of establishment conservatism, the other a mass, overcrowded College of Advanced Education (CAE) formed only in the 1960s. Yet at both campuses radical activists emerged wanting to change the world.

Established in 1966, WAIT was one of seven universities or CAE's built across the country in the 1960s as part of that decade's expansion of higher education. It was an isolated suburban campus set in the Perth suburb of Bentley, a site that was chosen after a section of the Collier Pine Plantation burnt down in the late 1950s. WAIT grew rapidly, from only 2000 students in 1966 to 10 000 ten years later. This rapid expansion, a certain rawness and some brutalist architecture, lent themselves to expressions of radicalism around social justice issues, while a lack of facilities caused grievances to arise.

UWA, by contrast, was and is an elite sandstone university. It is the sixth oldest university in Australia and was Western Australia's only university for six decades. Largely drawing its students from the middle and upper classes in Perth, its early expressions of radicalism were few and far between. In 1932, workers building the Reflection

Pond in front of Winthrop Hall, a beautiful old sandstone building with stain glassed windows and a metres high organ inside, went on strike; students became strike breakers by digging the hole themselves. To this day, that action is celebrated by UWA Guild presidents as a gesture of goodwill to the university, not condemned as undermining solidarity between students and workers. By the 1970s, as some faculties hired new, young, radical staff and radicalism penetrated the student population it had begun to change.

Together in the 1960s and 1970s, students at WAIT and UWA campaigned against the Vietnam war, supported the National Liberation Front, openly defied conscription, disrupted two apartheid South African sporting tours, opposed censorship, campaigned for women's and gay liberation, protected WA's native forests; many agitated for an end to capitalism and for a socialist future. Student activism was internationalist and national but it was also local as students sat in, occupied and disrupted their campuses to fight for initiatives such as student parking, longer library hours, lower food prices and, at UWA, an underpass under Stirling Highway.

This activism can partly be explained in the context of the worldwide flowering of political and industrial activism in the 1960s and 1970s. *National U*, the newspaper of the Australian Union of Students (AUS) wrote in 1968 about 'the year of rage': the student–worker rebellions that rocked France, the Tet offensive in Vietnam, the Prague Spring, the uprisings in the USA and revolts in numerous other countries. It asserted that 'overseas inspiration has fused new energy … into Australian student activism, nevertheless, it is local conditions that provide the basis for student hostility and frustration'.

At home in 1969, Left wing unions defeated the federal Liberal government's anti-strike penal powers with a nationwide strike against the gaoling of tramways union official Clarrie O'Shea. This began a period of working class militancy. Frequent union strike actions won big gains, and the workers' movement intersected with student militancy and social movements. This period saw a rejuvenation of and reorientation on the Left. The Communist Party of Australia became more open, moving away from its previously unquestioning loyalty to the Soviet Union. A youthful New Left emerged, socialist in orientation but critical of Moscow as well as Western capitalism. After the Sino–Soviet split in 1963, many adopted Chinese communism. Others became Trotskyists or anarchists. In the early 1970s at UWA, a large broad Left centred around the Guild and Labor Club. Peter Boyle founded the (Trotskyist) Socialist Youth Alliance in 1974. At WAIT from the early to mid 1970s, Maoists had a strong influence in the Student Guild and *Grok*, an important student newspaper.

The campus press was an important mouthpiece for student radicals through the 1960s and 1970s. The pages of UWA's *Pelican* and Curtin's *Grok* quickly became reflections and promoters of campus radicalism. In Sydney, a June 1972 conference of student newspaper editors, including the editor of *Grok* Rod Cole, set out what it regarded as the role of the student press, which was to 'give priority to information of a consciousness raising nature', as well as to 'consider [the student press] as an important instrument for radical change … and highlight the sickness of the entire system'. Regular columns by socialist feminists, communists and anarchists graced the pages of *Grok* every year between 1972 and 1976. At UWA, 1973 *Pelican* editor Rene Le Miere wrote: 'Students have both the opportunity and the need to mount a radical protest – a protest against the whole – not just some feature of society.'

For campus radicals and many others, the brutal war in Vietnam epitomised all that was rotten about the system. As historian and former student activist Mick Armstrong wrote in 2001, it was 'the cause [that] mobilised a generation of radicals ... [that] symbolised the irrationality and inhumanity of capitalism'. Students organised and took part in many demonstrations against the war, including the three big moratorium marches in 1970 and 1971, which they also attempted to radicalise by staging sit downs and breakaway marches in the city. At the 1971 moratorium march, 500 students staged a protest outside the offices of the *West Australian*, a strong supporter of the war.

UWA and WAIT student guilds, *Pelican* and *Grok*, became centres of draft resistance. Conscription – the draft – meant that twenty year old men would have their names drawn in a birthday ballot for compulsory conscription in the Australian army, which, for some, culminated in active service in Vietnam. Students formed the Draft Resisters Union. Members felt that conscientious objection, where conscripted young men would apply for an exemption on the basis of conscience, accepted the legitimacy of the law. A 1972 article in *Grok* described this process as 'merely an escape clause for the individual [that] in no way resists the draft'. Instead, they argued, it actively 'helps to maintain conscription by making it [appear] superficially fair and respectable'. By contrast, draft resisters openly defied the law, attempting, in the words of one *Pelican* cover, to 'Smash the Draft'.

Radical WAIT student activists distributed anti-conscription literature, encouraged students to publicly resist the draft and openly supported the Vietnamese fighters of the National Liberation Front (NLF). Activists also advocated filling in 'falsies', false draft cards that would help frustrate the system. Students harassed police who came onto campus in search of draft resisters. In 1972 WAIT Student Guild's welfare department and *Grok* put out a special appeal for funds to provide draft resisters a place to hide. The front page of a 1973 *Grok* issue depicted armed fighters declaring victory of the people and the army in the south.

At UWA, 1970 Guild Public Affairs Officer Bill Thomas went to jail for a week, and then went underground for a year to avoid National Service. *Pelican* pledged in 1971 to 'actively support, aid and abet all acts of resistance to the obscenity of the draft'. These words were attributed to the staff of *Pelican* as editor Derek Schapper had himself gone underground to avoid the draft. Every issue of *Pelican* that year carried an advertisement inviting students to the Guild reception for advice on conscientious objection or draft resistance. Then, on Orientation Day 1972, Peter Boyle recalled that

> The Army Reserve tried to set up a recruiting stall and brought in a van, but it was quickly surrounded by large numbers of us shouting antiwar slogans ... [Then] someone/some people let the air out of the tyres ... and it was abandoned for the day. The effective rule of the day was no military or police on campus.

Another incident involving UWA students illustrates the depth of feeling over the war and conscription. In a 1991 interview UWA activist Rupert Gerritsen, revealed that in 1972 he planted a bomb inside the St Georges Terrace offices of the Department of Labour and National Service, which administered the conscription system, to destroy the files containing details of eligible youths. Not wanting to hurt anyone, he programmed the bomb to explode in the early hours of 24 August 1972, but when it didn't, a friend anonymously tipped off authorities. Arrested, Gerritsen skipped bail and fled to New Zealand, but was found, extradited, convicted and served a year in Fremantle Prison. Another UWA activist, Julian Ripley, was allegedly framed for the bombing. Rene Le Miere, in a *Pelican* article entitled 'Ripley is innocent', wrote that the jury that convicted Ripley relied on a confession made in the presence of Detective Robert 'Bob' Kucera (later WA Assistant Police Commissioner and subsequently a minister in the state Labor government) – a confession that was not witnessed, not made in the presence of a lawyer, and which Ripley denied making. According to Le Miere, Ripley's fingerprints were not found on the bomb, whereas Gerritsen's were; in fact Ripley was working in Midland at the time the bomb was allegedly planted. In that 1991 interview Gerritsen further alleged that 'They threatened to throw him [Ripley] out of the fourth storey unless he signed a statement which they prepared for him'. Ripley was sentenced to five years imprisonment and his supporters have never managed to clear his name. A poster campaign with the slogan 'Kucera lied, Free Ripley' was conducted in vain.

Fighting apartheid in South Africa was another major cause. In 1971, students played a role in the Perth leg of national demonstrations against the Springbok rugby tour, which featured an all white South African rugby team. Activities included a public debate, leafleting and a demonstration outside the hotel housing the team and a sports stadium. The Springboks tour was heavily disrupted across the country and was the last South African team to visit Australia because the Whitlam government banned sporting tours in 1972. They didn't return until the fall of apartheid.

Extending the campaign against apartheid, the June 1971 Apartheid issue of *Pelican* urged students to boycott 'Polaroid apartheid'. Polaroid cameras were used to manufacture UWA student cards and South Africa's notorious pass cards, which restricted the freedom of movement of non-white people. In solidarity with the anti-apartheid campaign, which called for a boycott of South African businesses, the UWA Student Guild in 1979 banned the sale of Rothmans cigarettes on campus. Rothmans International formed part of the large South African-based multinational Rembrandt group of companies.

When student radicals were confronted with the reality of Aboriginal people's lives in Australia, they realised that apartheid did not occur only in South Africa. Aboriginal people were not allowed into a number of Perth nightclubs, so boycotts were organised in protest. In 1969, then UWA Guild Aboriginal Affairs Officer Charles Poynton organised a novel protest action. A local building merchant had gained permission to mine and sell a red and white stone that was sacred to the local Aboriginal community. The community lost a court appeal that would have resulted in the mining permit being withdrawn. The Guild then successfully applied for a permit to mine sand, limestone and gravel and proceeded to peg out their claim over the Kings Park war memorial. After the ensuing controversy, the builder's mining permit was revoked.

Pelican carried articles condemning apartheid in WA towns, as well as celebrating the famous Aboriginal Tent Embassy protests outside Canberra's Parliament House in 1972. *Grok* carried similar articles, with many after 1975 targeting the gutting of Aboriginal services by the Fraser government, while others covered local protests for housing and land rights. As a result of student campaigning UWA introduced Aboriginal studies units.

The UWA Guild established a Race Relations Department in the early 1970s and alongside local Nyungar activists, quickly set to work on campaigns for Aboriginal land rights. A similar portfolio was established at the WAIT Guild, with two workers employed to do fieldwork among the Aboriginal and Papua New Guinea communities. In 1979 students supported the Noonkanbah Aboriginal community's attempt to stop oil exploration on their land in the Kimberley region of WA. Police arrested student activists at an occupation of the responsible company's office in St Georges Terrace.

Student support for international causes extended well beyond the campaigns against the Vietnam war and apartheid. In late 1972 the WAIT Guild passed a motion supporting the Palestinian resistance, stating its 'belief that the Palestinian Arabs have a right to regain the territory taken from them over 70 years by the Zionist movement'.

WAIT was home to a number of international students, many of them from Malaysia. Debates concerning the legacy of British colonialism in the country and the need for democracy were common in *Grok*. The WAIT Guild also grappled with the question of how to include international students in campus politics and activism, given that some students feared reprisals when they returned home. Eventually, a proposal that the Guild Council should appoint an international student representative in order to circumvent the risks posed by students nominating for a position and standing in an election was narrowly passed at a Guild meeting.

Students also participated in demonstrations against the Indonesian invasion and occupation of Timor Leste (East Timor). These demonstrations took place under the threat of repression by the Court Liberal state government, which had passed legislation outlawing public meetings in Forrest Place. So police laid charges against two activists for posting signs to promote a demonstration and against five others for addressing a public meeting without police permission. (The government banned all meetings in WA in early 1976.) Also, in 1975, a UWA Guild general meeting voted to grant 10 cents per member to an appeal for a printing press for African liberation group ZANU in Rhodesia (now Zimbabwe). The money was donated and the press was purchased, but was allegedly confiscated by government troops within a week of arrival in Rhodesia.

The student Left also led the charge on gay liberation in Western Australia. In 1973, *Pelican* carried a five page 'Gay Front' supplement announcing the formation of a Campaign Against Moral Persecution (CAMP) university society, more radical and activist than the central CAMP organisation that had been set up in Perth in 1971 and explicitly seeking liberation. It condemned the WA Labor government because it had reneged on its promise to repeal laws against gay sex, and because Labor Premier John Tonkin remarked that homosexuality 'made him sick'. It described extreme oppression for homosexuals in Perth, 'where few venture out' and 'the majority remain fixed to the idea that they are sick individuals'. The following year the UWA Guild Council backed homosexual law reform, while in 1979 it established a Homosexual Information Office (now the Queer Department) and held the first Gay Pride week.

Students such as the Socialist Women group at WAIT took part in the women's liberation movement. Eager to draw links between women's liberation and other struggles for social justice, in 1975 activists invited African American civil rights advocate and feminist activist Florynce Kennedy and London-based cleaner and union activist May Hobbs to campus. At UWA, socialist student Deb Shnookal described university as 'an institution maintaining and perpetuating the capitalist status quo' and argued that the family was the source of women's oppression. In 1974 a collective of UWA feminists set up *Sybil*, the radical feminist journal that, over the next nine years, discussed a vast array of feminist issues. The dominance of men in student politics was one of these; indeed, the first female Guild president at UWA, Sue Boyd, was elected only in 1968. In 1975 Guild Council and AUS established a Department of Women's Affairs.

Pelican articles campaigned for legal abortion, not available in WA until 1998.

Environmental campaigns also featured prominently at the two universities. In 1975, WAIT students joined the Campaign to Save Native Forests, established to challenge the clear felling of forests around Manjimup. Over the decade long process nearly 375 000 acres of native Karri forest would disappear, reduced to wood chips for use in the manufacture of paper and cheap furniture. Students stressed to workers the importance of the forests and natural spaces, arguing that 'Workers need these natural spaces and national parks for social activity and relaxation'. They were also quick to counter the companies' claims that reducing overcutting would result in job losses, arguing that the same companies were already undermining conditions by 'looking to import workers during a period of high unemployment'. This argument paid off when the WA Trades and Labour Council joined the campaign in 1976. Students welcomed the union support, writing, 'It is apparent that the union action offers the only real hope of confronting the powerful and vested interests which are destroying the public forests for private profit'.

Students also fought censorship, campaigning against bans on books such as *The Marijuana Papers* and *Portnoy's Complaint* but the threat of censorship also hung over the heads of student newspaper editors. *Pelican* was censored every year between 1969 and 1973. The September 1969 issue, dedicated to the cause of free speech, featured a banned poster of a local production of *Othello* on its cover as well as explicit passages from *Lady Chatterley's Lover* inside. Consequently, editor Alistair MacKinlay and the Guild were convicted of 'making an obscene publication'. The October 1973 issue of *Pelican* also faced censorship. Featuring illustrations of naked anthropomorphic creatures the issue eventually had to be printed in Melbourne after Perth printers, the Independent Newspapers, who had reserved their right to censor any material that was, in their opinion, libellous or obscene, refused to print it.

Student activism was not confined only to issues of social justice. Many student radicals found the skills they had learnt off campus could be used just as effectively on it. One of the earliest successes was at UWA in 1969. During peak hour on 29 March hundreds of students staged a sit-in on Stirling Highway to demand an underpass be built after two students had been killed crossing the road. The underpass was completed eighteen months later and remains open today.

WAIT students also enjoyed success with the sit-in tactic. In 1971, activists organised successful sit-ins at the library and the administration foyer to force WAIT to extend library opening hours. Buoyed by their success with the library campaign, they then organised a sit-in at and boycott against a price hike at the local cafeteria, Joe's Caf, the following year. The cafeteria backed down on an immediate price rise and had to enter into negotiations with the student guild. Rod Cole wrote in *Grok*: 'Solidarity expressed in the caf boycott has reinforced student confidence in direct actions as a means to gaining their aims for a better deal for students.'

Throughout 1971 and 1972 the segregation of campus parking at WAIT came under fire from a sustained campaign by students. Parking was determined by a parking committee, with four members representing staff (a broad mix of academics, management and workers) and two students. This inequitable committee was charged with forcing students to the periphery of campus while claiming the best spots for staff.

In 1972 the Guild Welfare Committee launched the Open Parking

Campaign, recommending that students employ 'radical action as a method of exposing the injustice' of the parking system. Students were encouraged to park in staff bays and parking signs were blanked out. When the Institute repaired the signs, students tore them out of the ground. The Academic Staff Association claimed that segregated parking was the privilege of senior staff and academics; its opposition was so strong that when protesters occupied the administration building to force a decision on the matter, the staff shut the parking committee down. This removed the students' only avenue for communications. Eventually, student tenacity won out. When threatened with the campaign restarting the next year the Institute was forced to make concessions to students.

Throughout the 1960s and 1970s radical students at UWA and WAIT joined millions of others around the world to collectively shape history. They were very consciously part of a wider national and international movement. Drawing on radical politics and inspired by events elsewhere, they made an important contribution to struggles for social change, struggles that reshaped Australian society. Student unions and the student presses played an important role in organising and carrying the arguments for these actions at a time when the *West Australian* still called Indigenous people 'natives', rape in marriage was still not illegal, police entrapped gay men, people could not read what they wanted, and the Vietnam war raged on. Yet the vision of a truly liberated society driving many of the radicals of yesteryear is just as relevant now as it was then. Today's radicals can look to the past for inspiration for the many causes they need to rally around.

Cover of UWA student newspaper *Pelican* August 1971

Around the Cauldron cover page. Published by Wimin's Liberation Press, 1980.

31
Wimin Writing: Perth's Radical Feminist Publications
Bri McKenzie

It has long been suggested that second wave feminism skipped Perth altogether. It will come as no surprise to readers of this book, however, that Perth had a vibrant radical feminist movement during the 1970s and 1980s. The legacies of this period of women's activism included significant and lasting changes to state legislation on abortion and the passing of equal opportunity laws. Perth feminists were also instrumental in setting up health and support services for women across the state and, through the Women's Electoral Lobby (WEL), were central in campaigning for better representation of women in state parliament, on boards and in the judiciary.

But Perth's radical feminists left behind another legacy, one that emphasises the important steps made during the 1970s and 1980s towards a radical reimagining of wimin's place in the world. A significant part of their work was in awareness raising and in challenging themselves and others to deeply explore feminist ideas.

Enter the radical feminist magazine. While Perth's feminists, working both as on the ground campaigners and as femocrats in the state government did much to improve the provision of services for WA women, they also provided an outlet for radical feminist thought and discussion through their magazines and newsletters. During this period, Perth's feminists produced three important publications that added to the radical history of the city: *Liberation Information, Sibyl* and *Around the Cauldron*. These publications provide a rich commentary on radical feminist thought and help to highlight the work of Perth's feminists in bringing about social change.

The women's movement in Perth during the 1970s was broadly organised into two groups – the more conservative collectives that ultimately formed into the WA branch of the WEL and the more radical women's liberation groups. The radical feminist ideas held by members of these latter groups were distinct from traditional feminism in a number of important respects. For radical feminists of the 1970s gender was the defining factor in determining social, political, economic and physical disadvantage. Importantly, gender was considered more significant than class or race in understanding the oppression of individuals. Unlike traditional feminists, who generally focused on the importance of women's mothering role, radical feminists identified the family as the primary site of women's subjugation to men. This was borne out quite starkly across Australia at the time through a feminist focus on domestic violence and the provision of the first refuges for women and children who wanted to escape violent relationships. Nowhere was the new feminism's catch cry, 'The personal is political', more relevant than in these first efforts to shine a light on domestic violence. The new feminism also differed from feminist campaigns of the past because it had a dual purpose: to not only agitate for the better provision of services for women, but also to change society itself.

The 1970s was a time of great excitement and change for Australian women. The feminist movement of this decade was born out of the growing discontent of white middle class women, trapped in the paradox of domesticity and the desire for full time work. Domestic arrangements, lack of childcare and social expectations limited women's ability to gain access to the job market at the same time as more women were graduating from universities and looking for work. It was obvious that systemic change was necessary. Women's issues began to come to prominence at government level through the agitation of early feminist groups who campaigned for better access to childcare, equal opportunity legislation and a broader range of women's health services.

The election of the Whitlam government in 1972 added a sense of enthusiasm and expectation to the Australian feminist movement. In Perth, the change in government was received with great excitement. In a 1990 interview, author Dorothy Goodrick recalled:

> It was like take off! Suddenly here were all these exciting creative ways of looking at a whole range of issues that had been damped down or closeted for years. It was like a breath of fresh air being let into the portals of Parliament.

For Dot Goodrick and other Perth feminists of the time, the change in Canberra would have a significant effect on their ability to put their plans for change into action. Suddenly, there was more money available to fund women's health initiatives and allowances such as the single mother's pension became available for the first time. With domestic violence on the agenda and the introduction of the *Family Law Act*, it became easier for women to leave violent relationships. The new prime minister employed a women's adviser, Elizabeth Reid, who visited Perth in 1974 and inspired the local women's groups to set up the Women's Centre Action Group that went on to found Perth's first women's refuge, which was run on radical feminist principles. In 1975 during the UN's International Women's Year, the federal government established a Women's Year Secretariat. Staffed entirely by feminists, the secretariat distributed federal grants to women's organisations across the country.

It is within this context that Perth's radical feminist groups formed and began their efforts to raise the status of women's issues in the state. Perth Women's Liberation was one of the earliest groups to start campaigning. Established in 1971 and working with the motto 'We're all experts – every one of us can teach the rest, and all can learn', the group held regular weekly meetings at a house on Rokeby Road, Subiaco. Perth Women's Liberation was the first of Perth's radical feminist collectives to put out a publication, the newsletter *Liberation Information*. Produced on and off between March 1972 and May 1975, the newsletter provided women with information about Perth's feminist movement and contained articles on sexist products and advertising, planned feminist agitations around the city and recommended product boycotts. But the newsletter also involved its readers in deeper existential discussions about the nature of feminism and what it truly meant to identify as a radical feminist. The September 1973 edition, for example, challenged its readers to look beyond women's mere equality with men and question underlying patriarchal structures that placed objective value on maleness:

> Liberation implies freedom *from* an oppressor or an oppressively structured society. If woman frees herself by becoming man's equal, surely she is reinforcing all male values. And so it must become important for us to question the values to which so many of us aspire.

This was a common theme running through much of the radical feminist literature of the time. It reflected a radical ideology that challenged women to see their own complicity in perpetuating the patriarchy by merely seeking 'equality'. Indeed, the man question was something that created much debate within feminist circles everywhere at the time and Perth Women's Liberation was no different. The October/November 1973 edition of *Liberation Information* detailed a long discussion in which members debated the merits of allowing men to attend their meetings. Some members felt that when men came to meetings the quieter women remained silent while the more confident women engaged in loud debates with their male counterparts. Mike Miller, the lone male contributor to the newsletter, understood the need for women only meetings but noted that he hated being shut out. Debate on the issue was ongoing with no ultimate decision being reached.

One of the more humorous anecdotes to come out of the September 1973 issue of *Liberation Information* was a report on a protest held in that month by members outside the Perth Concert Hall. The Miss Australia Quest was an ideal forum for radical feminist resistance, so thirty-five members of Perth Women's Liberation, adorned in fancy dress, picketed the entrance to the event and distributed pamphlets to attendees. Some of the protesters held placards proclaiming 'I would like to be in the Miss Australia Quest, but I'm too ugly' or 'I'm Aboriginal'. On another occasion, in the wake of the rejection of an abortion Bill in federal parliament, Perth Women's Liberation members produced pamphlets on family planning and contraception and distributed them outside city high schools. The issue also recalled the media reaction to members of the group who they labelled 'disciples of Satan' and 'wolves in lamb's clothing'. Newspapers suggested the collective had produced sex pamphlets and accused them of pushing sex onto young people.

Broader public (and, indeed, government) reaction to Perth's women's liberation collectives was a reflection of the groups' radical agendas. There was very little understanding at that time of women's issues within the broader community, which resulted in a corresponding enmity towards women who spoke out against the established order. Radical feminists were understood by many a Western Australian to be sex obsessed, lesbian, man haters bent on ruining traditional families. As late as 1977, by which time Perth's feminist movement was firmly established, the WEL was in full swing, Perth-based action groups had strong links with Canberra, and WA Premier Charles Court was still supported in his traditional view, stated in a radio interview at the time, that the recipe for a successful marriage was a tolerant and patient wife.

For some members of Perth's Women's Liberation Movement, drawing attention to and deconstructing the sentiments of men such as Premier Charles Court was one of their most powerful tools. This was the approach taken in the first issue of Perth's first radical feminist magazine, *Sibyl*. Under the title 'Words on Women', the magazine pulled apart the writings of Nietzsche, and others, making a powerful statement about the power of the female intellect.

Distributed by a women's collective run out of The University of Western Australia, *Sibyl* started life in June 1974 as a pamphlet that discussed topics similar to those in *Liberation Information*. By the 1980s *Sibyl* had grown, into a well-known glossy magazine that looked more deeply at international feminist issues and had a distinctly academic feel. Collective members were drawn from the female undergraduate and graduate populations of the university. The group worked together to type, print and collate the magazine. *Sibyl* was produced quarterly, its last edition appearing in spring 1983.

Many of *Sibyl's* early contributors went on to become significant Western Australian feminist agitators and legislators. One of the magazine's early editors and collective coordinator Anne Giles was the daughter of prominent WEL member, women's activist and later Australian senator Pat Giles. Anne's co-editor Marcelle Anderson later became head of the Department of Premier and Cabinet under Western Australia's first female premier, Carmen Lawrence. Between 1974 and 1983 the magazine boasted contributions from prominent feminists such as Irene Greenwood, Maureen Davies, Dot Goodrick and Pat Giles.

Topics covered in *Sibyl* over its nine year history highlight this diversity. In 1975 alone the magazine examined a huge range of issues within the broader sphere of feminist interests, including the politics of rape, intrauterine devices, women and the law, family planning, Australian women's history, the Christian Women's Association, homosexuality, sex discrimination, abortion, women and doctors, childcare workers and the lives of Palestinian women. The magazine also contained book and product reviews, recommendations for how to avoid sexist language in speech and writing, poetry, artwork, cartoons and even critiques of radical feminism. Such variety was representative of the wide range of issues Perth's radical feminists were involved with during the 1970s and 1980s.

Sibyl is interesting on a number of fronts. It was Perth's longest running feminist magazine and appears to have been the magazine with the biggest readership and most diverse group of contributors. It was certainly a magazine with a broad outlook because it regularly looked to international developments in feminism and women's rights as well as covering the activities of the more mainstream of Perth's women's organisations like the WEL and Christian Women's Association. But in a subtle way, *Sibyl* also highlighted a number of important differences between the ideologies of Perth's women's liberation collectives, which can be seen in the shift to the use of the feminist term 'wimin'. Radical feminists of the 1970s often rejected the word 'women' because of its apparent derivative status from the word 'men'. The social custom of defining females and femininity with reference to a male norm was something that radical feminists fought against; challenging the use of male normative language conventions was one powerful way to draw attention to patriarchal power structures. Contributors to *Sibyl* thus occasionally toyed with the use of alternative terms such as wimin in their writing. This shift in language usage was not universal, neither within the group of *Sibyl* contributors nor within the Perth radical feminist movement as a whole. Indeed, writers to *Liberation Information* never used the term 'wimin' and persisted with 'woman' and 'women' throughout the publication's history.

In this respect, Perth's other radical feminist publication took a decidedly different approach. What stands out most about *Around the Cauldron: A Perth Wimin's Liberation Magazine*, is its purposeful and consistent dedication to the higher ideals of radical feminism. Through its title, the magazine shows a commitment to the contemporary nomenclature of radical feminism and an emphasis on the localness of feminist resistance: it was a Perth wimin's liberation magazine. Unlike *Sibyl* and *Liberation Information, Around the Cauldron* consistently used the term wimin in its articles (not the alternative spelling) and, in a rejection of organisational hierarchies, no one individual was selected for special mention such as might be expected for a magazine editor, for example. All contributors were identified only by their first name, another form of resistance to conventional labels of ownership and possession.

Published only once (in 1980), *Around the Cauldron* took seven months to produce because it had to be funded by donations from collective members and fundraising dances. When it was finally published, *Around the Cauldron* tapped into the mystical aspects of feminist thought. It was a revolutionary publication with anarchist overtones that read as a call to arms at a time when some Perth women worried that the feminist revolution may never happen. The magazine thus walked a fine line between espousing radical ideologies and expressing the power and pain of being a woman in 1980s Perth. It was not unusual for the magazine to feature articles on feminist witchcraft next to an exposé of class inequity in Perth's housing market. Sad and emotive feminist poetry featured prominently alongside rousing commentaries on lesbian separatism and the mistreatment of women by the media.

Very little is known about the group of women who produced *Around the Cauldron,* but its publisher is listed as the Wimin's Liberation Press. It was certainly a magazine produced by women for women (its cover features the comment 'For Women Only') and it published ideas that were truly radical, even by the standards of the time. Many Australian feminists who agitated and campaigned during the 1970s and 1980s held a highly deterministic view towards men and maleness based on a central understanding that men and women were different and that, at core, men were bad and women good. Within this discourse, radical feminism understood the world as being run by bad men and espoused an ideological position that located men and women as opposing combatants in an endless fight. Not all feminists adopted these ideas and even radical feminists varied in their attitudes to men and the patriarchy. Thus while *Liberation Information* challenged the limits of seeking mere female male equality, *Around the Cauldron* sought to highlight what its authors felt was the true extent of male power and dominance over women. In an article titled 'Rape from the perspective of wimin's liberation', the author suggests that 'All men reap the rewards of rape and all men must therefore be complicit in the crime'.

Such suggestions were – and continue to be – challenging. Members of the WEL and many other feminists were not comfortable with the idea that all men, by their nature, were rapists, as was first suggested by an American feminist. But Perth's radical feminist movement was diverse; its newsletters and magazines offer a glimpse into this diversity, showcasing the breadth and depth of feminist thought in the city during this period. The publications have also been influential in the contemporary context. Radical anarchist magazines such as Perth's *Avenue* follow in the footsteps of *Around the Cauldron* and *Sibyl* and show a marked similarity in their presentation and ideas. Indeed, Perth's radical feminist magazines appear to be localised versions of international publications such as the UK feminist magazine *Spare Rib* and eastern states publications such as *Scarlet Woman* and *Vashti's Voice*. Thus *Liberation Information*, *Sibyl* and *Around the Cauldron* were part of the national and international cultural shift that sought to reimagine wimin's place in the world. These unique publications are a physical record of the thoughts and experiences of the women involved in Perth's radical feminist movement. As such they are artefacts of a radical past not often appreciated or fully understood.

32
Hope in the Wasteland: East Perth City Farm
Andrea Gaynor

In an awkward little corner of the city, wedged between carparks and train tracks, lies the East Perth City Farm. Unsurprisingly, it's an unconventional farm. Focused on growing people and sustainability amid the instability of boom and bust Perth, the farm's crops and livestock have been symbols as well as tools for its educational and community development aims. While forming part of a vision of inner city renewal in a deindustrialised landscape, since 1993 it has kept gathering the resources to drive its own education and sustainability agenda, bending government schemes to its own ends and generating revenue through conventional and unconventional means. In doing so easy categorisation has eluded it and challenged us to rethink what a city can – and should – be. In 1996 farm manager Neal Bodel told a journalist: 'When we first started people said, "You can't grow food in the city", but we begged to differ.'

East Perth had previously combined an industrial district and largely working class residential suburb, but during the 1970s industry had moved out and by the 1980s East Perth was widely seen by outsiders as a derelict post-industrial wasteland. Residents, including those in twelve hostels in the area, were generally poor and marginalised: Aboriginal people, the homeless and alcohol affected, and women escaping domestic violence. The land, too, was damaged, with some serious contamination a legacy of prior industrial occupants.

In 1983, the newly elected Burke state Labor government established an Urban Lands Council to investigate the redevelopment of East Perth. The resulting detailed reports reflected a vision of a diverse and vibrant inner city community, an urban village that would include public housing while capitalising on the area's prime riverfront land.

The East Perth Project Outline Development Plan was released for comment in 1990. The following year, the federal Labor government of Bob Hawke established the Building Better Cities Program, which sought economic efficiency, sustainability and social justice through better planning and coordination of urban development. East Perth was one of its waterfront rebirth area strategies, funded to the tune of $31 million. In 1992 Carmen Lawrence's Labor government established the East Perth Redevelopment Authority (EPRA) to undertake the project. Its forward thinking operations manager was Reuben Kooperman. Among his ideas for innovative land uses in East Perth was a city farm, though he was yet to find a group to take it up.

At the same time, in the early 1990s, sustainability exponents Roseanne Geddes and Chris Ferreira were running a group called Planetary Action Network, the youth wing of Men of the Trees (MOTT). Founded in Kenya in 1922, MOTT was an international organisation dedicated to the planting and protection of trees. A branch established in Western Australia in 1979 operated a nursery in Hazelmere dedicated to growing and providing tube stock trees to farmers and gardeners. Roseanne had joined MOTT in 1989 and in the early 1990s she and Chris began to run Landcare and Environment Action Programs (LEAP), which funded long term unemployed youth to undertake literacy, numeracy and environmental skills training programs. They hoped to not only provide education, but also to boost motivation and self-esteem.

One of those young people was Neal Bodel. Fresh from the forest blockades in the deep southwest of the state, Neal was looking for a way to create positive change. As part of Roseanne's LEAP program he completed a Permaculture Design Certificate with Linda Grigg, then completed a Greenskills Landcare and Communication course in Boyup Brook before returning to the city. During his time at the MOTT nursery, Neal, along with his comrade Clayton Chipper, had talked with Roseanne about the idea of a city garden that would grow and produce food for an onsite soup kitchen. This and other conversations encouraged Roseanne to write to a range of businesses and organisations about the city farm idea.

One of those letters landed on the desk of Mike Toobey, an architect with EPRA; he took it to Reuben, who met with Chris and Roseanne and talked to their students about urban renewal. Chris, Roseanne, Neal and Clayton subsequently wrote up a proposal for EPRA, who in late 1993 agreed to lease the old Vacuum Oil Co. premises to MOTT for a peppercorn rental for two years while more permanent plans for the 3100 square metre site were made. Neal and Clayton were the first managers. They moved in and lived on the site in very basic conditions among industrial detritus from December 1993.

This part of East Perth hosted office workers and students by day but by night it was deserted and unsafe. Neal kept an axe handle under his bed and one night used it to intervene in an attempted sexual assault taking place on the lot next door. It was a challenging setting for an exercise in building community and sustainability.

A city farm was, by this time, not a novel idea. While there were long

Andrea Gaynor's partner Jamie Moir with an Australian game fowl

traditions of productive urban gardening in many parts of the world, the city farm as a deliberate strategy to ameliorate a range of urban ills was a twentieth century phenomenon. Farm gardens were established in New York City from 1902 to expose children to the reforming influence of nature and impart productive skills. The Scandinavian countries in the early twentieth century established animation farms and city farms with the aim of bringing children, teenagers and adults together in a healthy farm environment where they could learn through physical interaction with plants and animals. Enthusiasm for the city farm idea increased in the wake of the twin postwar processes of rapid urbanisation and industrialisation of agriculture, and the rise of modern environmentalism. In the Netherlands, a children's farm movement emerged amid concerns over children's diminishing knowledge of where their food comes from. The first city farm in an English-speaking country was established in Kentish Town, London, in 1972 by a group called Inter-Action, which also had interests in experimental theatre and community development. The first city farm in Australia, Collingwood Children's Farm, was established in 1979 to enable inner city children to have contact with nature and farm animals.

A consistent thread in the history of urban agriculture has been the value of the positive influence of nature on human character, and the East Perth City Farm proposal was no exception. But first, nature had to be returned to the site. This was no small undertaking for a site that had previously served as a tram workshop and foundry and in 1993 was still a functioning scrap metal yard. Much of the site was covered in thick concrete paving and most of the exposed soil was heavily contaminated. While EPRA paid for remediation works, Neal and Clayton were responsible for establishing the extent of contamination. They took surface and 1 metre subsurface samples into a lab for analysis; the results included lead levels more than 800 times the maximum safe limit. The warehouses were full of salvaged machinery, pipes, wood, old carpet and lost things. Researchers from UWA came out with Geiger counters after it was reported that radioactive copper salvaged from the Montebello Islands by crayfish fishers had been stored on the site (fortunately no radiation hazard was found). An environmental audit was completed and a bulldozer took 1 metre of soil off the top of the entire garden site to the west of the compound, revealing the sterile white sand below. Once it passed a leachate test, the gardening could begin.

City Farm, in association with Midland TAFE, started running LEAP courses in early 1994. The students worked with Neal and Clayton to establish garden beds in used tyres in the main compound and transform the cluttered and dilapidated buildings into useful spaces for working, learning and playing. For many of the students this was an opportunity to make their mark as part of an exciting new project while developing some useful networks and skills; for a few, particularly in later LEAP programs, it just seemed like forced labour. All of the first LEAP participants went on to work or further education, as did the majority of later participants. Some were inspired by City Farm's example and went on to do social and environmental work, others took their new sense of purpose and confidence into unrelated careers. Over time the list of city farmers grew to include people on community service orders, truancy and rehabilitation programs, and disabled adults and children. Volunteers – myself included – joined in on weekends.

After ten months the site was looking much greener. Though the interior was, as journalist Alison Farmer put it 'shabby in the extreme', this detracted little from 'the atmosphere of harmony that permeates the farm'. Other changes were also taking place. Neal and Clayton had noticed that new graffiti pieces would appear overnight. One night they awoke to the sound of cans being rattled and sprayed, so they went out to talk with the redecorators. This was the start of an urban art program at the farm. Local street artist Stormie Mills lined up support; a grant from the Urban Art Fund paid for the paint used by the emerging street artists for their pieces on the farm's abundant

City Farm gardens showing graffiti on wall

wall space. Some of the artists, drawn in by the farm's passion for sustainability, in time ended up completing permaculture courses.

I took an eye opening job at the farm teaching literacy to LEAP students and helped obtain needed resources from the city and beyond, including a windmill donated by Wannamal farmer Tom King. My partner Jamie and I had completed Permaculture Design Certificates and had been developing an interest in purebred poultry that was outstripping the capacity of our small Highgate backyard. While chooks arrived early on the City Farm scene, we saw an opportunity to educate people about the dazzling variety of poultry available and how to choose a breed that was right for their situation. Using Jamie's welding skills we gradually built a large undercover area using materials salvaged from a North Fremantle urban redevelopment, and brought eggs and even goslings in from Jamie's aunt, Australian poultry guru Megg Miller. Our small business – Tomfowlery – ran poultry workshops, built mobile pens and supplied poultry to households all over the state, including heat tolerant Transylvanian Naked Necks to the Pilbara.

The farm also established a nursery that waxed and waned over time, serving to develop horticultural skills as well as some income. As the warehouses were tidied up, gigs, festivals and workshops added to the income stream. The eastern warehouse was divided up into studios and made available for rent to artists who, by the mid 1990s, included a painter, a dressmaker, a sculptor and a blacksmith, who became an important part of the City Farm community.

Working with troubled youth in an area that was still home to many damaged people meant that things didn't always go smoothly. There were thefts, discarded syringes, sporadic outbreaks of violence and vandalism. One night some malefactors got into the poultry yards, where they beat several birds to death and wounded others. Jamie and I sent our remaining birds to safer homes and left the farm, broken hearted. As in many small groups with big ambitions and few resources there were rivalries, disagreements and power plays, clashing visions and burnout. At times the cosiness became a pressure cooker. Neal left City Farm in 1996 to pursue youth and community mental health work. He took with him an environment award in the Young Australian of the Year Awards for his work at the farm. Thom Scott took over as farm manager.

City Farm's original two year lease was renewed but plans for another use for the site were emerging. In 1999 Thom and Roseanne were told that the farm would need to be wound up by mid 2000, when the site would accommodate the second wing of Central TAFE's Advanced Manufacturing Technology Centre. A group called the Save City Farm Action Group sprang up in defence of the farm, and Roseanne and Thom lobbied hard, with community and media support, to retain the East Perth site. In February 2000 their efforts were rewarded when Premier Richard Court and Minister for Employment and Training Mike Board announced that the lease would be extended for another two years while a new site for the farm was found. In 2002, the somewhat more green ALP government gave the farm a forty year peppercorn lease over much of the new site. The lesser used western section would later be developed for St Bartholomew's house, which provides accommodation and support for homeless men.

Further farm initiatives followed. A Saturday farmers' market was established in 2004 and in the following year the farm was awarded organic certification, a remarkable achievement given its highly contaminated beginnings. Venue hire became a more prominent part of the farm's activities and in 2010 long held plans to open a cafe on the site finally came to fruition. Continuing City Farm's education and training mission, the cafe was begun as an enterprise that provided training opportunities for TAFE work experience students and people with learning disabilities on work programs. In 2010 manager Luke Durcan said: 'We make it very clear that we are a not for profit organisation and are a training facility, and the customers are understanding, and very patient.' By 2017, the endeavour had evolved, with a new emphasis on local and ethical sourcing, including from the farm's own organic gardens.

In the wake of the redevelopment East Perth has been repopulated with a new class of city professionals and managers occupying upmarket apartments and townhouses. In 2000, a former Nyungar resident said, with forgivable overstatement, 'In the old days all you needed was two bob in your back pocket to live in East Perth. Now you need two million dollars.' In 2017 median house prices remained in the order of $1 million. In contrast to the established middle class western suburbs, only one-third of people living in East Perth were born in Australia. The redevelopment of East Perth admirably succeeded in capitalising on the real estate potential of waterfront property, though its commitment to social housing was watered down and its present diversity is more cultural than socioeconomic. In this context the City Farm, with its Work for the Dole labour and ramshackle ambiance, still occupies a liminal and somewhat challenging position, between reform and empowerment, money and ideals.

I wish to acknowledge Neal Bodel for sharing his memories and archival material from City Farm, and his comments on a draft of this chapter. Any errors or omissions are entirely my own.

33
The Pioneer Bookshop and *Portnoy's Complaint*
Geoff Davis

My first acquaintance with Perth's Pioneer Bookshop was in 1952 when, as a 16 year old new member of the Eureka Youth League, I took on the role of picking up the Communist Party newspaper *Tribune* for the customers of the CPA's Applecross Branch while on my way home from school. I was in what was then called Fourth Year of my studies at Perth Modern School in West Perth; the CPA office and bookshop were close to the bus stop to my new home in Applecross where we had moved earlier that year.

The Party headquarters, with the bookshop occupying one room, was on the third floor of London Court overlooking St Georges Terrace. I was fascinated by what I found there: magazines from the Soviet Union and counties of the Soviet bloc, and China, all kinds of CPA pamphlets, novels by Soviet writers and other favoured writers such as the American Howard Fast, works of the 'saints' – Marx, Engels, Lenin and Stalin – and all kinds of other materials that met the needs of CPA members, supporters and neophytes like me.

Although the Party was by then free from the threat of illegality after the failure of the Menzies government's 1951 attempt to ban it by changing the constitution, I cannot recall ever seeing many people there other than those I presumed to be CPA members and supporters. This was still the period of the Cold War and the anti-communist propaganda of the time would have frightened away prospective buyers of such material, so during my weekly visits I had plenty of time to chat with Connie Sideris, the comrade in charge. Connie was a Macedonian from Greece married to a building worker who was also a CPA member. From her I learnt a lot about the situation of Macedonians in Greece, including the ban on the use of the Macedonian language.

Early in 1954, the first visit of Queen Elizabeth to Perth was announced and it was decided that the bookshop (and the CPA headquarters) would be closed for the duration. The Party feared that its position overlooking the Terrace, along which the Queen might travel, could be a cause for some kind of provocation. Nothing happened, of course, and the premises reopened when things returned to normal.

As I was a very new and young CPA member I had no idea of Party finances or discussions in the following couple of years, especially as much of my time in 1956 and 1957 was spent away from Perth because I was working in a small town about 200 kilometres distant. But early in 1957 I learnt of plans to move the headquarters and bookshop to a new site. This was necessary as the premises in London Court was becoming too expensive to maintain. Dr Roy Stanton, a long time CPA member, had acquired a small and very old cottage on the corner of Bulwer and Stirling Streets that he was making available to the Party.

Members with suitable building skills, including my father, a bricklayer by trade, then set about the work of renovation that included the addition to the Bulwer Street frontage of a narrow room with plate glass windows to serve as the bookshop. Behind it were one large room suitable for small meetings where full time workers had

Communist Party Secretary John 'Rivo' Gandini selling copies of *Portnoy's Complaint* outside the Swanbourne Hotel

their desks, a small kitchen, a workroom for secretarial support and an office for the CPA state secretary. A small separate building, formerly a washhouse and toilet, was fixed to create a room to serve the needs of the resident caretaker, Bertie Lake, an old CPA member who had been in the Middle East with the British Army during World War 1.

The stock in new bookshop for the first few years after the move was little different from what it had been before. The main difference was that the shop was now accessible to passers-by. Also, as the changes of the 1960s began to manifest themselves in sleepy Perth, the bookshop's greater visibility meant that on a number of occasions the plate glass windows were smashed, requiring heavy metal screens to protect them. This was a chore that I often had to help with until the insurance companies refused to pay out for replacements and grills were fixed in place. The fact that the bookshop and the CPA headquarters were now at street level also meant that surveillance became much easier for ASIO; photos released with the dossier of a deceased CPA member indicate that this was the case.

Change was to come to the Communist Party itself. In 1956 Soviet Premier Nikita Khrushchev made his 'secret' speech to the Soviet Party Congress exposing and condemning the crimes of Stalin. While the leadership of the CPA for some years condemned the publication of the speech in the *New York Times* as a forgery, they knew that it was genuine. Despite their efforts to deny its veracity, they could not stop the departure of some long standing members of the Party and the opening up of more discussion of issues not previously acknowledged. Previously hidden differences between the Soviet and Chinese communist parties became public in the early 1960s leading to more open discussion of all the issues in the Australian Party.

As I was by this time a member of the WA state committee, I had to read all the polemical material that arrived from Moscow and Beijing. Turgid it might have been but the differences in approach were scary, and in fact some Victorian CPA members who supported China, split and formed the CPA-ML (Marxist-Leninist). Pioneer Bookshop carried its weekly paper, which was filled with dreary articles that I am sure had few readers. By the middle of the decade open criticism of some developments in the USSR, such as the sudden overthrow of Khrushchev in 1964 and the gaoling of two Soviet writers for publishing their works abroad, saw the CPA starting to look more closely at the Soviet Union than it had ever done before and to openly question the Soviet Party about these events.

The great causes of the 1960s were impacting more everywhere. The Vietnam war, the US civil rights movement, women's liberation, gay liberation, the Aboriginal land rights movement and the CPA's opposition to the invasion of Czechoslovakia in 1968 by the USSR and its allies to prevent democratic reform were inspiring young people in all kinds of ways. The CPA was affected positively and negatively by all of these events.

Young people were becoming more critical about all kinds of things and the CPA itself was not immune from their impact. By 1967 CPA members, especially the younger ones, were openly criticising not just old Party policies but the very basis of some of its organisational principles. A new openness about issues enlivened the organisation at a time when more and more emphasis was being placed on democratising the Party to make it more attractive.

The result was that Pioneer Bookshop, while still carrying the same political materials as previously, began to extend the range of materials in stock. It dared to sell materials by and about Trotsky, for so many years condemned by communist parties everywhere. It established accounts with Australian publishers and importers and began to stock a much wider range of materials. It began to take orders for books customers wanted, often buying a few extra copies to put on the shelves. For a short period it was even stocking some pornography. To meet the interest of teachers who were becoming interested in alternative approaches to education we also started stocking paperbacks by gurus of new approaches to teaching and learning that were eagerly snapped up by those tired of the old educational paradigms.

It was in these conditions that, in 1970 the Pioneer Bookshop decided to stock a few copies of a new American novel, *Portnoy's Complaint*. At that time, books printed in Australia were not subject to official censorship, but imported material was carefully scrutinised by the Customs Department for evidence of pornography (political ideas seem to have been quite acceptable). After D. H. Lawrence's *Lady Chatterley's Lover* had been successfully defended against charges of obscenity against the publisher, Penguin Books, in London, copies had been reprinted in Australia. To follow this up, Penguin Australia decided to reprint the book by Philip Roth, which featured, among other things, descriptions of the masturbatory activities of the book's main character, Alexander Portnoy.

The major bookshops in Perth, fearing prosecution under the state's *Indecent Publications Act 1902*, decided not to put the book on sale, but Pioneer Bookshop, along with a few other small bookshops, purchased the usual few copies for sale. Within days, the bookshop was flooded with orders, and before long, bookshop manager Joan Broomhall, along with the other booksellers, was charged under the *Indecent Publications Act*. The response was even greater demand. Soon, boxes of books were being stashed at the homes of various comrades and friends of the Party prior to being placed on sale at UWA, hotels and elsewhere. On 11 September 1970 the police raided the bookshop to seize copies, even climbing up through a ceiling manhole to search for more. Party Secretary John 'Rivo' Gandini, who was doing some part time studies at the university, was selling copies to students when word came through that the police were on their way. With the help of the students, all copies were spirited away and the police left empty handed.

After an earlier case was indefinitely adjourned, in the last days of 1970, by agreement with the other booksellers, Joan Broomhall and Pioneer Bookshop became the test case before the Perth Magistrate's Court. With then CPA member and barrister Lloyd Davies donating his services for the defence, the case eventually got under way. As the Act allowed for literary merit as a defence, this was the basis of the defence. We did not have to seek witnesses to assist us; they volunteered. The defence called seventeen witnesses, all of whom swore to the book's literary merit. Among them were local literary figures such as Tom Hungerford, Peter Cowan, Fay Zwicky, Gerald Glaskin and Hal Colebatch, a UWA psychologist who wanted to use the book in courses on abnormal psychiatry, even a truck driver who told the court that after reading it he didn't feel depraved and corrupted. Clearly, people were sick and tired of the paternalistic way in which they were being treated and many were glad that someone was taking on the authorities.

I attended only a couple of sessions of the trial, as I was rarely free from work when the case was being heard. Those I did attend were entertaining. One such was when the prosecutor asked UWA's Professor of English, W. A. Edwards: 'And professor, what do you understand by this reference to "the puzzled penis" '? (There was a fictitious article with this title supposedly from an academic journal at the front of the book.) 'Well,' replied the professor. 'I suppose it didn't know whether it should go in or out.' There were loud guffaws around the courtroom and even the magistrate covered his mouth to hide his own snicker. On another occasion the prosecutor was reading examples from the text filled with crude language of all kinds. As I listened I could not help wondering if the police would charge the reader reciting these same sections on the street with some obscure offence like offensive language or disorderly conduct. In the court context it was all clinically pure.

With the kind of support we received, it was no surprise that, in early 1971, the magistrate came to a not guilty verdict, declaring that though he thought the book *was* obscene it also had literary merit. Faced with this verdict, the federal government saw the writing on the wall and six months later allowed the free importation of *Portnoy's Complaint*. This particular episode in the battle against literary censorship was over. The Communist Party and the bookshop came out of the exercise well, and gained prestige in some new circles, but it proved merely a small tear in the generally anti-communist fabric that surrounded us.

In the following fifteen years, and in part based on the profit from the thousands of copies of Roth's book, the bookshop did reasonably well financially. Students began to appear in the shop more frequently, some of them interested in politics and keen to discuss issues with the manager or other available CPA workers. Left wing people began to come in to check the bookshelves or to suggest or order books, including on progressive approaches to education. Occasionally, there would be bulk orders from other bookshops, schools or other organisations.

In 1971, Pioneer began selling *The Little Red Schoolbook*, which was based on Mao Zedong's *Little Red Book*. *The Little Red Schoolbook* was an Australian version of a tiny book originally published in Denmark. It encouraged young people to resist, however mildly, oppressive situations in schools, frankly discussed all kinds of issues relating to sex and drugs and gave advice on how to work for change in non-violent ways. I was a member of the executive of the Teachers Union at the time. At one meeting, conservative members raised the issue and demanded that the union call for a ban of the book. As none of them had even read it themselves, one of the union officers proposed that copies be purchased first. I was asked to buy twenty copies from the bookshop for executive members. After the copies were circulated, not another word was heard about the issue.

To further supplement its income, the bookshop also acted for a number of years as a drop-off and pick-up centre for dry cleaning to serve the needs of local people and, of course, to encourage people to browse and sometimes buy books. The shop began also to carry original language materials from the Soviet Union and regular customers continued to come in to pick up their Russian copies of *Pravda*.

By the middle of the 1980s, the tide had ebbed. There had been several changes in the bookshop management after Joan Broomhall's retirement, with younger CPA members, all women, taking the post. But the élan of the 1970s was disappearing. Local membership of the CPA was dropping despite the arrival on the scene of some enthusiastic students; the democratisation of the CPA and its policies meant little change in its political fortunes. A new manager failed to follow the policy of limiting unsolicited book orders to a financially viable size, with the result that the shop ended up with a debt of several thousand dollars.

One night I was called to go to the bookshop as there had been a fire. By the time I arrived, the fire was out and in the bookshop was mass of water and smoke damaged books. Fortunately, everything was insured. No one was ever caught or charged with setting the fire, but the insurance payout solved the debt problem. To this day, I cannot help thinking that this was no act of providence. At the time we had a number of very intelligent and serious university student members and the thought occurred to me that perhaps one of them, knowing of our debt problem, came up with that solution. I will never know.

In any case, the last days of the bookshop were not far off. By 1991 the CPA was no more. Its membership and political situation had declined to a point where the national leadership's proposed dissolution of the Party was adopted. As part of the process, the building that the former owner's widow had previously turned over to the national office of the CPA was sold and came eventually into the hands of the Western Australian Lotteries Commission, which demolished it, along with a neighbouring building, to make way for a new set of offices for a number of ethnic community organisations.

34
The Women's Peace Camp
Suellen Murray

The land along Point Peron Road in Rockingham, 50 kilometres south of Perth, has remained remarkably unchanged since the 1980s. Ramshackle holiday cabins and camping grounds still sit among the windswept, scrubby sand dunes. According to a tourist brochure, the area is 'ideal for carefree holidays'. Forming part of a regional park, the area has been largely protected from the southwards push of Perth's suburbanisation. There are now extra carparks and a lookout over the bay, hinting that perhaps this sleepy locality is busier than it once was. In the past Point Peron came alive only during the long school summer holidays when it was frequented by young families, attracted by the cheap accommodation and calm, cooling waters of the Indian Ocean. Point Peron was awakened in the first two weeks of December 1984 when it became the site of a women's peace camp, an event that was largely resisted by the local Rockingham community and that brought international attention to the adjacent Stirling Naval Base on Garden Island. The naval base is accessed by a causeway from the mainland at Point Peron and provided a site of major symbolic importance for the protestors.

The WA women's peace movement was part of a much larger national and international movement comprised of women and men.

Over time there have been many concerns of the peace movement; a key aspect in the 1980s was opposition to nuclear weapons. In WA there were numerous People for Nuclear Disarmament (PND) groups, as well as older peace groups associated with various political positions and professional identities. While varying to some degree in their motivations, they all shared a common concern at this time about the mounting stockpile of nuclear weapons held by the USSR and the USA and the dreadful harm that they could cause. Out of the Cold War had come a shared nuclear weapons policy of mutually assured destruction, aptly know as MAD. The outcome of this policy of deterrence was supposedly that, as both sides had nuclear weapons, neither would ever use them. Peace groups were concerned that they would be used, and that this might occur intentionally or accidentally. Moreover, the production of nuclear weapons was an enormous waste of resources and a huge risk to people across the world, not just those countries ideologically at war. Australia, while far distant from both the USA and the USSR, would still feel the effects of such nuclear explosions and was implicated as it was tied to the USA through the long standing ANZUS treaty. During the 1980s, demonstrations were held throughout Australia, including in Perth, the largest being the Palm Sunday rallies at which up to 20 000 people marched in opposition to the threat of nuclear war.

US ships and submarines berthed in Australian ports; in the 1980s, Fremantle received the highest number of these visits. In 1980, Prime Minister Malcolm Fraser had proposed Stirling Naval Base as a homeport to the US Navy. Amid public opposition, this offer was not taken up, but the *Sydney Morning Herald* reported in September of the following year that '[the base] will be heavily used', as it has been.

The Western Australian peace movement opposed these visits for a range of reasons. First, there was concern that these vessels were nuclear powered and carried nuclear weapons, a point that the US Navy refused to confirm or deny. A nuclear accident would produce devastating effects on local communities. Second, the visits by US ships made HMAS *Stirling* and Fremantle Soviet nuclear targets. The City of Fremantle had become a nuclear free zone in 1980, seemingly to no avail. Third, the women's peace movement in particular was concerned about the impact of thousands of sailors on rest and recreation taking advantage of what Deryn Thorpe, in the *West Australian* of 23 July 1985, described proudly as the ready availability of 'booze, a bed, broads and a bath'.

While the Western Australian women's peace movement was in part made up of the older women's peace groups such as the Women's International League of Peace and Freedom (WILPF), there were many other women involved. Younger women were protesting in a social and political environment that built on the activities of the women's liberation movement of the 1970s. They were worried not only about the potential for harm to women, children and men from nuclear war, but they also had other concerns that reflected their wider political interests, including environmental damage from the use of nuclear power and weaponry, social injustice and, in particular, violence and exploitation of women and other systemic gendered inequalities. The 1980s women's peace movement was also part of blossoming women's cultural developments in art, music, film and scholarship. At the time, that these activities, including a peace camp, would be for women only was a radical concept.

At the end of 1983, activists who had participated in the women's peace camp at the gates of the Pine Gap US military installation in central Australia brought news that the Australian women's peace movement would support another camp, this time in Western Australia. In many ways this was a surprising decision. By sheer force of numbers, the Australian women's peace movement was mainly located in the eastern states, and few of these women had ever ventured so far west. Some saw it as an opportunity to make their way to a place that could only be the wild west. Even though the peace activists previously had set up camp in central Australia, much of this work had been done in close collaboration between feminist activists in Canberra, Sydney and Alice Springs. But there were few – if any – close connections with Perth activists at this time, even though a national network of women's peace groups had been established. Known as Women for Survival, the network existed for some years, then faded away as the Cold War ended in the late 1980s.

Point Peron is located at the western end of Cockburn Sound and it was Cockburn Sound that gave its name to the camp: the Sound Women's Peace Camp, or just Cockburn Sound. It was, of course, a play on words: 'sound' women protested against the threat of nuclear war, and the women would make a 'sound' about it. The actions of many who were involved in organising the camp – and others who came – were informed by radical feminism. There was great diversity among the women, reflecting the widespread concern about war and nuclear weapons at this time. In Western Australia, the most radical of the women's peace groups, and the one that organised the Cockburn Sound camp, was Women's Action for Nuclear Disarmament (WAND). WAND had been formed in early 1983 and had organised a number of protest actions, including the first women's peace camp at Cockburn Sound on the Mother's Day weekend that year.

By the end of 1983, there was already a strong nucleus of activists committed to doing the hard yards of creating a campsite for up to 1000 women. There was also an expanding membership from across the Western Australian community. Once WAND committed to organising the camp it leased an upstairs office in High Street (later in Pakenham Street) in downtown Fremantle; it became a centre of political activity. The rent was paid for with donations from supporters, some of whom were union members, reflecting a key membership of the wider peace movement. The office was staffed by WAND members, who took time out from their paid jobs; others were students, unemployed, retired or otherwise not in paid work and had time to dedicate to the cause. Here in the WAND office in Fremantle, women gathered, with the occasional dog and sometimes children too. Many meetings were held. Women wrote press releases, produced newsletters, made badges, created posters and banners, organised fundraising events and payed attention to all the logistical issues to establish the campsite. Use of Crown land at Point Peron had to be secured from the state government, but approval was granted only on the day before the camp was set to start. Regardless, the women had unanimously agreed to proceed with the peace camp. Consistent with their radical approach to political action, there were no leaders as such. Instead, the women opted to be involved in open collectives based around the various tasks that needed to be done. Groups of women took responsibility for working with the media, staffing the office, fundraising and public speaking. Others arranged various aspects of the camp's infrastructure. This governance structure was to be replicated at the camp; spokeswomen reported on behalf of each collective to the large campwide meetings that were held.

At the Point Peron campsite there was no water or toilets, no ready access to food supplies and there was little shelter from the blazing sun. WAND women set about sourcing and installing these essential requirements. Fire safety regulations had to be met and first aid facilities put in place, as well as security measures to protect women from marauding young men who were to come at night to harass them. Although it was a national peace camp, it was very much organised by WAND members and a small number of other women who were an advance party from the eastern states and some who came from overseas, having made the long journey from the women's peace camp at Greenham Common in the UK to support the Western Australian women's peace movement. There was contact with the interstate women's peace groups during the period leading up to the camp, advising of progress via a monthly newsletter, infrequent phone calls and one meeting that was held in Adelaide some months before the event, but that was about all. Today it is hard to imagine how limited the communication actually was and how much was achieved with so little.

During this lead-up period, WAND paid attention to informing the Western Australian community about the reasons for the camp and the practicalities of setting it up, but there wasn't time for much else, other than the ongoing need to protest against the ship visits. Fortunately, the eastern states women had time to plot the various protest actions on their three day trip to Perth. The women mostly came in a convoy of buses; the possibility of a peace train had been investigated but found to be unaffordable, even with the support of the Australian Railways Union. On 1 December, the day of the federal election on which the Labor Party led by Bob Hawke was returned and Western Australian senator Jo Vallentine was elected on an anti-nuclear platform, the buses arrived at East Perth terminal. They then joined a cavalcade of cars driving through the city to Fremantle and on to Point Peron. The cars and buses were adorned with banners and stickers announcing the camp and its goals. The women further made their presence known by singing, chanting and yelling loudly and blowing car horns. As a pointer to what was to come, they were greeted by cheering as well as jeers. Another indication of the hostile reception they were to receive was the fires lit near the campsite the night before by those who opposed their presence. In tinder dry conditions, the fires were frightening for the women who were staying there in preparation for the commencement of the protest. While the camp remained safe, a large nearby area was burnt out.

The protest actions had a strong aquatic theme, sited as the camp was at the seaside. One day a group of women did a well-orchestrated display of water ballet at the beach near the naval base. On an earlier occasion amid street theatre at the car park near the causeway to Garden Island, the women requested a meeting with the commander of HMAS *Stirling*, the US naval attaché and later, the minister for defence so they could put forward their concerns. While they waited to have these meetings, a vigil was maintained at the gates to the causeway. Another action and the one that received the most media attention was given the title 'Breaking the sound barrier' by the protesters. It involved a large group of women storming the gates to the naval base. Some women climbed over the gates, others swam past and clambered up the rocks that formed the causeway banks onto the military land. They were met by heavy handed police. Meanwhile a flotilla of boats and a range of smaller craft floated, paddled and sailed unimpeded along the bay adjacent to the causeway into naval territory. Women decorated the gates with ribbons, banners, children's toys, mementos and heartfelt messages demanding peace and social justice. As a way of explaining their actions to the wider public, the women delivered a statement to the media on 6 December, which they reproduced in the

December issue of their camp newsletter, *Primordial Scream*:

> Militarism creates barriers, divides people, claims to protect us whilst exposing us to violence. Barriers of nuclear militarism create distrust of nation for nation, fear as a way of life, and secrecy as normal government practice. We women at Cockburn focus on the gate as symbolic of such barriers. Our water action makes a mockery of fences; we reclaim the land and the sea. We accept our responsibility to act against the injustice, the immorality, the affront to humanity represented by these barriers. In this action we link with women all over the world who want to reclaim earth's resources to affirm life rather than destroy it.

This protest continued the long tradition of creative actions that reimagined these barriers, as had happened at Greenham Common, Pine Gap and at other women's peace camps around the same time in Italy and the USA. There were further protests at the Fremantle police station where the seventy-five arrested women were held overnight and at the Fremantle Magistrate's Court when they were fined up to $75 for trespassing on Commonwealth land. In court, many attempted to speak of their concerns about nuclear war and social injustice. Later, other women appeared in court after having been arrested when they staged a sit-in while waiting to meet with the US naval attaché in his city office.

These activities were largely greeted with distaste by the Western Australian community. Newspaper commentary was overwhelmingly negative. Deservedly, the press observed, some of the women were arrested and dealt with by the courts. Such unruliness, not to mention their unkempt appearance, was not to be tolerated. Indeed, some said the camp should be shut down. Despite political pressure on Premier Brian Burke to act, the camp remained in place for the planned two weeks. While it is unimaginable that most Western Australians did not support the most obvious aims of the camp – peace and the elimination of nuclear weapons – what many did not like was the way the women went about attempting to achieve these goals. Despite this rancour, there were also expressions of support for the women's activities from the Western Australian community and further afield. Telegrams congratulating the women on their efforts came from around the world. Many people visited the camp to donate food and other forms of material assistance as ways of showing their approval of the women's message and the means by which they were trying to achieve it.

The women's peace camp at Point Peron occurred at a very specific point in time. In many ways that time has passed. In other ways it is still very much with us. There is still a huge international stockpile of nuclear weapons. Even though the shape of some political conflicts has changed, there continues to be major wars worldwide. Women are still subjected to unacceptably high levels of violence in their daily lives. While the peace camp did not bring an end to the possibility of nuclear war, world conflict or gendered violence, it demonstrated the strength of Western Australian women's desire for change and showed that they were willing to take radical action to achieve it.

SELECT BIBLIOGRAPHY

INTRODUCTION

Bennett, James, Cushing, Nancy and Eklund, Erik, *Radical Newcastle* (Sydney: NewSouth Books, 2015).

Bolton, Geoffrey, *Land of Vision and Mirage: Western Australia since 1826* (Nedlands: University of Western Australia Press, 2008).

Davidson, Ron, *Fremantle Impressions* (Fremantle: Fremantle Arts Centre Press, 2007).

Evans, Raymond and Ferrier, Carole, *Radical Brisbane. An Unruly History* (Melbourne: Vulgar Press, 2004).

Fox, Charlie, 'The View from the West', in M. Lyons and P. Russell, eds, *Australia's History: themes and debates* (Sydney: UNSW Press, 2005).

Gregory, Jenny, *City of Light. A History of Perth Since the 1950s* (Perth: City of Perth, 2003).

Gregory, Jenny and Gothard, Jan, eds, *Historical Encyclopedia of Western Australia* (Nedlands: UWA Publishing, 2009).

Harcourt, John, *Upsurge: A novel* (London: John Long, 1934).

Irving, Terry and Cahill, Rowan, *Radical Sydney: Places, Portraits and Unruly Episodes* (Sydney: UNSW Press, 2010).

Macintyre, Stuart, A Concise History of Australia (Melbourne: Cambridge University Press, 2009).

Roth, Philip, Portnoy's Complaint (London: Jonathan Cape, 1969).

Sparrow, Jeff and Jill, Radical Melbourne: A Secret History (Melbourne: Vulgar Press, 2001).

Sparrow, Jeff and Jill, Radical Melbourne: The Enemy Within (Melbourne: Vulgar Press, 2004).

Stannage, C. T. The People of Perth (Perth: Perth City Council, 1979).

Williams, Justina (Joan), The First Furrow (Willagee: Lone Hand Press, 1977).

'Perth: The New West', Bulletin, 5 March 1977, p. 62.

CHAPTER 1

Atkinson, Anne, 'Chinese Labour and Capital in Western Australia, 1847–1947', unpublished PhD thesis, Murdoch University, Fremantle, 1991.

Atkinson, Anne, 'Some Socio-Economic Aspects of the Chinese Community in Perth 1900–1920', *Early Days*, vol. 9, no. 2, 1984.

Atkinson, Anne, 'Placing Restrictions Upon Them. Controlling "Free" Chinese Immigrants and Capital in Western Australia', in Gothard, Jan, ed., *Asian Orientations. Studies in Western Australian History*, no. 16, 1995.

Chung Wah Association Hall (1911), 128 James Street, Northbridge. *Western Australia Register of Heritage Places*, no. 020027 – Permanent Entry & Assessment Documentation, accessed at inherit.stateheritage.wa.gov.au/Public/, n.d.

Chung Wah Association, ed., *Chung Wah Association 1910–85. Commemorative Book* (Perth: Chung Wah Association, 1985).

Tian Ming Cai, 'Astride Two Worlds. The Chinese response to changing citizenship in Western Australia (1901–73)', MA thesis, Edith Cowan University, Perth, 1999.

Western Australia Parliamentary Debates, 1905.

CHAPTER 2

Carberry, Graham, *Towards Homosexual Equality in Australian Criminal Law: A brief history* (Melbourne: Australian Lesbian and Gay Archives, 2010).

Davis, Geoff, *Causes*, self-published DVD, 2015.

Gay Call, Western Gay Images, Westside Observer, Campaign Circular / *West Campaigner*, SLWA.

Gay Liberation Archives, SLWA,

Interview with David Lamb, SLWA oral history collection.

Perth Gay Liberation meeting, 29 February 1980.

Plunkett, Reece, 'Making Things Otherwise, An Ethnogenealogy of Gay and Lesbian Social Change in Western Australia', unpublished PhD thesis, Murdoch University, Fremantle, 2005.

Report of Honorary Royal Commission into Matters Dealing with Homosexuality, 1974.

West Australian, November 1989.

West Campaigner, 1985, 1987.

Willett, Graham, *Living Out Loud: A history of gay and lesbian activity in Australia* (Sydney: Allen & Unwin, 2000).

CHAPTER 3

Beresford, Quentin, *Rob Riley: An Aboriginal leader's quest for justice* (Canberra: Aboriginal Studies Press, 2006).

Black, Selena, 'Big CHOGM march launches Occupy Perth', *Green Left Weekly*, 29 October 2011.

Gregory, Jenny, *City of Light. A History of Perth Since the 1950s* (Perth: City of Perth, 2003).

Johnston, Peter, 'Litigating Human Rights in Western Australia: Lessons from the past', *University of Notre Dame Australia Law Review*, no. 15, 2013.

Lubin, Judy, 'The "Occupy" Movement: Emerging protest forms and contested urban spaces', *Berkeley Planning Journal*, vol. 25, no. 1, 2010.

Lunn, Julie, 'Unemployed protests in central Perth 1928–1934: Analysing place and occasion', Honours thesis, Murdoch University, Fremantle, 2007.

Northern Times, 21 April 1932.

Reid, D. D., *Commonwealth Parliamentary Debates/Senate*, 2 April 1974.

Smith, Howard, 'Public Assembly in Western Australia: section 54B and the civil liberties campaign', *Legal Service Bulletin 291*, December 1980.

United Nations, *International Covenant on Civil and Political Rights*, adopted by the General Assembly of the United Nations on 19 December 1966, no. 14668, accessed 16 July 2017 at United Nations Human Rights, Office of the High Commissioner; also accessed 24 August 2017 at ohchr.org/EN/ProfessionalInterest/Pages/CCPR.aspx.

CHAPTER 4

Chibber, Vivek, 'Developments in Marxist Class Analysis', in *Critical Companion to Contemporary Marxism*, Jacques Bidet and Stathis Kouvelakis, eds (Leiden and Boston: Brill, 2008), pp. 353–67.

Everett, Nick, 'CHOGM protest defies intimidation, launches occupation', *Direct Action*, 37, December–January 2012.

Holloway, John, *Change the World Without Taking Power* (London: Pluto Press, 2002), 2010 edn.

Norton, Emma, email correspondence with author, 31 July 2015.

Oxfam, 'An Economy for the 1%', Oxfam briefing paper, January 2017, accessed 31 July 2017 at oxfam.org/sites/www.oxfam.org/files/file_attachments/bp-economy-for-99-percent-160117-en.pdf.

Refugee Council of Australia, 'Timeline of major events in the history of Australia's Refugee and Humanitarian Program', accessed 11 May 2016 at refugeecouncil.org.au/getfacts/timeline/; address no longer active.

Taylor, Daniel, 'The crisis of leaderless movements', presentation at Marxism conference, Melbourne, 2–5 April 2015.

Wood, Miranda, interview with the author, 21 October 2015.

CHAPTER 5

Brown, Margaret, 'Western Australia and the World: Anti-war organisations as a case study, 1919–39', MA thesis, The University of Western Australia, Perth, 1981.

Kalgoorlie Miner, March 1935.

Macintyre, Stuart, *The Reds* (Sydney: Allen & Unwin, 1998).

Murray, Kaye, 'Irene Greenwood: A voice for peace', unpublished PhD thesis, Edith Cowan University, Perth, 2002.

Prichard, K. S., *Women of Spain*, in possession of the Katharine Susannah Prichard Writers' Centre, Greenmount.

Prichard, Katherine Susannah, *Straight Left: Articles and addresses on politics, literature and women's affairs over almost 60 years, from 1910 to 1968*, collected and introduced by Ric Throssell (Sydney: Wild and Woolley, 1982).

Sydney Morning Herald, 19 November 1934.

Throssell, Ric, *Wild Weeds and Wind Flowers: The life and letters of Katharine Susannah Prichard* (Sydney: Angus & Robertson, 1975).

Wells, Julie, 'The political commitment of Katharine Susannah Prichard: Political activity 1930–40 and the writing of the goldfields trilogy', BA Honours History dissertation, Murdoch University, Fremantle, 1984.

Williams, Justina (Joan), *The First Furrow* (Perth: Lone Hand Publications, 1976).

Williams, Joan, *Anger and Love* (Fremantle: Fremantle Arts Centre Press, 1993).

CHAPTER 6

Australian Government, Geoscience Australia website, accessed 24 August 2018 at ga.gov.au/oracle/nuclear-explosion.jsp.

Barker *v* Carr, *WA Law Reports*, vol. 59, 1957–58.

Cope, Madge, 'Skirts', *Our Women*, UAW national journal, March and May 1964.

Cope, Madge, interview with Linda Coleman, 2000. OH3212 SLWA.

Gilchrist, Roma, 'A Chronicle of the Union of Australian Women Western Australian Branch', c. 1990, typescript, SLWA.

Hartley, Noelene, interview with Sarah Johnson, 2002, OH3304 SLWA.

Northbridge History Project: Shaping the future with history (CD-ROM) (Perth: Department of Premier and Cabinet, 2007).

Prichard, K. S., 'History of a Women's Organisation [Notes on the Modern Women's Club]', in Kay Daniels and Mary Murnane, eds, *Australia's Women: A Documentary History* (St Lucia: University of Queensland Press, 1980), document 276.

UAW Perth, *Good Cooking* (Perth: Union of Australian Women, 1968).

CHAPTER 7

Alcorn, Graham, *The Struggle of the Pilbara Station Hands for Decent Living Standards and Human Rights* (Sydney: Max Brown, 2001).

Biskup, Peter, *Not Slaves, Not Citizens: The Aboriginal problem in Western Australia, 1898–1954* (St Lucia: University of Queensland Press, 1973).

Brown, Max, *The Black Eureka* (Sydney: Australian Book Society, 1976).

Davies, Lloyd, ' "Protecting Natives?": The Law and the 1946 Aboriginal pastoral workers' strike', *Papers in Labour History*, no. 1, 1988.s

Healy, Leah, Secretary, Western Australian State Committee, Australian Communist Party, to Minister for Justice Emil Nulsen, 20 May 1946, State Records Office of WA (SROWA), 1945/0800/110.

Hess, Michael, 'Black and Red: The Pilbara pastoral workers' strike', *Aboriginal History*, vol. 18, no. 1, 1994.

Healy, Leah, Secretary, Western Australian State Committee, Australian Communist Party, to Minister for Justice Emil Nulsen, 20 May 1946.

Lew McBeath to Francis Bray, 29 May 1946, and Francis Bray to Acting Premier Frank Wise.

McLeod, Don, *How the West Was Lost: The Native question in the development of Western Australia* (Perth: self-published, 1984).

Minister for North West, 30 May 1946, SROWA, 1945/0800/137–40, 142.

Prichard, K. S., flyer, issued by Rev. P. Hodge, secretary, Provisional Committee for Defence of the Native Rights, May 1946, SROWA, 1945/0800/117.

Williams, Joan, *Anger & Love: A life of struggle and commitment* (Perth: Fremantle Arts Centre Press, 1993).

Wilson, Deborah, *Different White People: Radical activism for Aboriginal rights 1946–72* (Nedlands: UWA Publishing, 2015).

Wright, Tom, *New Deal for Aborigines* (Sydney: Modern Publishers, 1939).

Western Australian Native Administration Act 1936.

Workers' Star, December 1937, May 1946, July 1949.

CHAPTER 8

Kolic Peisker, Val, ' "Ethnics", "Cosmopolitans" and Others: Croatians in Western Australia at the beginning of the twenty-first century', in Raelene Wilding and Farida Tilbury, eds, *A Changing People: Diverse contributions to the state of Western Australia* (Perth: Office of Multicultural Interests, 2004).

Layman, Lenore and Fitzgerald, Criena, eds, *110 in the Waterbag: A history of life, work and leisure in Leonora, Gwalia, and the Northern Goldfields* (Perth: Western Australian Museum, in Association with the Leonora Historical Research Project, 2012).

Srhoy, Bart, *Journey Beyond Origin* (Perth: Hesperian Press, 1998).

Sutalo, Ilija, *Croatians in Australia: Pioneers, Settlers and Their Descendants* (Adelaide: Wakefield Press, 2004).

West Australian, November 1934.

Workers' Star, May 1935, September 1937.

CHAPTER 9

Bevir, Mark, 'The Labour Church Movement, 1891–1900', *Journal of British Studies*, vol. 38, no. 2, 1999.

Fry, Eric, 'Australian Worker, Monty Miller', in E. Fry, ed., *Rebels and Radicals* (Sydney: Allen & Unwin, 1983, pp. 178–93)

Gill, Andrew, *'God gave the Land to the People': Single taxers in Western Australia, 1898–1914* (Perth: Blatellae Books, 2016).

Miller, Monty, *Labor's Road to Freedom* (Melbourne: Andrade's Bookshop, 1920).

Scates, Bruce, *A New Australia: Citizenship, radicalism and the first republic* (Melbourne: Cambridge University Press, 1997).

Westralian Worker, September 1901.

Williams, Victor, ed., *Eureka and Beyond: Monty Miller, his own story* (Perth: Lone Hand Press, 1988).

CHAPTER 10

Daily News, May 1971.

Historic Rock Mass for Love in Perth Western Australia, youtube.com/watch?v=tLbdavET_Ms.

Rock Mass for Love, celebrated at St George's Cathedral, Perth, 1971, LP record, Astor Records, Melbourne.

Marcuse, Herbert, *An Essay on Liberation* (London: Allen Lane, 1969).

Marks, Ian and Macintyre, Iain, *Wild About You! The Sixties Beat Explosion in Australia and New Zealand* (Portland: Verse Chorus Press, 2010).

Marwick, Arthur, *The Sixties: Cultural revolution in Britain, France, Italy and the United States* (Oxford: Oxford University Press, 1998).

Putland, Rowena, ' "God gets his groove on": the Perth rock masses, 1970–71', BA Honours, The University of Western Australia, 2011.

Neville, Richard, *Hippie, Hippie, Shake: The dreams, the trips, the trials, the love-ins, the screw ups … the Sixties* (Melbourne: William Heinemann, 1995).

Tonkin, John, *Cathedral and Community: A history of St George's Cathedral* (Nedlands: University of Western Australia Press, 2001).

YouTube, Bakery's *Rock Mass for Love*, posted by Frank Hill, September 2013.

CHAPTER 11

Bolton, Geoffrey, *A Fine Country to Starve In* (Nedlands: University of Western Australia Press, 1978).

Fox, Charlie, 'The Unemployed and the Labour Movement: The Western Australian Relief and Sustenance Worker's Union, 1933–34', *Studies in Western Australian History*, no. 5, 1982.

Graves, H. E., *Who Rides? Events in the life of a West Australian police officer* (London: Lovat Dickson, 1937).

Interview with Syd Foxley, Oral History Collection, SLWA.

Williams, Justina, *The First Furrow* (Perth: Lone Hand Publications, 1976).

CHAPTER 12

Craig, Terry, 'Radical and conservative theatre between the wars', *Studies in Western Australian History*, no. 11, 1990.

Daily News, November 1936

Entries for Lachberg, Maurice Derek, McClintock, Herbert, Poignant, Harald Emil Axel, Prichard, Katharine Susannah, Vike, Harald in *Australian Dictionary of Biography* (Melbourne: Melbourne University Press, various dates); see also *Australian Dictionary of Biography* at adb.anu.edu.au.

Goddard, Julian, 'The Workers' Art Guild', Artworks Group of the Operative Painters and Decorators Union and the Association for the Study of Labour History, oral recording, SLWA.

Hyde, Dylan, ' "We present this play not for your entertainment but for your chastening", The Workers' Art Guild, 1935–42', *Papers in Labour History*, no. 18, 1997.

Krantz, Dorothy, interviewed by Chris Jeffery, 1980, in oral history collection, SLWA

Layman, Lenore and Goddard, Julian, eds, *Organise!: A Visual Record of the Labour Movement in Western Australia* (Perth: Trades and Labour Council of WA, 1988).

Poole-Johnson, Walter, interviewed by Chris Jeffery, 1976, in oral history collection, SLWA.

Worker's Star, 17 June 1938.

CHAPTER 13

Chapman, Ron, 'The Radicalisation of Forest Protest in Western Australia', in A. Gaynor and J. Davis, eds, *Environmental Exchanges. Studies in Western Australian History*, no. 27, 2011.

Davidson, Dianne, *Women on the Warpath. Feminists of the First Wave* (Nedlands: University of Western Australia Press, 1979).

Elston, Kylie, 'The Origins of the Conservation Council in Western Australia 1955–67', Honours dissertation, Murdoch University, Fremantle, 1993.

Gregory, Jenny, 'Remembering Mounts Bay: The Narrows Scheme and the internationalisation of Perth planning' in A. Gaynor and J. Davis, eds, *Environmental Exchanges. Studies in Western Australian History*, no. 27, 2011.

Hawkins, W., *River Reclamation and Foreshore Freeways, Pelican Point – Hackett Drive – Point Resolution Bridge* (Nedlands: Nedlands–Crawley Residents Association, 1967).

Lutton, Nancy, 'Rischbieth, Bessie Mabel (1874–1967)', *Australian Dictionary of Biography*, vol. 11 (Melbourne: Melbourne University Press, 1988); see also *Australian Dictionary of Biography* at adb.anu.edu.au/biography/rischbieth-bessie-mabel-8214.

Map, 'Perth Central Area Development Proposals' 1955 Atlas – 'Plan for the Metropolitan Region' (Stephenson & Hepburn)', plate 14, accessed 23 August 2017 at planning.wa.gov.au/5462.aspx.

Serventy, Vincent, *An Australian Life: Memoirs of a naturalist, conservationist, traveller and writer* (Fremantle: Fremantle Arts Centre Press, 1999).

CHAPTER 14

Burgmann, Verity, *Revolutionary Industrial Unionism: The Industrial Workers of the World in Australia* (Cambridge: Cambridge University Press, 1995).

Daily News, 5 January 1905.

Erickson, Rica, 'Tracey, Eliza (1842–1917)', *Australian Dictionary of Biography* (Canberra: National Centre of Biography and Australian National University, 1990), accessed 14 July 2017 at adb.anu.edu.au/biography/tracey-eliza-8838/text15507.

Erikson, Rica, 'Eliza Tracey, a woman with a grievance', *Early Days*, 1983.

Fry, Eric, *Rebels and Radicals* (Sydney: Allen & Unwin, 1983).

Scutt, Tom, ' "Kicking Like Hell". The Industrial Workers of the World in Western Australia', *Papers in Labour History*, no. 11, 1993.

Summers, Lise, 'From Wasteland to Parkland: A history of designed open public space in the City of Perth, Western Australia, 1829–1965', unpublished PhD thesis, Curtin University, Perth, 2007.

Sunday Times, September 1889, August 1915, February 1937.

Williams, Victor, ed., *Eureka and Beyond: Monty Miller, his own story* (Perth: Lone Hand Press, 1988).

CHAPTER 15

Bishop C. L., Riley Papers, SLWA.

Gregory, Jenny, *City of Light: A history of Perth since the 1950s* (Perth: City of Perth, 2003).

Gregory, Jenny, 'Development Pressures and Heritage in the Perth CBD 1950–90', *Australian Economic History Review*, no. 49, 1, 2009.

Gregory, Jenny, 'Remembering Mounts Bay: The Narrows scheme and the internationalisation of Perth planning', in Andrea Gaynor and Jane Davis, eds, *Environmental Exchanges: Studies in Western Australian History*, no. 27, 2011.

Gregory, Jenny, 'Stephenson and metropolitan planning in Perth, Gordon Stephenson Special Issue, *Town Planning Review*, vol. 83, no. 3, 2012.

Parks and Reserves Amendment Act 1954, no. 59.

Rischbieth, Bessie, Papers, SLWA.

Stephenson, Gordon and Hepburn, J. A., *Plan for the Metropolitan Region of Perth and Fremantle: Report prepared for the Government of Western Australia* (Perth: Government Printing Office, 1955).

Walker, Lucy (aka Dorothy Sanders), *Monday in Summer* (London: Hodder & Stoughton, 1961).

CHAPTER 16

Bailey, Janis, 'Blue Singlets and Broccoli: Culture in the service of union struggle', *Labour History*, no. 79, November 2000.

Bailey, Janis, 'A Sociocultural Study of the Third Wave Ca*mpaign*', unpublished PhD thesis, Murdoch University, Fremantle, 2001.

Bailey, Janis and McAtee, Di, 'The Workers' Embassy Scrapbook', special issue of *Papers in Labour History*, no. 20, 1998.

Heritage Council of Western Australia, Register of Heritage Places, Permanent Entry, Data Base No. 15850, Solidarity Park (1997), accessed 20 September 2017 at inherit.stateheritage.wa.gov.au/Admin/api/file/

d03ff132-0d29-1aec-bb02-86328db42a16.

CHAPTER 17

Ansara, Martha, *Always Was, Always Will Be: The sacred grounds of the Waugal*, Kings Park, Perth (Balmain: self-published, 1989).

'Collection of material relating to issue of Swan Brewery site', third floor, Ephemera stack, SLWA.

Jacobs, Jane, *Edge of Empire: Postcolonialism and the city* (London: Routledge, 2002).

Mickler, Steve, 'The battle for Goonininup', *Arena*, no. 96, 1991.

State Library of Western Australia photo and ephemera collections.

Weir, Isobel, *Narrative: A play for voices*, sound recording, 1990, SLWA, Perth.

Watkins, Amanda, 'Redevelopment of the Old Swan Brewery Site: A case study of state, local capital and inter union politics', *Papers in Labour History*, no 13, 1994.

Vinnicombe, Pat, 'An Aboriginal site complex at the foot of Mt Eliza, which included the Old Swan Brewery building', *Historic Environment*, vol. 9, nos. 1–2, 1992.

CHAPTER 18

'Aboriginals want native title over 185 000 sq. km of State', *West Australian*, 20 September 2006, p. 1.

Biskup, Peter, *Not Slaves, Not Citizens: The Aboriginal problem in Western Australia 1898–1954* (St Lucia: University of Queensland Press, 1973).

Brunton, Ron, 'A Bombshell in the Centre of Perth: An anthropologist considers the single Noongar judgment', Bennelong Society, Occasional Paper, January 2007.

Host, John with Owen, Chris, *'It's still in my heart, this is my country': The Single Noongar Claim History* (Nedlands: UWA Publishing, 2009).

Moore, G. F., 'A Descriptive Vocabulary of the Language of the Aborigines', in G. F. Moore, *Diary of Ten Years of an Early Settler in Western Australia and also a Descriptive Vocabulary of the Language of the Aborigines*, first published in

1884 (Nedlands: University of Western Australia Press, 1978).

'Perth hit with Native Title win', *Australian*, 20 September 2006, 1.

Rowley, C. D., *The Destruction of Aboriginal Society* (Ringwood: Penguin, 1970).

Single Noongar Claim, Bennell v State of Western Australia [2006] FCA 1243, accessed 22 April 2017 at jade.io/j/#!/article/113153.

Single Noongar Claim Appeal, Bodney v *Bennell [2008] FCAFC 63* (23 April 2008), accessed at austlii.edu.au/au/cases/cth/FCAFC/2008/63.html, Pt 95, n.d.

State Library of Victoria, 'Native Title and the Yorta Yorta', *Ergo*, accessed 5 January 2017 at ergo.slv.vic.gov.au/explore-history/fight-rights/indigenous-rights/native-title-yorta-yorta.

White, Isobel, ed., *Daisy Bates: The native tribes of Western Australia* (Canberra: National Library of Australia, 1985).

CHAPTER 19

Barker, Anthony and Jackson, Lisa, *Fleeting Attraction: A social history of American servicemen in Western Australia during the Second World War* (Nedlands: University of Western Australia Press, 1996).

Cottle, Drew, 'Forgotten Foreign Militants: the Chinese Seamen's Union in Australia, 1942–46', accessed 29 May 2019 at colouredcolonials.yolasite.com/chinese-seamen-refugees-1942-1946.php.

Daily News, September 1925.

Fitzpatrick, Brian and Cahill, Rowan, *The Seamen's Union of Australia, 1872–1972* (Sydney: Seamen's Union of Australia, 1981).

Gifford, Peter, '*No winners*': *The British Seamen's Strike of 1925* (Perth: Hesperian Press, 2005).

Loh, Morag and Winternitz, Judith, *Dinki – Di: The contributions of Chinese immigrants and Australians of Chinese descent to Australia's Defence Forces and War Efforts 1899–1988* (Canberra: Australian Government Publishing Service, 1989).

'China – Shooting of Chinese Seamen by Australian Guards at Fremantle, 28

January 1942', National Archives of Australia (NAA) Canberra, A981, CHIN 7.

'Report on Organisation and Activities of Security Service – Perth branch, 1943', NAA, Canberra, A373/1,7431.

'Shooting of Chinese Seamen by Dutch at Fremantle, 31 March 1942', NAA, Canberra, A981, CHIN 8.

Ward, Liam, 'Radical Chinese Labour in Australian History', *Marxist Left Review*, no. 10, 2015.

CHAPTER 20

ABC *News*, 20 and 22 April 1998.

Bramble, Tom, *War on the Waterfront* (pamphlet), Brisbane Defend Our Unions Committee, October 1998.

Fox, Charlie, email to the author, 24 May 2016.

Combet, Greg, *The Fights of My Life* (Melbourne: Melbourne University Publishing, 2014).

ICFTU Bulletin, 8 April 1998.

LeftPress Collective, *After the Waterfront. The workers are quiet* (Brisbane: LeftPress Printing Society, 2007).

Left Link, 22 April 1998.

Mulheron, Rachel, 'Maritime Union of Australia (MUA) v Patrick Stevedores Pty Ltd: Marrying injunctive relief and labour supply contracts', *JCU Law Review*, 1999/8, Case Note 153, 152–64, accessed 22 April 2017 at austlii.edu.au/au/journals/JCULawRw/1999/8.pdf.

Oliver, Bobbie, *Unity is Strength: A history of the Australian Labor Party and the Trades and Labor Council of Western Australia* (Perth: API Network, 2003).

O'Neill, Stephen, 'The Waterfront Dispute: From High Court to settlement – summary and comment', *Current Issues Brief 1*, 1998–99, 14 September 1998, Parliament of Australia, accessed 22 April 2016 at aph.gov.au/About_Parliament/Parliamentary_Departments/Parliamentary_Library/Publications_Archive/CIB/cib9899/99cib01.

'War on the Wharfies', news summary, April 1998, accessed 21 April

2016 at takver.com/wharfie/apr98.htm#apr98027; originally published on the Maritime Union of Australia, WA Branch website at mua.org.au/western_australia_branch.

CHAPTER 21

ALF State Executive, *The Fremantle Wharf Crisis of 1919* (Perth: Australian Labor Federation, 1920).

ALP State Executive Correspondence Files, State Library of WA (SLWA), Accession No. 16881A, files 40, 166, 177.

Hopper, Peter, 'The Fremantle Lumpers' Strike', BA Honours dissertation, The University of Western Australia, Perth, 1975.

Oliver, Bobbie, *Unity is Strength. A history of the Australian Labor Party and the Trades and Labor Council in Western Australia*, 1899–1999 (Bentley: API Network, 2003).

Oliver, Bobbie, *War and Peace in Western Australia. The social and political impact of the Great War* (Nedlands: University of Western Australia Press, 1995).

Police Department Files, State Record Office of WA (SROWA), Accession No. 4092/1918.

Premier's Department Files, SROWA, Accession No. 1496, files 33/19 and 111/19.

West Australian, May 1919.

Westralian Worker, 9 May 1919.

CHAPTER 22

Black, David, 'Biography of John Curtin', accessed 15 February 2016 from John Curtin Prime Ministerial Library at john.curtin.edu.au/resources/biography/details.html.

Oliver, Bobbie, 'Shaping the Nation: John Curtin and Australia', accessed 16 February 2016 from John Curtin Prime Ministerial Library at john.curtin.edu.au/shapingthenation/essay/index.html.

Oliver, Bobbie, *Unity Is Strength. A history of the Australian Labor Party and the Western Australian Trades and Labor Council 1899–1999* (Perth: API Network, 2003).

People's Printing & Publishing Company, *Minutes of Annual General Meetings 1915–28*, John Curtin Prime Ministerial Library, Curtin University, Series no. JCPML01263/3.

Westralian Worker, editorials, various dates, 1917–28.

CHAPTER 23

Burgmann, Verity, 'The social responsibility of labour versus the environmental impact of property capital: The Australian green bans movement', *Environmental Politics*, 9, no. 2, 2000, pp. 78–101.

Burgmann, Verity and Milner, Andrew, 'Ecotopians in Hardhats: The Australian Green Bans Movement', *Utopian Studies*, 22, no. 1, 2011, pp. 125–42.

Colman, James, *The House That Jack Built: Jack Mundey, green bans hero* (Sydney: NewSouth, 2016).

Davidson, Ron and Davidson, Dianne, *Fighting for Fremantle: The Fremantle Society story* (Fremantle: Fremantle Press, 2010).

'Green Bans Travel West to Perth', *Tribune*, 29 January 1974, p. 12.

Gregory, Jenny, 'Development Pressures and Heritage in the Perth Central Business District 1950–90', *Australian Economic History Review*, 49, no. 1, 2009, pp. 34–51.

Layman, Lenore, 'Development ideology in Western Australia 1933–65', *Historical Studies*, 20, no. 79, 1982, pp. 234–60.

Lesh, James P., 'From Modern to Postmodern Skyscraper Urbanism and the Rise of Historic Preservation in Sydney, Melbourne and Perth, 1969–88', *Journal of Urban History*, 45, no. 1, 2019, pp. 126–49.

'Peninsula Hotel Gets a Reprieve', *West Australian*, 14 May 1976, n.p.

'Residents call for halt to pub demolition', *Tribune*, 6 August 1974, p. 12.

Thomas, Athol, 'A plan to preserve the Palace', *Canberra Times*, 8 October 1973, p. 2.

Thomas, Athol, 'The Palace guard begins to stir', *Canberra Times*, 26 January 1974, p. 2.

Thomas, Athol, 'Support from the Palace Guard', *Canberra Times*, 1 June 1974, p. 9.

'W.A. Builders Labourers' Bans', *Tribune*, 9 April 1974, p. 12.

CHAPTER 24

Appeal between Desmond Phillipson (Appellant) and the Minister of State for Labour and National Service (Respondent) in the Supreme Court of Western Australia, Appeal No. 51 of 1968, Vivienne Abraham Papers, in private possession.

Davies, Lloyd and Davies, Joan, interviewed by Bobbie Oliver, Cottesloe, November 2000.

Gregory, Jenny, *City of Light* (Nedlands: University of Western Australia Press and Perth City Council, 2003).

Laufer, Beatrice, 'All who do not resist participation are guilty: Draft resistance in Western Australia between 1970 and 1972', Honours dissertation, The University of Western Australia, Perth, 2006.

Oliver, Bobbie, *Unity is Strength: A history of the Australian Labor Party and the Trades and Labor Council in Western Australia* (Perth: API Network, 2003).

Oliver, Bobbie, 'What kind of democracy is this?' Conscientious objectors to the National Services Schemes, 1950–72 in Bobbie Oliver and Sue Summers, eds, *Lest We Forget? Marginalised aspects of Australia at war and peace* (Perth: Black Swan Press, 2014).

Papers in Labour History, no. 29, 2005.

Peacemaker, various issues, 1966–71.

Pointon, Tony, interviewed by Bobbie Oliver, Perth, 31 October 2000.

Thomas, Bill, interviewed by Alexis Vassiley, Perth, 28 April 2008.

Vassiley, Alexis, ' "Smash the Draft!" and Other Tales: A snapshot of student activism at The University of Western Australia, 1969–71', The University of Western Australia. Institute of Advanced Studies, *The New Critic*, issue 13,

December 2010, accessed 25 January 2017 at ias.uwa.edu.au/new-critic/thirteen/vassiley.

Worth, David, 'Peace Movement', in Jenny Gregory and Jan Gothard, eds, *Historical Encyclopedia of WA* (Nedlands: University of Western Australia Press, 2009).

CHAPTER 25

Layman, Lenore and Goddard, Julian, eds, *Organise!: A visual record of the labour movement in Western Australia* (Perth: Trades and Labor Council of WA, 1988).

Macintyre, Stuart, *Militant: The life and times of Paddy Troy* (Sydney: Allen & Unwin, 1984).

Maritime Worker/Maritime Workers Journal, various dates.

May Day file, Fremantle History Centre, Fremantle City Library.

Photo collection at the State Library of Western Australia (SLWA).

West Australian, May 1897, May 1902, May 1912, May 1922.

Westralian Worker, May 1925.

CHAPTER 26

Aveling, Harry, *The Laughing Swami: Australian sannyasin disciples of Swami Satyananda Saraswati and Osho Rajneesh* (Delhi: Motilal Banarsidass Publishers, 1994).

Davidson, Ron, *Fremantle Impressions* (Fremantle: Fremantle Arts Centre Press, 2007).

O'Brien, Paula, 'The Rajneesh Community in Fremantle', MA thesis, Murdoch University, Fremantle, 2008.

Rajneeshee File, Fremantle History Centre, Fremantle City Library.

Stork, Jane, *Breaking the Spell: My life as a Rajneeshee and the long journey back to freedom* (Sydney: Macmillan, 2009).

Wild, Wild Country, Netflix, March 2018

CHAPTER 27

Archer, Jan, 'The 1952 Metal Trades Strike in Western Australia: a War of Attrition', *Papers in Labour History*, no. 25, 2001.

Hicks, Dave, interviewed by Julie Rogers, 2002, Midland Government Railway Workshops Project, SLWA Oral History Collection.

Oliver, Bobbie, *Unity is Strength. A history of the Australian Labor Party and the Trades and Labor Council in Western Australia*, 1899–1999 (Perth: API Network, 2003).

Read, Jolly, *Marksy. The life of Jack Marks* (Perth: Read Media, 1998).

Recollections of former Workshops employees: Fred Cadwallader, Rod Quinn, Ted Zeffert, Neil McDougall, Denis Day, Jack Coleman, Philip Bristow-Stagg, Ron Wadham, Patrick Gayton, Jack Emery, Alan Bright, Frank Bastow and Kevin Mountain, Midland Government Railway Workshops History Project, SLWA Oral History Collection.

Wadham, Ron, interviewed by Richard Noyelle, 2002, Midland Government Railway Workshops Project, SLWA Oral History Collection.

CHAPTER 28

Donaldson, Gwen, Snake Pit file, Mt Flora Museum, City of Stirling.

Drewe, Robert, *Swimming to the Moon* (Fremantle: Fremantle Press, 2014).

Gracie, Murray and Mills, John, eds, *Jive, Twist and Stomp: WA rock & roll bands of the 50s and 60s* (Fremantle: Fremantle Press, 2010).

Grey, Patricia, 'Leopard Skin Bikini' and 'The Snake Pit', *Chronicle Scarborough*, accessed 24 August 2017 at chroniclescarborough.com.au/story/snake-pit/.

'History of Rock'n'Roll in Western Australia', accessed 24 August 2017 at members.optusnet.com.au/perthrocks/History%20of%20rocknroll%20 in%20Western%20Australia.htm.

Mirror, December 1952, June and July 1956.

Report of the Police Commissioner, year ended 30 June 1956, in *Votes and Proceedings of the Western Australian Parliament*, 1957.

Stratton, Jon, 'Bodgies and Widgies', *Journal of Australian Studies*, vol. 8, no. 15, 1984.

Sturma, Michael, *Australian Rock'n'Roll: The first wave* (Sydney: Kangaroo Press, 1991).

'The Snake Pit', *Hindsight*, ABC Radio National, 23 October 2011.

Weekend Mail, July 1960.

Wordley, Dick, ed., *The Gap: A book to bridge the dangerous years*, Western Australian edition (Perth: West Australian Newspapers, 1959).

CHAPTER 29

Annual Reports of the Director of Mental Health Services, *Votes and Proceedings of the Western Australian Parliament*, for the years 1965 to 1982.

Cocks, Errol, et al., *Under Blue Skies: The social construction of intellectual disability in Western Australia* (Perth: Centre for Disability Research and Development, Faculty of Health and Human Sciences, Edith Cowan University, 1996).

Ellis, Archie, *Eloquent Testimony: The story of mental health services of Western Australia, 1830–1975* (Nedlands: University of Western Australia Press, 1984).

Foley, Marcia, 'Social Policy in Western Australia', *Studies in Western Australian History*, no. 25, 2007.

Fox, Charlie, 'Debating Deinstitutionalisation: The fire at Kew cottages in 1996 and the idea of community', *Health and History*, vol. 5, no. 2, 2003.

Laffey, Paul, 'Antipsychiatry in Australia: Sources for a social and intellectual history', *Health and History*, vol. 5, no. 2, 2003.

Martyr, Phillipa, unpublished manuscript on the history of mental health services in Western Australia. I wish to acknowledge Dr Martyr's considerable help in the research for this essay.

Pyke, Alicia, 'Deinstitutionalisation of the Western Australian mental health care system: A critical examination of community health care', MA in Community Development, Murdoch University, Perth, 2007.

Sunday Times, 7 January 1968.

CHAPTER 30

Armstrong, Mick, *1, 2, 3, What Are We Fighting For* (Melbourne: Socialist Alternative, 2001).

Aspect, 1969–71.

Boyle, Peter, email correspondence with Alexis Vassiley, 27 May 2017.

Cornish, Patrick, ed., *Two and Sixpence, A student century* (Perth: The University of Western Australia Student Guild, 2013).

Duckham, Ian, *Power and Persuasion: A history of The University of Western Australia Academic Staff Association and its predecessors 1913–2013* (Perth: University of Western Australia Academic Staff Association, 2013).

Fraser, Ronald, *1968: A Student Generation in Revolt* (New York: Pantheon Books, 1988).

Gerritsen, Rupert, interview with Stuart Reid, 10 January 1991.

Grok, various issues, 1972–78.

Hastings, Graham, *It Can't Happen Here: A political history of Australian student activism* (Adelaide: Flinders University Students' Association, 2002).

National U, 1968.

Pelican, various issues, 1969–79.

Quinlivan, Julie, ed., *Student Days: The University of Western Australia Student Guild – A collection of memoirs* (Perth: The University of Western Australia Guild of Undergraduates, 1988).

Shervington, Christine, *University Voices: Traces from the past* (Nedlands: The University of Western Australia Press, 1987).

Thomas, Bill, interview with Alexis Vassiley, 28 April 2008.

Vassiley, Alexis, 'Smash the Draft!' and Other Tales: A snapshot of student activism at UWA, 1969–71'; *The New Critic*, no. 13, December 2010.

Walker, Sue, *Western Australian Parliamentary Debates, Legislative Assembly*, p. 794, 11 September 2002.

White, Michael, *WAIT to Curtin: A history of the Western Australian Institute of Technology* (Perth: Paradigm Books, 1996).

CHAPTER 31

Around the Cauldron: A Perth Wimin's Liberation Magazine, 1980, held at SLWA.

Brankovitch, Jasmina,,'Burning Down the House? Feminism, politics and women's policy in Western Australia, 1972–98', unpublished PhD thesis, The University of Western Australia, 2007.

Eveline, Joan and Hayden, Lorraine, eds, *Carrying the Banner: Women, leadership and activism in Australia* (Nedlands: University of Western Australia Press, 1999).

Goodrick, Dorothy (Dot), interviewed by Criena Fitzgerald, 1990, SLWA Oral History collection.

Hopkins, Lekkie and Roarty, Lynn, *Among the Chosen: The life story of Pat Giles* (Fremantle: Fremantle Press, 2010).

Liberation Information, September 1972–May 1975, SLWA.

McFerren, Ludo, 'Interpretation of a Frontline State: Australian women's refuges and the state', in Sophie Watson, ed., *Playing the State: Australian feminist interventions* (Sydney: Allen & Unwin, 1990).

Murray, Suellen, 'Breaking the Silence: Nardine Women's Refuge and the politicisation of domestic violence in Western Australia during the 1980s', *Women Against Violence: An Australian feminist journal*, issue 7, December 1999.

Murray, Suellen, 'Taking Action Against Domestic Violence in the 1970s: Nardine Women's Refuge and Radical Feminism', *Studies in Western Australian History*, no. 19, 1999.

Sibyl, June 1974–October 1983, SLWA.

CHAPTER 32

Bodel, Neal, private archive and personal communication with the author.

Davies, Kayt, 'City Farm – Paradise Reclaimed', accessed at kayt.info/article5.html, n.d.

Dickie, Joe and Mairs, Jessica, *Kentish Town City Farm: How it all began* (documentary film), 2012, accessed 24 August 2017 at 40years.ktcityfarm.org.

uk/the-first-40-years/.

Farmer, Alison, 'Farm in the City Inspires Jobless', news clipping, n.d. (c.1994), in Neal Bodel's private archive .

Gaynor, Andrea, *Harvest of the Suburbs: An environmental history of food production in Australian cities 1880–2000* (Nedlands: University of Western Australia Press, 2006).

Gregory, Jenny, 'Obliterating History?', *Australian Historical Studies*, vol. 39, no.1, 2008.

Hillyer, Vivienne, 'Bennett House: Aboriginal heritage as real estate in East Perth', *Urban Policy and Research*, vol. 19, no. 2, 2001.

'It's cool down on the farm', *Sunday Times*, 12 September 2010.

New York City Department of Parks and Recreation, 'History of Farm Gardens in NYC Parks', accessed 29 September 2017 at nycgovparks.org/about/history/community-gardens/farm-gardens..

Rankin, Amanda, 'Perth's Permaculture Celebration', *Nova Holistic Journal*, vol. 3, no. 7, September 1996.

CHAPTER 33

Blears, Barrie, 'Together with us. A personal glimpse of the Eureka Youth League and its origins, 1920–70 (Sydney: self-published, 2002).

Davis, Geoff, *Causes*, DVD, self-published, 2013.

Davis, Geoff, 'A Communist Remembers', *Papers in Labour History*, no. 29, 2005.

Roth, Philip, *Portnoy's Complaint* (London: Jonathan Cape, 1969).

Thornberry, Berit, trans., *Little Red Schoolbook* (Wellington: Alister Taylor, 1972).

CHAPTER 34

Green, Gail, *Nuclear Menace in our Backyard: Why US military bases in Australia and the Indian Ocean threaten world peace* (Sydney: Australian Peace Committee, 1983).

Murray, Suellen, 'Mixed Messages: Gender, peace and the mainstream media in Australia, 1983–84', in M. Abbenhuis and S. Buttsworth, eds, *Restaging War* in the Western World: Noncombatant experiences, 1890–today (New York: Palgrave Macmillan, 2009).

Murray, Suellen, ' "Make Pies Not War": Protests by the women's peace movement of the mid 1980s', *Australian Historical Studies*, vol. 37, no. 127, 2006.

Sound Women's Peace Camp, 'Breaking the Sound Barrier', press release, 6 December 1984, reproduced in *Primordial Scream*, December 1984, p. 13.

Thorpe, Deryn, 'Perth women dial S for sailor', *West Australian*, 23 July 1985, p. 59.

Williams, Justina, 'A Significant Event: Cockburn Sound Women's Peace Camp, 1–15 December 1984', in Charlie Fox, ed., *Papers in Labour History*, no. 10, 1992.

PICTURE CREDITS

pp. 12-3 and p. 128: Courtesy State Library of Western Australia, 00775d.

p. 16: Courtesy State Library of Western Australia 76899P.

p. 33: Courtesy State Library of Western Australia with kind permission of Geoff Davis, former President of Campaign Against Moral Persecution.

p. 43: Courtesy State Library of Western Australia B3820684/1 380762PD.

p. 50: Courtesy Desire E. M. Mallet.

p. 53: With kind permission of Sam Cavallaro.

p. 62: Courtesy J.N. Rawling collection, Noel Butlin Archives Centre, ANU N57/2353.

p. 63: Courtesy State Library of Western Australia. BA/898/24.

p. 74: Courtesy State Library of Western Australia 5700B1

p. 85: Courtesy State Records Office of WA, cons993_1945/0800_f.117.

p. 96: Courtesy Maurice Grubisa.

p. 106: With kind permission of Wendy Wood.

p. 119: With kind permission of St. George's Cathedral.

pp. 120-1: Courtesy Ric Chan with assistance of Jim King.

p. 138: Courtesy Gilchrist Collection, State Library of Western Australia BA501/10, with kind permission of Mrs Lesley Fleay.

p. 146: Courtesy the Daily News.

p. 154: Courtesy State Library of Western Australia 2442B, with kind permission of the Library Board of Western Australia.

p. 158: Courtesy Erin Gothard-Fox.

p. 173: Courtesy of the Daily News and Peter Rigby.

p. 176-7: Courtesy Di McAtee.

p. 180: Courtesy Janis Bailey

p. 181: Courtesy Janis Bailey.

p. 194: Courtesy Erin Gothard-Fox.

p. 206: Courtesy Toni Wilkinson.

p. 209: Courtesy Margaret Owen.

pp. 210-1 and p. 239: Courtesy West Australian Newspapers, WAN-0031387.

p. 218-9: Courtesy State Library of Western Australia, 5323D/1557.

p. 220-1: Courtesy State Library of Western Australia, 5323D/1558.

p. 240: With kind permission of Mrs Moya Sherlock.

p. 253: John Curtin Prime Ministerial Library collection, 'Records of the J S Battye Library of West Australian History, Westralian Worker Office, Stirling St Perth, 1930' (JCPML00139/10).

p. 258: Courtesy Erin Gothard-Fox.

p. 264: Courtesy Erin Gothard-Fox.

p. 267: Courtesy Erin Gothard-Fox.

p. 270: Courtesy Erin Gothard-Fox.

p. 277: Courtesy Gilchrist Collection, State Library of Western Australia BA501/2175, with kind permission of Mrs Lesley Fleay.

pp. 282-3: Courtesy West Australian Newspapers WAN-0031385.

p. 300: Courtesy State Library of Western Australia 048485PD.

p. 301: Photo Greg Quail, reproduced with kind permission of Dr Kathryn Shine, Journalism, Curtin University.

p. 307: Courtesy Erin Gothard-Fox.

pp. 316-7 and p. 330: Courtesy City of Stirling History Collection.

p. 320: Courtesy Barry Watts and the Midland Workshops History Project.

p. 340: Courtesy Erin Gothard-Fox.

p. 350: With kind permission of Conrad Hogg, President, UWA Student Guild.

p. 363: With kind permission of Conrad Hogg, President, UWA Student Guild.

p. 364: Magazine held at State Library Western Australia. All reasonable attempts have been made to contact the copyright holder. Any person wishing to claim copyright please contact the publisher.

p. 378: Courtesy Andrea Gaynor.

p. 381: Courtesy Andrea Gaynor.

p. 387: Courtesy the Daily News.

EDITORS AND CONTRIBUTORS

EDITORS

Charlie Fox taught Australian History at the University of Melbourne and The University of Western Australia before retiring at the end of 2011. He has published widely on histories of work, unemployment, intellectual disability, and radical political and cultural movements. At present he does occasional walking tours of radical Perth and Fremantle.

Alexis Vassiley is a postgraduate researcher at Curtin University. His dissertation examines the rise and fall of trade unionism in Western Australia's Pilbara mining region. He has published in *Labour History* on trade union solidarity with Aboriginal rights at Noonkanbah, as well as on establishing militant trade unionism in the Pilbara.

Bobbie Oliver is an Honorary Research Fellow at The University of Western Australia. Prior to retiring in 2018, she was Associate Professor of History at Curtin University. Her most recent book is *A Natural Battleground: The fight to establish a rail heritage centre at Western Australia's Midland Railway Workshops*.

Lenore Layman is a Western Australian historian. Among her publications are *Organise! A visual record of the Western Australian labour movement, Powering Perth: The East Perth Power Station and the electrification of Perth* and *110 in the Waterbag: A history of life, work and leisure in Leonora, Gwalia and the Northern Goldfields*. She was also the historian member of the team that produced the Australian Asbestos Network website on the health disaster of asbestos use in Australia.

CONTRIBUTORS

Janis Bailey is Adjunct Associate Professor in the Department of Employment Relations and Human Resources at Griffith University. Previously, she taught at Edith Cowan University. She participated in the Third Wave protest in 1997. Her research interests include vulnerable workers, industrial relations in hotels, retail, community services and universities, and union strategy and culture.

Riley Buchanan recently completed an MPhil at the University of Notre Dame in Fremantle in which she explored artistic representations of atrocities committed during the Spanish Civil War. She is the host of Radio Fremantle's *Out of the Woodwork*, in which she interviews researchers from a range of disciplines about their work.

Geoff Davis is a teacher with a strong interest in history, politics, education and social and political activism through the State School Teachers Union, the Communist Party of Australia, gay groups and peace and friendship organisations. He pioneered the teaching of Chinese in WA schools and founded WA and national organisations of Chinese language teachers. He was a committee member of the Australian Society for the Study of Labour History Perth for many years and published his autobiography, *Causes*, in 2013. He was made a Member of the Order of Australia in 2006 for his service to education.

Nick Everett is a learning adviser at Murdoch University. He has also worked as a sessional academic at Curtin University and the University of Notre Dame, teaching in the fields of Australian history, Aboriginal studies and human rights. In 2016, Nick completed a Masters of Human Rights at Curtin University. His research explored the contribution of the Australian labour movement and Australian Communist Party in building solidarity with the Pilbara strike, as well as the strike's significance in forging a national Indigenous rights movement.

Andrea Gaynor is Associate Professor of History at The University of Western Australia. An environmental historian, she seeks to use the contextualising and narrative power of history to address contemporary problems. She is co-editor, with Nick Rose, of *Reclaiming the Urban Commons: The past, present and future of food growing in Australian towns and cities*. At UWA she is chair of the History Discipline Group and director of the Centre for Western Australian History. She also convenes the Australian and New Zealand Environmental History Network and endeavours to inform policy as a member of the Beeliar Group: Professors for Environmental Responsibility.

Jenny Gregory AM is Emeritus Professor of History at The University of Western Australia. Among her books are *City of Light: A history of Perth since the fifties* and the edited collections *The Historical*

Encyclopedia of Western Australia (with Jan Gothard), *Seeking Wisdom: A centenary history of The University of Western Australia* and *A Man for All Seasons: Essays for Geoffrey Bolton* (with Stuart Macintyre and Lenore Layman).

Chris MacFarlane is a Perth-based activist involved in local anti-fascist organising. He is an undergraduate student studying journalism and literary and cultural studies at Curtin University. He has written about anti-Indigenous racism and workers' rights for Socialist Alternative's *Red Flag*, as well as anti-fascism for the Curtin student paper *Grok*.

Bri McKenzie is a lecturer at Curtin University and coordinator of Curtin's history program. Her research specialty is the history of Western Australian midwifery and maternity services. Her other areas of research interest include Australian feminism, LGBTQI+ history and Australian environmental histories of colonialism.

Suellen Murray is Associate Dean (Research and Innovation) in the School of Global, Urban and Social Studies at RMIT University. In the 1980s Suellen was involved in the peace movement and was an organiser of the Sound Women's Peace Camp.

Dr Chris Owen is a historian and Honorary Research Fellow in the School of History at The University of Western Australia. His most recent publication is *Every Mother's Son is Guilty: Policing the Kimberley Frontier of Western Australia 1882–1905*.

Alex Salmon has written extensively on Western Australian labour history. He holds a Bachelor of the Arts in history with honours from Murdoch University. His thesis topic was *The Communist Press in Western Australia 1932–50*. In 2012 his essay on the 1931 Perth Treasury riots was awarded runner up prize in the City of Perth history contest.

Red Swan Series
WESTERN AUSTRALIAN RADICAL LABOUR HISTORY AND POLITICS

The Red Swan Series in radical Western Australian labour history and politics, published by Interventions, brings to life stories from the workers' movement and social movements that need to be told. It offers a perspective on the state's history and politics that challenges the status quo.

Series Editor: Alexis Vassiley

ALSO BY INTERVENTIONS Red Swan Series

A NATURAL BATTLEGROUND
THE FIGHT TO ESTABLISH A RAIL HERITAGE
CENTRE AT WESTERN AUSTRALIA'S MIDLAND
RAILWAY WORKSHOPS
Bobbie Oliver
Red Swan Series 1
2019

'Often those in power would prefer us to forget yesteryear's struggles, the easier to mould tomorrow to their interests. Bobbie Oliver brilliantly illuminates why we must not forget the Midland Railway Workshops – and so lights a way forward for Western Australia and other challenging sites around the post-industrial world.'

**Colin Divall Emeritus Professor of Railway Studies
University of York, UK**

When the Government Railway Workshops at Midland closed on 4 March 1994, Western Australia lost a major trainer and employer of skilled tradespeople and much of its heavy industry. Former workers feared that their history of industrial achievements on the factory floor and through union action would also be lost. Despite expending considerable resources and promising to honour a "proud history" and create an "exciting future", the development authorities have done little to redevelop the site. A Natural Battleground is the story of the fight to save the buildings from demolition and dedicate space in them for a rail heritage centre to preserve the Workshops' history. The first aim was achieved, the second is merely a hope. As the author says, "Somewhere in these buildings, decency dictates, there must be space to tell the whole story of what happened here, including what happened to those workers whose lives were irrevocably changed by their closure." Whether you are interested in the history of trade unions, heritage or railways this book will engage and inspire you.

Red Swan Series
WESTERN AUSTRALIAN RADICAL LABOUR HISTORY AND POLITICS

ALSO BY INTERVENTIONS

**REVOLUTION IS FOR US
THE LEFT AND GAY LIBERATION IN AUSTRALIA**
Liz Ross
Reprinted 2019

'The homosexual is essential to the sexual revolution; there can be no revolution, no liberation, without us.'

Australia's Gay Liberation movement arose at a time when revolution was in the air and gays wanted to be part of it. It was the Left which had a theory and practice of revolution – Marxism. But it is often asserted that the Left was backward and even hostile, that Marxism had no tradition of dealing with sexual oppression. This book challenges those claims and shows that the Left – and the working class – was involved in the earliest gay rights movements and was integral to the new Gay Liberation Movement. It also refutes the claim that the Left has no intellectual tools to explain the oppression of women and gays. The book uncovers the rich history of the Left and Gay Liberation in Australia, an inspiration for activists today.

ALSO BY INTERVENTIONS

**AGAINST THE STORM
HOW JAPANESE PRINTWORKERS FOUGHT
THE MILITARY REGIME, 1935-1945**
By Masao Sugiura
Edited by Kaye Broadbent
Translated by Kaye Broadbent and Mana Sato
English edition 2019

'In doing what is normal for any trade union activist today – recruiting, arguing and organising – my comrades and I were made to suffer persecution, imprisonment and death'

This inspiring memoir tells how young Japanese print and publishing workers maintained links and sustained organisation between workers during the height of Japanese military aggression before and during World War II. It destroys the myth that all Japanese people all supported the war, and provides a thrilling account of worker organising in conditions of repression that has lessons for up-and-coming unionists of today.

ALSO BY INTERVENTIONS

**LOSING SANTHIA
LIFE AND LOSS IN THE STRUGGLE
FOR TAMIL EELAM**
By Ben Hillier
With Anton Balasingham's: Liberation Tigers and
Tamil Eelam freedom struggle

'The smell of death lingers over the pages of Ben Hillier's Losing Santhia'

It is confronting but necessary to read what happened when tens of thousands of Tamils were corralled on the Mullivaikal beach in so-called no fire zones. Hillier provides an honest appraisal of what happened to members of the Tigers in this period. While the setback for Tamil self-determination was massive, there is also a positive story from the heart of the struggle. And personal stories of love and happiness from the front line bring hope to the fore. The essay ends with the critical question – can the progressive left forces in Sri Lanka forge a common purpose?

– Lee Rhiannon, former Australian Greens federal senator